# THE NAKED EYE

# THE
# NAKED EYE

## MY TRAVELS
## IN SEARCH OF THE HUMAN SPECIES

# DESMOND MORRIS

500 616428

First published in Great Britain in 2000

1 3 5 7 9 10 8 6 4 2

Ebury Press
Random House, 20 Vauxhall Bridge Road, London SW1V 2SA

Random House Australia Pty Limited
20 Alfred Street, Milsons Point, Sydney, New South Wales 2061, Australia

Random House New Zealand Limited
18 Poland Road, Glenfield, Auckland 10, New Zealand

Random House (Pty) Limited
Endulini, 5A Jubilee Road, Parktown 2193, South Africa

The Random House Group Limited Reg. No. 954009

www.randomhouse.co.uk

Papers used by Ebury Press are natural, recyclable products
made from wood grown in sustainable forests.

A CIP catalogue record for this book is available from the British Library

ISBN 0 09 1878675

Edited by Alison Wormleighton
Designed by David Fordham
Typeset by MATS, Southend-on-Sea, Essex
Printed and bound in Great Britain by Cox & Wyman, Reading, Berks

# TABLE OF CONTENTS

# INTRODUCTION

———◆———

AS A YOUNG MAN I was a poor traveller. I rarely ventured outside western Europe. This was due partly to lack of funds and partly to a fear of flying. As a child I had been involved in an air accident and my memory of human body-parts, in the wreckage of two aircraft that had collided in mid-air above me, remained all too vivid. I took my first, unavoidable flight when I was thirty-seven, certain that it would be my last. Surviving it was such a pleasant surprise that I lost my fear and became addicted to the idea of soaring aloft. Even then, however, my scope was limited by a ridiculously heavy workload.

All this changed when, to my even greater surprise, a book I had written in four weeks, *The Naked Ape*, became a bestseller. The resulting windfall meant that, at last, at the age of forty, I was free to go anywhere, anytime. I gave up my desk job in London, where I was the director of the Institute of Contemporary Arts, and with my wife, Ramona, set off in 1968 to explore the world.

In the thirty years that followed I made up for lost time. According to my records I have now clocked up a total of 281 foreign trips and visited a total of seventy-six different countries. I developed – and still possess – an insatiable urge to see every aspect of human activity. Ideally I would like to visit every culture in the world, but as there are over a hundred left to go, I know I will never make it.

The reason for my wanderlust is more than mere curiosity. As I have set myself the task of observing and reporting on human behaviour, it is vital that I see it in all its many forms and patterns. Nobody can write about the human species if they have only studied their own society. It is this thought that keeps me heading for London's Heathrow airport, time after time.

The results of my observations of the human species have been published in sixteen books, from *The Naked Ape* of 1967 to *The Human Sexes* of 1997. But what is missing from those volumes is the more personal, anecdotal aspect of my travels. Many strange things have happened to me along the way, each of which has something to say about the place I was visiting and about the people I met there. In this book I will try to capture them in a series of brief sketches, of humanity as I have encountered it during my travels in search of the human species …

# EXPLORING THE MALTESE ISLANDS

## (1968–1974)

————◇◆◇————

WHEN WE CHOSE THE MALTESE ISLANDS AS OUR BASE FROM WHICH TO EXPLORE THE MEDITERRANEAN WORLD, RAMONA AND I KNEW REMARKABLY LITTLE ABOUT ITS SOCIAL HISTORY. WE HAD DASHED OUT THERE FOR A QUICK VISIT IN THE AUTUMN OF 1967 AND, FOLLOWING A WHIRLWIND TOUR OF AVAILABLE PROPERTY, HAD BOUGHT A VAST, THIRTY-ROOMED HOUSE, THE VILLA APAP BOLOGNA, IN THE VERY CENTRE OF THE MAIN ISLAND. IT WAS IMPULSE BUYING ON A GRAND SCALE.

LESS THAN FOUR MONTHS LATER WE WERE LIVING THERE, ENJOYING THE NOVELTY OF THE RELAXED, SUN-BAKED DOLCE VITA, A STARTLING CONTRAST TO THE HIGH-PRESSURE, WORK-DOMINATED LONDON EXISTENCE WE HAD LEFT BEHIND. HAVING MONEY FOR THE FIRST TIME IN OUR LIVES, IT WAS OUR CALCULATED INTENTION TO SPEND IT AS FAST AS POSSIBLE AND THEN GET BACK TO WORK IN LONDON. INSTEAD OF PLAYING SAFE AND HOARDING THE UNEXPECTED WINDFALL FROM A BEST-SELLER, WE WERE GOING TO USE OUR TEMPORARY FREEDOM TO EXPERIENCE ANOTHER CULTURE — ONE THAT WAS ENTIRELY NEW TO US.

(PLEASE NOTE THAT SOCIAL ATTITUDES IN MALTA HAVE UNDERGONE MAJOR CHANGES SINCE THE SIXTIES.)

## THE CLOCKWORK CENSOR

W HAT HAS ATTRACTED us to Malta are its friendly people, its impressive architecture, its glorious climate, its central position in the Mediterranean, and the fact that the English language is widely understood. What we have not bargained for, coming from London at the height of the 'swinging sixties', is the oppressive censorship and the sweeping power of Malta's religious leaders.

After arriving at the Villa, it does not take us long to discover that the Catholic Church in Malta, with the diminutive Archbishop Gonzi at its head, is almost medieval in its attitudes. Without realizing it, we have chosen to move to the only country in the world where my books are being systematically burned by the Church. At first this makes me uneasy, but as time passes it becomes clear that I will be left in peace. The Maltese people have such a generous nature that they are happy to have me as a visitor, despite the fact that my book *The Naked Ape* is officially banned. Intrigued by this double standard, I try to find out if there is a list of prohibited books. I am told that there *is* a kind of list, but that it is not publicly available. It does not set out all the forbidden titles in the world, but simply records those that have arrived in Malta, been confiscated and then been destroyed. In other words, a book is considered innocent until it is proven imported by a Maltese citizen. It is then subjected to trial by censor and, if found guilty, is thrown in a furnace.

So the 'Banned List' shows only books that have been caught in the censor's net, not those that might one day be found. I discover that Malta's Post Office Act 'empowers the Postmaster General to open mail other than sealed letters if he suspects it to contain anything indecent, obscene, impious or seditious and to destroy it if his suspicions are confirmed'. Since *The Naked Ape* views man as an animal, supports the theory of evolution and discusses human sexual behaviour in some detail, it qualifies for a triple burning if that were possible. No wonder it is on the infamous list.

I am fascinated to know the names of the other authors on the list. With whom do I share the honour of being a forbidden fruit? A local journalist, who shall be nameless, helps me out. He manages to have a copy of the list made for me and passes it to me with great secrecy, as if it contained the plans for a nuclear device. I cannot believe what I read. The names on the list are astonishing. Has the Church gone mad?

Instead of being insulted, I am now deeply flattered, for my disbelieving eyes tell me that I share the list with none other than Balzac, Stendhal, Voltaire and Zola. The Maltese authorities, in this modern age, the late sixties, have been burning copies of Stendhal's *Scarlet and Black* and my favourite book of all time, Voltaire's *Candide. Scarlet and Black* was first published in 1830, and *Candide,* even earlier, in 1759. The mind boggles.

What makes the list even more bizarre is that it is not in alphabetical order, but in order of book importation. The result is that, right next to some famous literary work, there is often a sleazy, soft porn title. The censor obviously had little doubt about what to do with *Keep it Kinky, Until She Screams, Young Topless, Sex Trap* or *Slaves to Sin.* Straight into the furnace with the lot of them. But mixed in among them, apart from literary classics, are recent novels by such established figures as Kingsley Amis, Mary McCarthy, Nicholas Monsarrat, Alan Sillitoe and even dear old Leslie Thomas, who beats them all by having *two* novels banned.

Educational sex manuals are also consigned to the flames. There they go ... watch them burn in hell ... *The Psychology of Sex, Sexual Responsibility in Marriage, Sexual Happiness in Marriage, The Search for Sexual Enjoyment, The Truth about the Pill, Sex Manners for the Single Girl, The ABZ of Love.*

I am so fascinated by this pious book-burning that I decide to make some further enquiries. I still find it hard to believe that the Banned List is real. It must surely be a joke played on me by the journalist who supplied the list. But sadly this proves not to be the case. When I visit the few bookshops that exist in Valletta and ask for certain 'tricky' titles, I am told that they cannot be ordered and sold to me, but that if, the next time I fly into Malta, I bring them with me for my personal use, that will be allowed. As a visitor I can read them, but the Maltese people themselves must not be allowed to see them. So it is true. In the literary sense, Malta is living in the Dark Ages.

I mention my feelings on this subject to a well-known Maltese author I meet at a party. He grins and taps the side of his nose. I expect him to share my irritation, but his only comment is that I should consider myself lucky to be banned, since it will dramatically increase the sales of my book in Malta. He explains that, as soon as word gets around that a book has been put on the list, everyone wants to obtain a copy, and dozens are smuggled in. He also impresses on me the need to keep quiet about the whole business and just get on and enjoy myself on the island. If I don't make a fuss, the authorities will leave me alone. I am not Catholic and I am not Maltese, so I am looked upon as a migratory bird, not a resident species. I avoid pointing out to him that the first thing the Maltese do with migratory birds is to shoot them down and have them stuffed by the local taxidermist.

Taking his advice to heart, I forget all about the infamous Banned List and set about enjoying myself. With the sun and the sea and the mellow rocks, this is easy to do, but I am still intrigued by the character of the Maltese Church, and especially its tiny overlord, the greatly revered Archbishop Gonzi. My first encounter with him occurs when I am exploring the capital, Valletta, admiring this brilliantly conceived city which, with its geometric grid of streets on a long spit of land, feels like a miniature prototype for Manhattan. As I approach the Archbishop's palace, there is a stir. People on the pavements are all turning to face in the same direction. Following their gaze I can see something long, black and shiny gliding silently towards me. It is a huge Cadillac driven with excessive care by a stiffly erect chauffeur. Its number plate is unique. Most of its black, letter-box shape is blank. There are no numbers, no letters. But in the very centre there is some kind of vertical emblem. As it comes closer this emblem turns out to be an archbishop's mitre. There can only be one occupant and, sure enough, perched like a parrot in the vast interior, is the minute figure of a fully bedecked Gonzi.

His impact on the citizens of Valletta is even more impressive. As the gleaming, elongated Cadillac creeps past, they not only stop dead in their tracks, but actually drop to one knee on the pavement. Down they go, one after another, creating a wavelike ripple down both sides of the street, as the car passes them. This is a class act. They know how to do religion here – none of your trendy, guitar-playing vicars, robbing the Church of its authoritarian dignity. This is the real thing.

As a totally non-religious observer I find myself fascinated by a Church that makes so few concessions to modern life. Malta offers me the gift of a time machine, taking me back several centuries to see religious obedience as it used to be. Even the incongruous Cadillac (a gift, I discover, from a group of Maltese who have emigrated to North America) is somehow transformed into a state carriage, lacking only a team of plumed, black horses to pull it.

Further investigation reveals that the Maltese Church spreads its influence to cover every aspect of social life. It refuses to allow politicians who are members of the opposition labour party to be buried on consecrated ground. It completely dominates the school system; when it discovered that some of the laboratories in the university did not have Christian emblems displayed on their walls, it had a collection of crucifixes rushed there immediately.

It is even rumoured that the Church demands a percentage of the earnings of Valletta's prostitutes, after the fleet has been in port, payment of which gains the girls holy forgiveness. And it is claimed that the Church also insists on the confiscation of any contraceptives imported into the island by these unfortunate ladies of pleasure.

On the beaches, modesty is legally enforced, it being an offence for a Maltese woman to display herself in a two-piece bathing suit. Away from the beaches, women are not allowed to wear shorts, and even female trousers are frowned upon. It is also forbidden for a man to be stripped to the waist in public in any of the towns or villages. (In the late sixties the non-Maltese are already beginning to ignore these restrictions, despite the fact that they are clearly spelled out in tourist guidebooks.)

In contrast to its excessive prohibitions, the Church also has several excessive enthusiasms. It loves to display the suffering of sinners. On Good Friday each year there is a marathon procession at the village of Qormi (pronounced 'or-me'). We are taken to watch this by a Maltese doctor friend who always enjoys the event because it brings him such good business. Men who have sinned during the year are able to atone for their wickedness by taking part in the procession, black-hooded and barefoot, with heavy leg-chains, and dragging full-scale crucifixion crosses for several miles. In each of these huge wooden crosses there is a cavity into which

are placed heavy lead weights, one per sin. This mea[...]
the extremely wicked will end the day in agony and with badly
blistered feet. 'There's old George,' cries our doctor friend
with a chuckle. 'He'll be in the surgery first thing tomorrow.'
Business is looking up already.

The Maltese Church also likes to let God know that it is still
there and sends Him repeated reminders in the form of loud
explosions. Each village has an annual festival at which, in
addition to the parading of the heavy statue of the local saint
through the decorated streets, there is also a salvo of ear-
splitting, window-rattling bangs. These bangs are manu-
factured in the local fireworks factories, where several lives
are lost each year in the process. Each of the fireworks has the
same, all-too-familiar rhythm, rather like a solemn drum-roll:
brrrrrrrrrrrrr – boom! It is the boom at the end that shakes the
foundations. These pyrotechnic expletives have only one
purpose: to produce a louder bang than those of the next-door
village. These are not the pretty, decorative fireworks we all
know and admire (although the festivals do have those as
well); these are serious proclamations of village status and are
aptly described as 'aerial bombs'.

By competing for loudness, each village aims to attract the
Almighty's attention and divert it away from rival villages. In
this way, the village hopes to be especially favoured in the
year ahead. There are those (including the owners of many
frightened dogs) who feel that, if God really could hear these
terrible explosions, He would quickly send a tidal wave to sink
the whole island and gain a little peace. But He seems to be
rather hard of hearing, and the contest cheerfully continues,
year after year, with the smell of gunpowder mingling with
burning incense to create an evocative fragrance that lingers
long in the memory after the festival is over. If a group of
animal-lovers decided to protect their terrified pets by starting
a Maltese Noise Abatement Society, the Archbishop would

undoubtedly declare it the work of the Devil and have them all excommunicated on the spot.

My second encounter with Gonzi the Magnificent occurs unexpectedly on a flight to Rome. The buzz around the airport is that the Pope has sent for the Archbishop to castigate him for being too – how can one put it? – too religious. It seems that Gonzi's medieval excesses have disturbed the Pontiff and he wants gently to insist that Gonzi cools it and tries to make at least a few concessions to twentieth-century progress. Judging by the twinkling high spirits with which Gonzi makes his splendid entrance into the waiting aircraft, the Pope is in for a wasted afternoon.

The first-class section of the regular Malta Airlines flight to Rome is very small, with only a few pairs of seats on either side of the central aisle. Having arrived early, I am the only occupant so far, when Gonzi appears. The Maltese air-hostess is flustered. In her short, tight skirt, she would find it hard to drop to one knee and has to make do with impromptu bobbing actions. Gonzi, accompanied by a large male bodyguard, surveys the empty seats and selects the one he likes best, next to a window. Nobody dares explain to him that there are such mundane things as seat tickets. He waves a jewelled glove out of the window at no one in particular.

His bodyguard must now depart and leave his overlord to the mercy of the skies. But before he can take his leave he must crouch on one knee before the Holy One and kiss the ring on his gloved finger. With Gonzi in a window seat this is no easy task, but the man has no choice. He kneels and leans across the aisle seat in a single, deft manoeuvre, reaching out for the Archbishop's gloved hand as he does so. He can't quite make it, but with one last effort does manage to bring his protruded lips to within an inch of the sacred ring. Sadly, in this final brave lunge forward, he catches his testicles painfully on the arm of the aisle seat and instead of kissing the ring, emits a silent scream over it. Withdrawing backwards in a slightly crumpled posture, he escapes from the aircraft and hobbles off across the tarmac.

Gonzi smiles beatifically about him, blissfully unaware of his faithful aide's little drama. At this moment the American ambassador and his wife make a briskly businesslike entrance. He is holding their first-class tickets in his hand and peering at the seat numbers written on them. He becomes agitated and shows them to his wife. Gonzi is sitting in their seats. He is not merely sitting in them, he is regally installed in them, his long, flowing robes arranged to convert a humble seat 2A into a sacred throne. The ambassador and his wife hold an agitated conversation, first with one another and then with an even more flustered air-hostess. I overhear them debating the alternatives: uprooting the aged Gonzi or sitting somewhere else. The catch with sitting somewhere else is that they do not know which seat Gonzi was originally allocated, so they may settle themselves in a stranger's seats and then have to face the ignominy of being turfed out themselves.

Gonzi at last becomes aware of their presence and of their obvious discomfort. He understands perfectly. These spiritually frail beings are terrified of flying. Their fear of dying in a hideous air crash has reduced them to gibbering wrecks. He must offer them his help. In a surprisingly loud voice for such a small frame he announces grandly to the tense couple standing before him: 'Have no fear, while I am on board, God will not dare to strike down this aeroplane.' That does it. Without further ado, the American couple sink into seats 1A and 1B. Luckily nobody else appears and they watch gratefully as the doors shut and we are at last on our way.

Why have I warmed to Gonzi? I dislike everything he stands for – institutionalized superstition and blind faith in place of scientific curiosity. And yet this brief encounter with him has made my day. I suppose it is the sheer oddity of the man that is so appealing. (According to the *Malta Year Book* for 1968, among Gonzi's many titles is 'Major General of the British Army' which, for a Maltese priest, makes him even odder.) But as someone once said, a colourful enemy is more fun than a colourless friend.

A few days later, back at the Villa again, I am explaining all this to a neighbour, over a glass of wine. He is one of my favourite authors, the delightfully chaotic Anthony Burgess, who has bought a splendid old house in Lija, the village next to ours. A brilliant wordsmith, he is living a second life, having unexpectedly survived the first one. Some years before, his doctor told him solemnly that he was suffering from a terminal brain tumour and that he had only one year left. His immediate reaction was to sit down and write six novels at breakneck speed, in order to leave sufficient funds for his shortly-to-be-bereaved wife. When the doctor was proved hopelessly wrong, and Burgess emerged in excellent health, it dawned on him that instead of writing one novel every six years, he was in reality capable of completing six in one year. What's more, they were good. They had not suffered from the speed at which they had been written. If anything, they had benefited from the intense flow of words. So he kept it up, and went on writing at a pace that his lazier friends considered almost obscene. Books poured from his study, and life was full of gusto again.

When his wife died he soon remarried. With his lively second wife and their small son, he has now moved to Malta where, like me, he is enjoying the escape from city pressure. But there is one big difference between us. I am a non-religious observer who looks upon Gonzi and Co as a baroque entertainment, while he is a good Catholic who takes Church matters seriously. As it turns out, he takes them much too seriously. When I tell him in a light-hearted way about the infamous Banned List, he explodes. How could they do that! They must be crazy!

To me, the Banned List is by now no more than an amusing anecdote and I rather enjoy the fact that my book is inflammatory in both senses of the word. But to Anthony it is scandalous that the Church, *his* Church, should be behaving in such a draconian way. He decides to make a stand on my behalf. I beg him not to do so. I have a bad feeling about what might happen. Burgess in full flood is a frightening prospect and all I want is to be left in peace, behind my high stone walls, on this fascinating little island. A social issue is something I do not wish to become. But there is no stopping him.

As a good Catholic, albeit a very modern one by Maltese standards, he feels that he can speak to the Maltese people as if he were one of them. He can proudly say 'we' when he addresses them as Catholic to Catholic. Big mistake. He decides that he will deliver a public lecture at Malta's Royal University. Huge mistake. He will tell them a few home truths about their ridiculous censorship restrictions. Enormous mistake.

He expects me to be there to hear him defending my book and demanding that it should be removed from the Banned List. In fact, he wants the Banned List removed altogether. I try once again to stop him, but it is no use. His brilliant literary and linguistic brain, which as a writer fills me with awe, is matched by an almost laughable unworldliness. He is like a genius child who hasn't yet learnt the social niceties. Whatever the opposite of street-wise is, he is it. He is library-wise and street-foolish. For me, it is part of his great charm, but for him it is about to prove costly. I decline his invitation to attend the great event and feel myself sinking in his estimation.

The day of the lecture arrives. Burgess is a famous figure and the turnout (as an eyewitness later tells me) is impressive. The cream of Maltese society is there, settling down to listen to what they fondly imagine will be a few choice literary gems. Instead they find themselves on the rack. Burgess castigates them at great length for their prudery and for their narrow-mindedness. He berates them for allowing the Maltese people to be treated as children and, reaching his climax, informs them that, unless human adults are allowed to come face to face with every kind of human experience, they will never learn to make up their own minds about what is good and what is bad, and from within themselves to resist the bad. If you treat people like naughty children, they will behave like naughty children. 'It is no wonder,' he storms, 'that when the Maltese emigrate to England they become the brothel-owners of Soho.'

His tirade is met with a stony silence followed by a politely subdued mass exit. Common courtesy is considered to be a major attribute in these small, heavily populated islands and, despite his best intentions, Burgess's abrasive remarks are deeply offensive to his cultured audience. He keeps saying 'we', assuming that his known Catholicism will enable him to treat them as 'family', but to them he is a revered visitor, a famous, foreign exotic, and the last thing they expect from him is a public 'family row'.

The following day he and his wife and son leave for a short trip to Italy. When they return to their Maltese home the following week, they find that all the doors have been padlocked. They are no longer welcome on the island. Stunned, they return to Italy and decide to settle there.

I feel terrible but there is nothing I can do. I tried my hardest to warn him off, but he refused to listen. There are other authors living in Malta – Nigel Dennis, Nicholas Monsarrat, Hunter Davies, Frederick Mullally – some, like me, on the Banned List, but all, like me, quietly minding their own business. We are visitors, and if we wish to live here, enjoying the Maltese sun, we must accept Maltese cultural traditions, even if we find some of them alien to our own. For me, personally, the fact that they are so very different is part of their fascination. It helps to give me new insights into human nature. I don't want them to be the same. I don't want to convert them.

People are always talking about the importance of bio-diversity, whenever rare species are threatened; in the same way, I long for cultural diversity, and relish the moments when I encounter some new human strangeness.

To give just one example, I cherish the thought that there exists in the censor's department of Maltese officialdom a specialized nipple-blotter. Each day this young man must rise from his bed, dress carefully and set off to his office. There he sits in front of huge piles of freshly imported magazines from Europe and America. He must laboriously turn the pages of each of these publications, one by one, scanning the glossy illustrations for any sign of an exposed female nipple. Once he has spotted one, or perhaps even a pair, he reaches out his right hand, picks up an ink-stamp, presses it into an ink-pad and then slams it down on the offending nipples. If his aim is good, he will have completely obliterated the sight of these obscene female appendages and saved tender Maltese eyes from the shock of seeing them when they innocently open their new copies of *Vogue, Harpers,* or *Life.*

I am carefully saving some my favourite nipple-blotted magazines, to remind me in the future of how very sexy a deliberately obscured nipple can be. My only concern is for the psyche of that poor young man who must spend hour after hour nipple-bashing. Imagine yourself in his position: nipple, bang – nipple, slam – nipple, crash – nipple, thump! At the end of his working day he has done nothing but brutally beat a thousand tender nipples into oblivion. The effect this must have on his mental state is hard to imagine.

There is a postscript to the story of Anthony Burgess and forbidden books. A few years later, Burgess himself is in trouble with the censor, but this time in England. His extraordinary novel *A Clockwork Orange* has been made into a film by the brilliant American director Stanley Kubrick. It is so outrageously violent that there is a public outcry and a demand that it should be banned from all cinema screens. Kubrick contacts me and asks for my help to prevent this from happening. At his invitation, Ramona and I attend a showing in London and we are both wildly impressed. It is a tour-de-force. True, it is violent, but the violence is presented with such style and cinematic elegance that the whole film becomes a great work of art. I agree, without hesitation, to defend it against its critics and appear on a TV debate, crossing swords with the venerable Malcolm Muggeridge. He is genuinely appalled by the film and I find it hard to sway him. But I do my best and Ramona and I are rewarded by an invitation to dinner with the Kubricks. This is a pleasant surprise because he is notoriously reclusive and secretive.

He gives us directions to his isolated home in a remote lane in Elstree and we drive there on a pitch-dark February evening. Turning into his drive we are confronted with what looks like a heavy farm gate on which is pinned a large notice. There is so much writing on it that I have to climb out of the car and get close to it to read the words that are illuminated by our headlights. The notice explains that somebody, on a recent visit, did not shut the gate fully and it swung slowly open after they had passed through. The Kubricks' dog had then wandered into the road and been killed by a passing car. It is therefore imperative to close the gate in a special way, giving it an extra pull-to after the first one has appeared to shut it. This first pull-to is deceptive, and the second, stronger pull-to is essential to ensure the full closure of the gate.

I am standing, bent over in the beam of the light, absorbing all these details in the cold night air, watched by a bemused Ramona. I am beginning to understand why Kubrick the director often needs a hundred takes of a shot to satisfy him. I open the gate, drive through and then return to perform the precise closing actions that are required of me. On the first take, I am not sure that I have performed well enough, so I open the gate again and close it once more – strong, first pull-to; then the crucial, second pull-to. I feel a little judder that was not there the first time. Success. Cut and print.

Back in the car, I drive on until the headlights pick out the shape of a door. On it there is another large notice. Once again, I get out and read my detailed instructions. This notice is concerned with categorizing the visitors according to the possible reasons for their calling at the house. Some are directed one way, others another. None of these instructions seems to quite fit our friendly, dinner visit. The closest category would have us turning right, so we move on again in that direction. Two further notices and we have arrived at what seems a good place to park the car. We get out and stumble though the darkness towards a lighted window. Finding a door, we knock and enter. Along a passageway we come upon a woman busily cooking in a kitchen. She looks up startled and enquires nervously what we want. At this point Stanley himself appears, realizes who we are, introduces his wife, and asks why we have chosen to come though the back of the house. I explain about the notices and that I have done my best to follow his instructions as carefully as possible. He winces and apologizes. 'Those were the daytime notices,' he explains. 'I forgot to take them down and replace them with the night-time ones. I am so sorry.'

There follows an engrossing dinner with a fascinating man, hospitable, quiet and complex. I discover that Burgess's story, *A Clockwork Orange,* is partly autobiographical. The character in the film who appears as 'the writer', and who has his expensive typewriter smashed by a gang of thugs, is Burgess himself. The writer's wife, who has a rubber ball stuffed in her mouth while she is raped by the gang, represents Burgess's own first wife who, when pregnant with his child, was brutally attacked by a gang of four American army deserters in a London alleyway. It was in a blackout during World War II, and she was beaten so badly that she subsequently miscarried.

The rest of the story is Burgess's way of working out his feelings about these thugs and what should be done with them. In *A Clockwork Orange*, when the leader of the gang is caught, the authorities set about reprogramming him. His eyelids are mechanically clamped open and he is exposed to prolonged aversion therapy. Every time he is shown a scene of rape, or some other form of violence, he is subjected to intense pain. Eventually the authorities are satisfied that he has been 'cured' and is no longer a threat to society. But in our final glimpse of him we realize that his ego is still intact and that he has somehow managed to resist them.

To our discomfort, as an audience leaving the theatre, we are forced to recognize that we enjoyed the moment when the gang-leader managed to beat the system. And yet this is the brutal, raping monster from the earlier part of the film. Burgess has been playing with us. He has forced us to face the fact that we prefer a figure who enjoys freedom, even if he is evil, to one who has been turned into a slavish automaton of the state.

This is an alarming conclusion and one that angers many people who see the film. But Burgess fervently believes that 'it is better to *choose* evil than to be *forced* to be good'. In a letter to me, Kubrick emphasizes his belief 'that the clockwork of a mechanical society can never counterfeit the organic vitality of moral choice; that goodness is nothing if evil is not accepted as a possibility'.

The point is that, once a man has been forced to be obedient to an authoritarian order, he can become so brainwashed that he is lost for ever. But if he has the freedom of choice and, today, uses it for evil, there is always the chance that, tomorrow, he may change his mind and use it for good. This last point is obscured in the film because Kubrick has based his script on the American edition of the book, an edition which omits its final chapter. In that chapter, Burgess allows his young thug to mature and to change, abandoning the violence of his youth. The American publisher considered this ending naïvely optimistic and, to Burgess's annoyance, removed it. But, with or without it, the author's essential message remains the same: 'a man who cannot choose ceases to be a man'.

With these thoughts in mind, it is now clear to me why Burgess felt so determined to deliver his unpopular message to the Maltese élite. By imposing a strict censorship on books, the Maltese authorities were robbing their people of the chance to make their own decisions. Better to give them their freedom, even at the cost of exposing them to controversial ideas, rather than stamp out all forms of personal rebellion. It is important to realize that alongside every destructive act of rebellion, there may be dozens of constructive ones, and it is these that give society its innovations and its triumphs. For a man whose wife had, in real life, been savagely attacked by young thugs, this is a remarkable assessment. But then Anthony Burgess was a remarkable man.

## NOTE

NOT LONG AFTER KUBRICK'S *A CLOCKWORK ORANGE* WAS RELEASED, IT WAS REPORTED THAT A GROUP OF FOUR BOYS, DRESSED IN THE STYLE OF THE THUGS IN THE FILM, GANG-RAPED A NUN IN POUGHKEEPSIE, JUST NORTH OF NEW YORK. PUBLIC REACTION WAS PREDICTABLE, AND THERE FOLLOWED DEATH-THREATS TO KUBRICK AND HIS FAMILY. ON POLICE ADVICE, HE WITHDREW EVERY COPY OF THE FILM AND REFUSED PERMISSION FOR IT EVER TO BE PUBLICLY SCREENED AGAIN. ALTHOUGH THIS IS UNDERSTANDABLE, IT IS A TRAGEDY THAT HIS MASTERPIECE HAS BEEN HIDDEN FOR SO LONG,

ESPECIALLY AS IT WAS LATER REVEALED THAT THE BOYS WHO GANG-RAPED THE NUN (A) HAD NOT SEEN THE FILM AND (B) WERE NOT, AS FIRST REPORTED, DRESSED IN THE STYLE OF THE THUGS IN THE FILM. PERHAPS, ONE DAY, KUBRICK'S ESTATE WILL RELENT.

KUBRICK HIMSELF BECAME INCREASINGLY WITHDRAWN, NOCTURNAL AND ECCENTRIC. IN 1978 HE MOVED FROM THE HOUSE, ABBOT'S MEAD, WHERE WE HAD VISITED HIM, TO A NEARBY MANSION, CHILDWICKBURY MANOR, WHERE HE INSTALLED ELECTRONIC GATES AND VIRTUALLY DISAPPEARED FROM PUBLIC VIEW. WHEN HE DIED IN 1999, HIS GARDENER WAS ASKED BY A REPORTER FOR HIS PERSONAL OPINION OF THE GREAT MAN. HE REPLIED: 'IN THE TWENTY-ONE YEARS I HAVE BEEN WORKING HERE, I HAVE NEVER ONCE SET EYES ON HIM.'

AS FOR MALTA, ITS TIGHT CENSORSHIP HAS LONG SINCE BEEN RELAXED AND THE 1990s GUIDEBOOKS NOW FEATURE TOPLESS BATHERS LYING ON THE ROCKS WHERE, IN EARLIER DAYS, THEY WOULD HAVE CAUSED AN UPROAR. HAD HE LIVED TO SEE THIS, THE DREADED ARCHBISHOP GONZI (RECENTLY DESCRIBED BY A MALTESE AUTHOR AS A 'MINI-PERSON WITH A MEGA-EGO') WOULD HAVE BEEN OUTRAGED, BUT HE WAS SPARED THIS HORROR, HAVING FINALLY GONE TO MEET HIS MAKER (AND NEAR-EQUAL) IN 1983, AT THE ADVANCED AGE OF NINETY-EIGHT.

## WHY BLACK MARY'S COFFIN IS SO SHORT

HAVING SPENT THE last twelve years living in the centre of one of the largest cities in the world, it comes as something of a shock to find ourselves on an island so small (only seventeen miles by nine) that one can drive right around it in an afternoon. Within a few months we know every shop there is, have visited every cinema and restaurant, and have travelled over every mile of every main road. After a while it feels a little claustrophobic and we soon decide that, in order to enlarge our horizons, we will have to buy a boat. An order is placed for a 30-foot twin-diesel cabin cruiser from an Italian shipyard and we wait patiently for it to arrive.

In the meantime, it has to be said that there are certain advantages in living in such a tiny country. Since everyone knows almost everyone else, the entire nation has the attractive mental outlook of a small village. It is not uncommon, even on a busy street, to see two cars, travelling in opposite directions, stop dead when they draw level with one another. As the traffic following comes to an abrupt halt, an arm emerges from the front window of each car, and the two drivers proceed to greet one another with a long, leisurely handshake. There is no impatient horn-honking from the cars behind. Everyone waits while the two friends exchange a little gossip and then the lines of traffic move off again.

Nobody bothers to lock their cars here. Theft is almost unknown. When describing the atmosphere in a Maltese town to first-time visitors, I use as an example the fact that, when we are buying provisions in our open sports car, we can place our bags of shopping in full view on the back seat and go off for a cup of coffee with the certain knowledge that they will still be there when we return.

There are few, if any, parking regulations, and such things as parking meters are unheard of. You leave your car wherever there is a space available. And there are few road signs, because every Maltese driver knows every square inch of the island. Approaching a roundabout is a dramatic experience because nobody recognizes the usual priorities. It is every man for himself and the roundabout becomes a kind of 'chicken run' in which the bravest driver goes first, in the hope that the driver of the other vehicle will slam on his brakes and give way to him. As this often acts as a challenge to the rival driver's manhood, the accident rate in Malta is worthy of a place in the *Guinness Book of Records*. Because small cars tend to suffer more in collisions that large ones, this does create its own special kind of priority system: the bigger your vehicle the more you are respected. Nobody in an ordinary saloon ever challenges a bus or a truck. Bus drivers know this and fling their wonderful old monsters into each roundabout with great abandon. Perhaps this is why every bus has a small shrine next to the driver, where passengers can cross themselves and gain a blessing as they climb aboard.

Another unique feature of driving in Malta is the milometer reading. If a car has been brought to the island when it is brand-new, and has been driven around regularly every day for the past, say, thirty years, it will still have a milometer reading that is unbelievably low. In any other country you could be forgiven for thinking that someone had tampered with the mechanism, but not here. It is simply impossible to clock up a large number of miles when the full length of the island is less than twenty miles. As a result, there are some fabulous old cars, still more or less in mint condition, of makes and types that have vanished to the scrap heap years ago in any large country. For those who are fascinated by antiquated motors in pristine condition, Malta is the place to explore.

Because of the village mentality, there is hardly any crime on Malta. There is a jail, but when I enquire about it, I am told that there are only three inmates and two of these are foreigners. I ask a Maltese policeman what he would do if he caught some young thugs breaking the law. 'I would ask them to stop, and if they ignored me I would then threaten to tell their mothers. That always works.'

The whole island is still abuzz with the scandal of the almost unheard-of event of a murder. But again, this involves a foreigner – a sailor who has attacked a prostitute with a knife. She was known in Valletta as Black Mary because of her long, jet-black hair, and her funeral is a strange affair. Her body has been placed in its coffin in her small house near the red-light district. As the pallbearers edge the coffin carefully out through the front door and into the street, to start its journey to the church, there is a scream from the watching women. This is because, as the coffin slowly comes into view, it is clear that it is an unusually short one. This would not have caused a scream had Black Mary been a short woman, but she was not. Indeed, she was exceptionally tall. The awful truth, which dawns on the onlookers as soon as they can see the whole length of the coffin, is that the knife-man, in his savagery, had not left a great deal of Mary for burial. The brutality of the killing shocks them to the core. It would be bad enough anywhere, but here, on this exceptionally friendly island, it seems beyond belief.

———◦◦◦———

Before long we are told that our boat has arrived from the Italian shipyard and is about to be launched in the yacht marina. We watch this event with a mixture of intense pleasure and some apprehension. The idea of enlarging our world by exploring the seas around Malta is enormously appealing, but the truth is that neither Ramona nor I know anything at all about the sea. Marine lore is as foreign to us as space travel. The sight of our new boat being lifted into the water by a huge crane is suddenly rather daunting. Below decks she has room to sleep several people. Her twin engines are immensely powerful. She has lifebelts, an anchor, fire-fighting equipment – this is not a toy, this is serious and when we are out there, at the mercy of the sea, with sudden storms blowing up, sharks circling us ... Calm down, this is ridiculous. All the same, I wish I were a good swimmer. The truth is, I have only just learned to swim. I was nearly drowned as a small child and have hated the water ever since. Arriving in Malta and having a private pool where I could struggle with my water phobia in private, I have forced myself to learn and have at last conquered my fears. But if something goes wrong out at sea, I won't have a hope.

These thoughts are passing through my mind as the shiny new boat, which we have christened the *Argo,* is eased gracefully down into the water. The experts who have launched her take her for a test run and proclaim her fit and well. She is ours. Now what?

An out-of-work ship's captain is found who will show us the ropes, in both senses of the phrase. We learn how to dock and undock. At one point, as we pull on a rope with a boat-hook, the rope suddenly stretches tight and, acting like a bowstring, fires the boat-hook, arrow-like, down the marina, narrowly missing the yacht at the next berth. We are learning. Eventually we set out to sea and our temporary captain decides to enter a bay and show us how to drop anchor. It soon becomes clear why he is out of work, because he drops the anchor onto some fishing nets which proceed to foul our propellers. We are now rapidly increasing our vocabulary of marine terms, some of which are even repeatable. At last we are free and return to port. Our marine mentor has decided he has had enough and returns to the sea-front bar where we had discovered him.

Now we are on our own. We enlist our wonderful Maltese driver, Domenic, as 'crew' and nose our way bravely out into the ocean. Being strictly a road man, he is ill-at-ease but, despite his misgivings, carries off the occasion in his usual quietly dignified way. Edging past the tall, sloping battlements of Valletta, we feel wonderfully independent – able to go anywhere, do anything. And the view is breathtaking. This is Malta at its best, as it must have been seen by every visitor to the island before the arrival of the international airport. It was built to be seen this way, and it is seriously impressive.

Another boat passes us, going into harbour, and its

occupants wave to us. We wave back, feeling almost cocky now. This reminds me of something I have been reading in a booklet about marine signals. It seems that, if you see someone sitting on a rocky outcrop, you can tell whether they are passing the time of day there or are stranded and need help. If they are happy, they wave; if they are stranded, they hold their arms straight down by their sides and then, keeping them straight, raise them and lower them sideways, several times. I hope I never have the chance to find out if this really works.

As the weeks pass, we become bolder and bolder, taking the *Argo* right round the island and across to Gozo. We quickly learn the constantly varying moods of the sea, and feel more and more at ease as we explore the coastlines. But when the British Navy enters port, we suddenly feel very small and insignificant. In the days before we had a boat of our own, destroyers and aircraft-carriers were picturesque and romantic, but now they are awesome and strangely repellent, especially when seen close-up from the deck of a small vessel. Painted in a dull, leaden grey, they loom over you with a curiously unnerving, silent menace. I try to imagine what it would feel like to be on board one of these weapon-heavy giants. I am about to find out.

## A RUM DO ON THE *HERMES*

ONE DAY IN VALLETTA, I walk past a young British sailor on shore leave. He turns and asks if I am the man he used to see on television, back in England. We begin a polite exchange of trivia and then, to my surprise, he invites me to visit his ship, which has just arrived for a short stay in Valletta harbour. The idea does not appeal to me, but I am not quick enough to invent a convincing excuse. It is clear to him that I am trying to think of the right thing to say, and I have to face the fact that now I must either accept his offer or risk insulting him. I hear myself agree to pay him a short visit the following morning. Why do we let small civilities get us into unwanted, embarrassing situations? I hate war, so why should I agree to set foot on a man-o'-war? But perhaps it will have some unexpected, minor reward.

On board the Royal Navy aircraft-carrier *Hermes* the following morning, drinking a pint of rum with the matelots (their word, not mine), there is an overpowering sense of peacetime boredom. Breaking this monotony must be one of the major rewards of going to war. In fact, as I perch here awkwardly in the narrow confines of this claustrophobic, armoured bunk-room, I am overpowered by the perverse thought that war is essentially an anti-boredom device, with all its other, more traditional functions having only a secondary role. The young sailors seem strangely haunted by the immense, latent power of their huge vessel, a power that is so deeply dormant that a fog of futility hangs over the great, grey ship.

One young sailor with a broken arm tells me that he dreamt last night that the Queen was in trouble for stealing six bottles of salad cream from a supermarket. I think he expects me to psychoanalyse him. I am tempted to give him a clue by asking him if the queen in question is one he knows personally, but decide to keep my mouth shut.

It soon becomes clear that their main aim is to ensure that I drink so much of their dark rum that I will be unable to walk steadily down the long, sloping gangway when I have to face the moment of leaving the ship. This may seem like a hostile act on their part, but it is not. It is clear from their body language that it is a friendly way of making me briefly one of them. Reluctance to have my glass filled yet again is noisily swept aside and what started out as a simple social encounter rapidly develops into a test of manhood. This has something to do with the fact that they are British, I am British, tots of rum are still an active British Navy tradition, and the American fleet is pathetically dry. My morning booze-up therefore becomes a matter of national pride.

At last I escape and, after the usual goodbyes, turn and confront the gangway. I know they are watching me and I must perform for them. Feeling only half in control of my legs, I decide on a flamboyant exit. Instead of stiffly shuffling down the long slope, I will boldly prance it. The rum is now in almost total control and I walk on cushions of air. Towards the bottom of the slope, with victory in my grasp, I feel my legs bend outwards, as if to accommodate a saddled horse. Only a superhuman effort gets me back onto the quayside and solid land. I turn, smile weakly, and wave. I am just able to detect that they are proud of me. I have passed the test.

My problem, of course, is that I am not a seasoned boozer with a reinforced gut-lining. In fact, apart from a social glass of wine, I rarely include ethyl alcohol in my diet. So a large quantity of hard liquor on an empty stomach cascades straight into my bloodstream and unravels me. When I was young I quickly learned – like so many teenagers – the penalty for a long night's slurping. The moment that the toilet floor starts to tilt and then slowly revolve is hard to forget. And the smell of vomit-stained clothing also tends to lodge itself firmly in the memory bank. After a few encores, the booze-up performance joins the 'never again' category of juvenile experiences. As least, for me, it did. But not, it would seem, for so many young men, and I can't help wondering why.

The lads-getting-pissed-together ritual is so immensely popular that rich brewers have been able to raise mansions on the strength of it. As a piece of human behaviour it is nothing more than competitive drinking accompanied by verbal trivia and followed by communal urinating. On one occasion I carried out the unpleasant experiment of joining a piss-up group and pretending to drink along with them while in reality remaining completely sober. (I would like to claim this was devotion to scientific, observational duty but the truth is that I had recently suffered a bout of hepatitis and was forbidden alcohol.) I was then able to watch the gradual changes that took place as the evening wore on. It was clear that, to the semi-sloshed, the loss of inhibition was a bonus. Their humour became more hurtfully intense and more pointed. But then, as fully sloshed members of the group, they began to change. Inside their minds, they became increasingly profound with their repetitive statements, even philosophical. In the outside world, however, they were becoming increasingly vacuous. When they finally reached over-slosh, they either vomited, fought, became maudlin or passed out.

The true appeal of this type of interlude lies in its shared pain – the cruel humour, the loss of self-control, the threat of violence, the nausea and the hangover. Members of any group that finds itself faced by a shared disaster experience a powerful emotional-bonding process. Kidnap hostages, shipwreck survivors, soldiers under fire, all become bonded more intensely than people enjoying relaxed relationships. Twenty-four hours of high drama is more powerfully bonding than twenty-four years of humdrum everyday life. So a quiet, carefully restrained drinking session would have far lower bonding impact than one that is spiralling rapidly into social danger zones. The shared hangovers give the drinkers the sense that they have emerged from a group trauma. And they feel strangely closer for it.

So, for modern young men, who have long ago lost the exhilarating risk-taking of the primeval hunting party, the hard-drinking party is there to tie them together, just as tightly as ever. Only loners, like me, seem to be immune.

## SHARKS ON THE ROCKS

———————◆———————

FOR ME, exploring Malta means investigating a culture alien to my own. I am becoming obsessed with recording all the minute differences between English and Maltese body language. I spend more and more time sitting in sea-front cafés observing the passing scene, jotting down notes, making quick sketches and taking photographs. But next week, with the arrival of a special party of house guests, my exploring will be diverted, for a few weeks at least, and will take a very different direction.

Our guests are David Attenborough and his family. We have been close friends for over ten years and Ramona and I are eagerly awaiting their arrival. Our first meeting, back in the fifties, was rather odd. David and I were on rival television channels, each in our way trying to do the same thing – to get people excited about animals. David was presenting *Zoo Quest* for the BBC and I was presenting *Zootime* for ITV. Our respective bosses had told us to keep apart. ITV had only just started, robbing the BBC of its British television monopoly, so there was considerable hostility between the old established channel and the new upstart. It was made clear to both David and myself that we were not, under any circumstances, to fraternize with the enemy. Needless to say, this only made us more determined to meet and compare notes.

It was Leo Harrison Matthews, director of the Zoological Society of London, who broke the embargo for us, inviting us both to lunch with him at London Zoo. On television we appeared as rather earnest young men, both intent on imparting our fascination with the animal world. So we were pleasantly surprised to discover that, in the flesh, we also shared an irrepressible sense of humour. In fact, from that day to this, I cannot think of any meeting between us that has not involved prolonged and uncontrollable laughter.

I am slightly alarmed, therefore, to see how tense and serious David looks as he arrives on the island. The explanation is not hard to find. David is so good at his work that he has fallen prey to the Peter Principle. This states that 'in a hierarchy every employee tends to rise to his level of incompetence'. David has made such supremely competent animal programmes that the BBC has rewarded him by promoting him to a level where he can no longer roam the world bringing back wonderful images, but must instead sit behind a desk in London and chair committee meetings.

Why on earth does a brilliant field naturalist take such a step? Why does something as destructive as the Peter Principle work so inexorably? The answer is that it is difficult to ignore a major compliment, no matter how unsuitable it may be. When David was offered the challenge of becoming Controller of a whole new channel – BBC2 – he found the idea irresistible. It would give him the power to influence television in ways he felt important. But it also meant that he himself would no longer be directly involved in the creative acts that he had instigated.

In fact, one of the first things he did, after taking charge of the new channel, was to give me a new, adult, animal series in which we would not only show viewers the wonders of nature, but would also, for the first time on television, discuss biological issues and controversies in detail in regular studio debates. It was his idea, but I, and others like me, had the pleasure of carrying out the work. David had to remain trapped in his impressive offices at Television Centre.

I presented fifty of those hour-long programmes before

deciding to leave England and explore other cultures. Now, here I am, living on a small island, and David, for a few weeks at least, is able to escape from his desk and join me 'on location'. I am hoping that he will be able to relax a little and enjoy his temporary freedom. I am sure that the tension I see in him will soon evaporate – and indeed it does. By the next day, the tough administrator/negotiator has vanished. He is unwinding rapidly and lies by the pool with his family, reading a book on the Maltese islands.

Once he has got the Controller out of his system, another change occurs. Relaxing by a pool is not enough. He disappears. We all wonder where he has gone. Then somebody spots him on top of the tall tower that protrudes from the centre of the Villa roof. He is staring at something in the distance through a pair of binoculars. We lazily debate what this might be – a bird of prey, perhaps? Now my own curiosity is aroused, and I start the long trek to the top of the tower. 'We are dying to know – what exactly are you looking at?' 'Phosphatic nodules,' is the enigmatic reply. It is typical of David that he already knows more about the natural history of the island than I do. I have been here for months and he has only been here for a few hours, yet it is he who is about to explain to me one of Malta's most exciting natural features.

He indicates some layers of rock in the far distance. Malta is one of the rockiest islands in the world. Everywhere you look you find dramatically beautiful geological formations, with the soft, mellow limestone looking so much like melting cheese that you feel you could eat it. David points out that in certain areas there are dark horizontal bands in this golden limestone, bands of nodules in which there are embedded (dramatic pause) the fossilized teeth of the extinct Giant Shark – the greatest predator the seas have ever seen, three times the length of the Great White Shark of today. Some of the biggest teeth are said to be almost as long as your hand, triangular in shape, with sharply serrated edges.

In earlier centuries these teeth were thought to have magical powers and were called 'St Paul's Tongues'. St Paul was shipwrecked on Malta in the year AD 60 and legend has it that, to show his gratitude for having been saved from drowning, he banished all the poison from the snakes of Malta. It was wrongly believed that these serpents kept their venom in their tongues and St Paul was said to have magically cast all their tongues into the rocks where, to this day, they can be found, protruding from the surface. And that is why all the snakes on Malta (unlike other Mediterranean islands) lack venom and are harmless to humans.

The truth, of course, is that Maltese snakes have always been non-poisonous, but it is a good story and, in earlier times, helped to maintain a lively trade in fossil sharks' teeth. Between the thirteenth and eighteenth centuries, almost every court in Europe had to have some of these teeth. They were used at feasts and banquets to test whether the wine had been poisoned. Fear of poisoning by rivals was widespread in those days and many protective devices were used to protect against this. The St Paul's Tongues were considered to be especially useful because of their association with the banishing of poison by St Paul. Sometimes the teeth were hung in special ornamental 'trees' that were placed on the table near the wine; sometimes the teeth were dipped into the wine. It is said that during the seventeenth century the export trade in these teeth reached such a level that no ship ever left Malta without some on board.

By the nineteenth century, the trade in these fossil teeth had died out and most people had lost interest in them. But not David. He is not superstitious, but he is an avid fossil-collector, and from their photographs it is clear that these particular fossils are not only remarkable natural-history specimens, but also, in a sinister way, strangely beautiful.

Back in 1909 the American Museum of Natural History had reconstructed the open jaws of the Giant Shark and then, for photographers, had asked people to sit inside them. It was obvious that this monstrous fish would have been capable of chomping down on an entire family of human beings and despatching them with a single gulp, had it not obliged us by becoming extinct. This fact adds a macabre thrill to the idea of possessing one of these teeth, and it is clear that a dramatic, Attenborough-led tooth-hunt is in the offing.

We are now rapidly moving into phase three of the David Attenborough metamorphosis. Since arriving on the island: DA the Tense Controller lasted about twelve hours; DA the Relaxed Holiday-maker held out for about six hours; now we are witnessing the final transformation into DA the Manic Explorer. His whole body language has changed. He is like a young wolf who has scented moose on the horizon. It is a joy to behold. The David we all know and love is triumphantly resurfacing from beneath the sea of selection committees, union meetings, political pressure-groups, budget debates and management seminars in which he has been so miserably submerged for months on end.

Descending hurriedly from the Villa tower, he wants to know how to find the nearest ironmonger's shop. Within the hour, we are all equipped with hammers and chisels and knapsacks and sally forth on an urgently organized tooth-hunting expedition. Because the island is slightly tilted and the rocks slope down towards the east, we head for the west, where the cliffs will be at their most dramatic. There we will have the best chance of finding the embedded sharks' teeth that, by now, we have come to view as the most essential acquisition on this planet.

Driving as far as the roads will take us, we park and strike off along a narrow track towards the distant clifftops. DA is now firmly in control and we all follow meekly behind him in single file, feeling rather like native bearers in search of King Solomon's Mines. At one point he stops to photograph a small wild flower. We pause while he does this and I can't resist a little experiment. Before he has finished I start slowly walking on, along the path. The others follow me. Gradually DA catches up and quietly, inconspicuously, reassumes his position at the head of the column. The experiment is a success. There is nothing pushy about the way he has done this. It is just that his boundless enthusiasm demands full expression and following along behind us will not suffice.

David's age is changing rapidly. With each footstep he sheds another year. When he arrived on the island he was physically forty-five, mentally fifty-five. Now he is physically twenty-five and mentally fifteen. This is the true Attenborough and I make two silent predictions: (1) that he will always be fifteen and (2) that he will give up his desk job. I say nothing about this, partly because David hates talking about himself and partly because I am so out of breath trying to keep up with him.

Finally, reaching the cliffs, we scatter, each searching for the perfect overhang where large, triangular teeth might be glinting at us from the curved slopes of golden limestone. Soon, the sound of hammering echoes through the landscape. We are all searching frantically and, when we do finally set eyes upon the small irregularity that is the tip of a tooth, we find ourselves hissing Yesssss! Then there is the careful tapping and chipping, as we break away the soft limestone that encases the tooth. From the tip alone it is hard to tells its size. Is it a monster or a baby? At last it crumbles free and we can clean it off and examine it. The last time this tooth was moved was millions of years ago, when its owner met a mysterious death in the primeval oceans. Mysterious because, when you think about it, what on earth could have exterminated a species of killer shark that was three times the size of the

Great White? If the Great White survived, then w
Giant Shark? It doesn't make sense. Another pro
solved one day.

The hours pass and, at last, we regroup to compare our trophies. We have been surprisingly successful and there is a great deal of happy banter about who has found the best tooth. Both size and quality have to be taken into account. The biggest one of all is badly blunted. The most perfect one is only of medium size. The most dramatic one has a crack in it. And so on. Anyone would think they were diamonds, the way we fuss over them. To us they are almost as good.

Resting on the clifftops afterwards, gazing out across the calm sea towards the mysterious little flat-topped island of Filfla, I feel lucky to have known David. Like me, he is profoundly uninterested in his inner self and profoundly fascinated by the world around him. Looking down at the fossils in his hand, he says: 'Two grown men, spending all day doing this ...' and he laughs. But the truth is, he's in his element, and he knows it.

## NOTE

MY PREDICTION WAS CORRECT. WITHIN A FEW YEARS, DAVID ATTENBOROUGH TOLD THE BBC THAT HE WAS LEAVING. YOU CAN'T GO, THEY SAID. HAVE ANOTHER CHANNEL — TAKE BBCI AS WELL. STAY. DAVID ACCEPTED AND BECOME THE DIRECTOR OF PROGRAMMES FOR THE WHOLE OF THE BBC. THE PETER PRINCIPLE HAD STRUCK AGAIN. BUT NOT FOR LONG. THREE YEARS LATER HE FINALLY BROKE FREE AND WENT BACK TO DOING WHAT HE LOVED — MAKING PROGRAMMES. IF HE HAD STAYED HE WOULD UNDOUBTEDLY HAVE ENDED UP AS DIRECTOR GENERAL BECAUSE HE WAS SO GOOD AT RUNNING THE PLACE, EVEN THOUGH HE DID NOT ENJOY DOING IT. BUT LUCKILY FOR THE REST OF US, THE FIFTEEN-YEAR-OLD INSIDE HIM WAS STRONG ENOUGH TO DEFEAT THE MIDDLE-AGED MAN THAT HE WAS BEING FORCED TO BECOME. HE WENT ON TO MAKE *LIFE ON EARTH, THE LIVING*

PLANET, TRIALS OF LIFE, THE PRIVATE LIFE OF PLANTS AND THE LIFE OF BIRDS, THE
FIVE GREATEST NATURAL-HISTORY SERIES EVER SHOWN ON TELEVISION. AND
IT IS NO ACCIDENT THAT THE THEME OF 'LIFE' FEATURES IN THE TITLE OF ALL
OF THEM, FOR HE IS ONE OF THE GREAT LIFE-ENHANCERS OF OUR CENTURY.

## THE SEARCH FOR THE FILFLA LIZARD

THIS MORNING David announces that we are all going to go
in search of Europe's rarest reptile – the Filfla Lizard. It is so
rare that it may even be extinct, and he wants to find out the
truth. I have heard of it but I have never seen it, and I am soon
just as excited about the prospect as he is. We start to make
our plans and, as always when David is on the hunt, a mood of
boyish enthusiasm spreads throughout the villa. His curiosity
is highly infectious and before long there is nothing any of us
wants more than to set eyes on the elusive *Lacerta filfolensis*.

There are two reasons for its extreme rarity. First, it lives
only on a tiny, flat-topped island three miles off the south-west
coast of Malta. Second, this treeless, uninhabited island has
had only one use in recent years – as a target for the Royal
Navy, who use it for bombing and shelling practice. It is
entirely possible that every single lizard there has been blown
to smithereens.

Filfla has a magic appeal. It juts out of the sea like a tiny
version of Conan Doyle's Lost World, with hostile, vertical,
200-foot-high cliffs all around it and a rocky plateau on top.
The plateau is less that 1,000 feet long and only about 150 feet
wide. This means that the entire surface of the island is about
the size of three football pitches. Not a generous habitat for a
whole species. Add to that the fact that it is barren and rocky
and it is clear that the Filfla Lizard needs all the help it can get

and can certainly do without Navy shells landing on it in large numbers.

I have often stared out at little Filfla, standing proud in the distance, but have never thought of visiting it. In fact, on one occasion, watching a huge warship firing its big guns at the sheer cliffs, I made a mental note to keep well clear of it. I was under the impression that it was out of bounds to small boats, although I had never seen this in writing or a formal announcement. It just seemed common sense to stay away from a naval bombardment zone. So, despite my interest, I had never pointed the *Argo* out to sea in Filfla's direction. Not until now.

In a small booklet about Filfla, published by local historian Charles Boffa, I read that in ancient times the island must have been visited by the Romans, some of their pottery sherds having been found there. Later, in the fourteenth century, a small chapel was fashioned out of a cave, and an emergency store of wine and food was left in the cave for shipwrecked sailors or storm-blown fishermen who might be driven to use the island as a refuge.

Surprisingly, there was a spring of fresh water on the island and at a later date this made it an attractive haunt for pirates. In the eighteenth century, the Knights of St John used gunpowder to blow up the rocks around the spring in an attempt to reduce Filfla's appeal to the buccaneers, but to no avail. The spring stubbornly continued to provide fresh water.

Everything changed when warships began using the island for target practice in the thirties. As the vertical cliffs began to crumble, the chapel vanished, the spring was at last destroyed and a pathway that led up to the plateau was also demolished. As a result, it would take ropes and grappling irons to climb to the top, and the ascent was dangerous because so many of the rocks had been loosened by the shelling. From a distance Filfla was as alluring as ever, but at close quarters it had lost much of its appeal.

That is the brief history of the island. All that Filfla offers today is its unique lizard, and no minor threat like a naval bombardment is going to dampen the enthusiasm of an Attenborough in full quest. We are lucky with the weather. The sea is unusually smooth as the *Argo* throbs along at full speed, circling Malta and then striking out towards the tiny, for-bidden island. And we are lucky with the Navy, too. There isn't a warship to be seen.

As we approach Filfla, its 'lost world' quality increases dramatically, and I quite expect to see a fleeting glimpse of a small dinosaur peering over the edge of the cliff. But a rare lizard will have to suffice. I decide not to go too close, because of jagged rocks in the shallows, and we drop anchor about 50 yards offshore. Ramona's elderly father stays on board while David and I swim ashore. It is an eerie, abandoned place. So many of the rocks on the shore have been blasted there by human intervention that they do not present a natural landscape. The island is more like a rubbish dump for large, malformed boulders. David disappears in search of his lizard, while I explore the shallows wearing my snorkel mask. I am somewhat alarmed by the sight of several large shells (the explosive variety, not the marine type) lying in the underwater rubble.

David returns and pronounces the lizard safe and well. He and I swim back to the boat side by side, peering at the marine life through our snorkels as we go. Then I see something that brings me to a sudden halt. Immediately below us is the boat's anchor. It is hooked around what, at first glance, appears to be a small rock, but at second glance is all too clearly not a rock, but a smooth, metallic object. The truth dawns on me – I have anchored the *Argo* on a huge, unexploded shell.

There is quite a strong current now, tugging at the boat, and the anchor is pulling against the shell with some force. I gesticulate urgently to David, and together we stare down at the scene beneath us. Breaking surface, I tear off my snorkel and shout out to Ramona's father, asking him to start the *Argo*'s engines and put her into reverse. This will unhook the anchor and free it from the shell. He is not too familiar with the *Argo*'s controls but manages to start her up and then throws her into gear. Unfortunately, instead of reverse, he plunges her full speed ahead. With my snorkel tugged on again, I am just in time to see the powerful engines of the *Argo* (the equivalent, the salesman said, of ten Rolls-Royces) put such pressure on the heavy shell that, to my horror, it is pulled clear off the rocky seabed and thrown up into the water. David and I watch, as if in slow motion, as the sinister metal object rises up towards us and then slowly falls back down again, landing on the rocks with such force that we hear a sickening 'clonk'. While it is rising in the water I am thinking to myself: 'We are going to die – this is it.' As it crashes back down again, I expect everything to go black. But we are still here. Miraculously, the shell must have been a dud.

Back on land that evening, we are at a party and I mention to a Maltese businessman that it seems a pity that Filfla Island should still be used as a naval target. He agrees immediately, saying, 'Yes, yes, I have always wanted to build a hotel on Filfla. Think how exotic it would be: a building standing on its own, rising up out of the sea, covering the whole plateau – so remote and romantic.' The conclusion is obvious: the naval shelling is not such a bad thing after all. It may kill a few of the lizards, but it also keeps the developers away. Conservation by bombardment. Not exactly a textbook solution for a rare species, but effective nonetheless.

**NOTE**

THE SHELLING HAS LONG SINCE BEEN PROHIBITED AND THE ISLAND DECLARED A NATURE RESERVE. IN 1987, THE LARGEST GREAT WHITE SHARK EVER CAUGHT WAS TAKEN NEAR FILFLA, A RECORD THAT MAKES OUR

CAREFREE SNORKELLING THERE IN THE EARLY SEVENTIES SEEM, IN
RETROSPECT, EVEN MORE HAZARDOUS THAN IT APPEARED AT THE TIME.

## MAY I HAVE A WORD WITH YOU?

RETURNING IN THE *ARGO* to the yacht marina after an exhausting trip, I make a cardinal error. I forget the unwritten rule of marine etiquette which states that you must always slow your speed down to a crawl when entering the harbour. The reason for this is that failure to do so will spill several gallons of gin and tonic. Most of the large, glamorous and obscenely expensive vessels in the harbour are floating gin palaces. They rarely if ever set out to sea. Instead they lie snugly safe along the length of the marina quay. If a small 30-footer like mine forgets itself and comes in at speed, all these millionaires' toys start to rock from side to side, and hundreds of brimming gin glasses cascade onto the immaculate decks and the elegant cabin floors. This is social sacrilege of the highest order and I have just committed it.

As I secure the *Argo*'s ropes, I can already see a wiry figure clambering out of a long, sleek vessel to my left. His deep red face contrasts vividly with the pure white of his hair and his long, white, drooping moustache. He is leaning purposefully forward as he walks, as if heading into a strong wind, and he is not a happy man. To my dismay I see that additional figures are now emerging explosively from other vessels and are heading in the direction of my mooring berth. From their expressions it is clear that keel-hauling is too good for me.

'I say, may I have a word with you?' – the dreaded words that mean a polite Englishman is seething with anger. This is clearly time for a small experiment in human behaviour. The last thing in the world that these approaching figures expect from me is a grovelling admission of (a) guilt, (b) remorse or (c) crass stupidity. What they do expect is (a) excuses, (b) defiance or (c) protestations of innocence. The secret in such situations is to give them the unexpected. So I go into full grovel.

David Attenborough, who is beside me on deck, realizes what I am doing and rapidly retreats below. He can't take the sight of his old chum in grovel-mode. This is a pity because I would like him to see the power of body language in action. The grovel, which I have used previously to avoid speeding tickets (until I carelessly mentioned the technique in a television interview, after which the police always recognized what I was up to), is working well. I have adopted the necessary posture – body slightly crouched, lowered head, sagging limbs, anxious facial expressions, hand-to-face auto-contact, weak voice-tonality and all the other subordination signals. I explain that I am a complete idiot, that I have no excuse for my disgusting behaviour and that, unlike them, I am a complete novice in all matters marine and am unfit to have a place in their magnificent marina. Before long, finding no soil in which to grow, their anger has withered and died. But even I am surprised by the way the encounter ends. They actually apologize to me for having accosted me.

I suspect that David has been listening to all this because, when he re-emerges after they have departed, he shakes his head and says: 'You cynical bastard.' I then have to apologize to him, but this time it is for real, because, even as a charade, such behaviour is unnerving for onlookers. It is also, I discover to my cost, unnerving for the performer. Demeaning myself, even though it has been a calculated experiment, leaves its mark. Body language is so powerful that it is almost impossible to enact something without the mood portrayed invading the brain of the actor. Laurence Olivier used to claim that he could think about his laundry while playing Othello. That trick is sadly beyond me and for the next few hours I am in a bad mood.

In the evening we are going out to dine at a small restaurant in Rabat. The food is good, but there is no air-conditioning and so we arrive in open-neck shirts. It is a hot night and we are sure that casual dress will suffice. We are wrong. An unusually overbearing head waiter approaches us as we are waiting to be shown to our table. David and I give him our best, cheery smiles. Our families are assembled expectantly behind us. The smiles are not working. The man insists we are breaking his dress code. I look around at the other diners, all sweating profusely in jackets and ties, and something snaps. I start shouting into the man's face.

In normal circumstances I would have retreated, because I hate making a fuss, but not tonight. Without realizing it, I have an emotional balance to restore. Earlier I over-grovelled. Now, to compensate, I must over-assert. I deliver a short lecture, at the top of my voice, so that the entire restaurant can hear what I am saying, about the Freudian significance of the male necktie, ending with the bellowed climax: '… and if you think we are going to put ridiculous penis-symbols around our necks just to please you, in your stuffy little restaurant, you are very much mistaken.' I then turn on my heel and usher our whole party out of the building. Behind me I can detect a stunned silence. The fact that most of the diners have recognized David, and that several of them are probably on his staff at the BBC, adds an extra piquancy to the incident.

We drive off, with me still fuming, and find a delightfully airy fish restaurant on the coast. To my surprise, David is not at all upset by my appalling behaviour. In fact, he is delighted. I have restored a balance, not only for myself, but also for him. I have been artificially submissive and uncharacteristically aggressive, in quick succession, and the two have cancelled one another out. We are back to normal balance again. I am de-grovelled.

The following day we all set off for another full day on the *Argo,* travelling right round the island to a tiny circular cove on the south-west coast. It has a narrow entrance and we manoeuvre the boat in with great care. After we have anchored and swum in the shallow water, we are just settling down to lunch when a huge, streamlined shape glides into view. It is not a vessel from Malta; I have seen nothing this glamorous here before. It must have come across from Sicily, which is only about 60 miles to the north. My suspicions are confirmed when we hear the Italian voices of its immaculately uniformed crew. They have spotted our little cove and, to our intense annoyance, have decided to ease their glamour-boat into it.

The cove is so small that there is barely room for the two boats. It is remote from anywhere. There are no other boats within miles and, until this moment, we were the sole owners of this minute, exquisitely private hole in the long, rocky coastline. We had travelled a long way around Malta to reach it, and now we are being invaded by some flashy Italian millionaire in his obscenely expensive and disgustingly impressive super-boat. Our sense of territorial intrusion – fuelled, if we would admit it, by a tinge of silent envy – is growing by the second.

The large boat, about three times the size of ours, is having trouble securing an anchorage without actually hitting us. Finally it does bump into us and that is too much for David. He decides we must take some sort of action. His decision is strengthened by the arrival on the intruder's deck of several blindingly beautiful young women wearing bathing costumes that consist of little more than coloured ribbons. They proceed to drape themselves in languorous, studio poses across the deck, watching the docking-struggles of the crew

with vacant expressions of the kind adopted by fashion
models on the catwalk. A middle-aged Italian in a dark blazer
and white trousers shouts some instructions, and the crew
lower protective floats around their vessel, to guard its
pristine paintwork from further clashes with the *Argo*.

David wants to know how I am going to deal with *this*
situation. Something aggressive is needed. I am enjoying my
lunch down below and am also enjoying the view, but I
suggest that, if he wants to drive the Italian and his harem
away, all he needs to do is to adopt the full primate threat-
stare. 'It works for dominant monkeys. All you have to do is go
on deck and stand facing them. Then just stare at them.
Remain expressionless and silent and don't take your eyes off
them. That should work.'

Seeing a pair of binoculars, David decides to go one better.
Slinging them around his neck he goes up on deck and, facing
the super-boat, he brings them up to his eyes. He is now
solemnly examining the intruders through his glasses across
a distance of about ten feet. He does not smile or frown,
merely stands there, immobile. The rest of us go on with our
lunch and wait to see what happens.

Suddenly there are some fresh orders to the crew, barked
in Italian. They immediately start pulling in their ropes and
raising their anchor. Then the deep throb of their powerful
engines is heard and the gleaming super-boat starts slowly
reversing out of our little cove. As it glides past, its owner
lowers his head and calls out to me: 'Bon appetit!' I wave and
smile. They are gone. David is exultant. The primate threat-
stare has worked. It is on the tip of my tongue to say 'cynical
bastard', but somehow it doesn't seem appropriate. Why is
that? His action was just as calculated as my grovelling in the
marina the day before. But for some reason, artificial
aggression is less disturbing than artificial appeasement. I
shall ponder on this. In the meantime David is in a high good

humour and we once again have our private territory to ourselves. Swimming in the bay after lunch, we all feel strangely elated. Body language has triumphed again.

## WHY IS IT SNOWING COCA-COLA?

PERHAPS BECAUSE OF the strong British influence, the Maltese are fanatical about football. Every town has its own club with devoted local supporters who, should their team enjoy a victory, travel up and down the local streets after the game, blowing their horns incessantly and waving huge flags from the windows of their cars. There are enough clubs to form a league, and winning the league carries with it massive local status. Towards the end of the season, when the championship is hanging in the balance, tempers become frayed and violence may erupt on a scale that makes English hooligans look positively angelic by comparison.

We are blissfully unaware of this when we decide to take Jason, our toddler (who was born here in Malta), to see his first-ever match. Unknown to us, it happens to be the game at which the championship for this year will finally be settled. Our local team, Birkirkara, are playing Valletta. The situation is complicated by the fact that if Valletta win they will become champions, but if they lose, Sliema, who have already played their last game, will take the crown. This means that there are not two, but three sets of supporters with a vested interest in the outcome of the game. And they are all there at the Birkirkara stadium, voicing their feelings with great energy.

The atmosphere is tense as we find our seats, up at the back of the main stand. The place is heaving with humanity, the three sets of supporters being squeezed into the space normally occupied by only two. The mood is approaching mass hysteria and the game has not even begun. Little Jason senses the importance of the situation and is duly impressed. It is clear to him that what he is about to see must be very, very important if grown-ups get this excited about it. He particularly likes the mounted police on their huge horses, lurking in the corners of the ground. And the sea of rival colours makes it feel like a carnival. His eyes are wide with eager anticipation.

Then the game begins and the crowd roars and bellows with every move. Jason thinks this is wonderful. He has never seen grown-ups behaving like this before. After a while the referee gives a dubious penalty to Valletta and they score. If it stays like this, Valletta will win the match and Sliema will lose the championship. A complicated, three-way warfare breaks out. The Birkirkara fans pour onto the pitch and try to attack the referee. The Valletta fans come to his defence and counter-attack. There is a stalemate and it looks as though everything will soon return to normal, but now the Sliema fans decide to join in. Because they have even more to lose than Birkirkara, they are intent on seeing the match abandoned. They manage to lift up a long concrete bench and use it as a battering ram. They are charging at the terrified referee, who flees into the grandstand at a point immediately below us. He leaps over the barrier and cowers beneath the low wall there. Jason thinks this is even better than the football. It's just like the movies. But where are the cavalry? Amazingly, here they come, in the shape of the mounted police, who are galloping up and down the pitch as though the Grand National has just started, sending groups of marauding fans scattering in all directions.

The combined efforts of the Birkirkara and the Valletta fans are winning the battle and, as the crowd surges forwards, the referee crouches a little lower in his inadequate hiding place. We are so engrossed in this that we have barely noticed that all the grandstand seats except ours have been vacated, the people around us wisely having beaten a hasty retreat to the exits. A hail of bottles is now raining down on the grandstand, as the outraged fans hurl missiles in the direction where they know the referee is hiding. Some of these bottles are aimed so high that they strike a concrete wall above us, shattering with such force that they explode into tiny flakes of glass. These flakes float gently down to settle like snow on our clothing. 'It's snowing Coca-Cola,' observes Ramona. 'I think it's time to go.' She is right, of course, but Jason and I, for our separate reasons, are reluctant to give up our ringside seats at what is rapidly turning into a latter-day Roman colosseum. I myself am busy making careful observations of human fighting actions, while Jason is enjoying what seems like the widest-screen movie he has ever set eyes on. It suddenly dawns on me just how irresponsible I am being and we, too, at last make our hurried exit, shaking our clothes free of the glassy snow as we go.

I do my best to explain to Jason that football matches are not always that thrilling, but I don't think he believes me. It is easy to see how young Romans could grow up thinking that the contests in the colosseum are normal games. Lions three, Christians nil. The only thing to do is to divert him onto other sports. Domenic, our driver, suggests horse-racing. Apparently our milkman has a trotting horse called Urzie III, who is showing great promise, and Malta has a fine harness-racing track. That should be exciting, and happily in a non-violent way.

This is even more successful than I have anticipated. Jason has exactly the right mentality for studying form. Although he is not yet four years old, he can already identify 112 different makes of motor car, and has collected in small notebooks the numbers of every taxi on the island, and the name of every decorated lorry and of every boat in the harbour. He also insists on being taken each day to count the number of vehicles being taken off and put on the Malta-to-Gozo ferry. It is a simple matter for him to adapt this insatiable appetite for fact-collecting to the task of studying race-form. He soon knows the name of every racehorse on Malta, how many times each one has won and lost, and when it last raced. At the racetrack he calculates the chances of each entry and is allowed to place a small bet. Retiring confidently to his seat, clutching his betting slip in his hand, he then proceeds to pontificate in his tiny voice, to everyone around him, about the outcome of the next race. Elderly Maltese gentlemen are charmed by this show of juvenile bravado, and pat him condescendingly on the head, giving knowing smiles to one another. They then place their own bets, unwisely ignoring Jason's advice.

The race is run. They lose, he wins, and proudly trots off to collect his money. This is not easy, because he is so small that, at the paying-out counter, he has to stand on tiptoe and raise his arm as high as possible while waving his winning slip in the air, in order to be noticed. Over the rim of the tall counter, all that the pay-out men can see is a small hand waving a piece of paper. The rest of him is invisible. They push his small winnings to the edge of the counter and watch with fascination as the little hand scoops up the money and disappears.

Back at the Villa after each visit to the racetrack, a special ritual has to take place. Every race has to be re-enacted with detailed commentaries and wild celebrations. On his best day, when he picks the winners in four consecutive races, the celebrations go on for hours. Will this prove to be a passing fad, or have we inadvertently imprinted him with a fascination for racing that will last a lifetime? How early do adult patterns get laid down in childhood? Time will tell.

## NOTE

ALTHOUGH HE SOON LOST INTEREST IN GAMBLING, JASON'S EARLY 'IMPRINTING' ON RACING STATISTICS TURNED OUT TO BE A POWERFUL

FORCE. A QUARTER OF A CENTURY LATER, AFTER OBTAINING A DEGREE IN EGYPTOLOGY AT OXFORD, HE HAS TURNED HIS BACK ON THE ACADEMIC WORLD AND IS NOW WORKING AT THE JOCKEY CLUB HEADQUARTERS IN LONDON, IN THE RACE-PLANNING DEPARTMENT OF THE BRITISH HORSE-RACING BOARD.

## WHATEVER HAPPENED TO THE DONKEY-FACED GIRLS?

THERE IS A MYSTERY at the Villa. In a corner of the wine cellar there is a large square lump in the floor. A small crack in this strange lump reveals a hollow beneath. There are no floorboards here, only solid stone flooring, so the dark crack is slightly sinister. Curiosity demands that I make the crack wider. After hammering away at it for a while, I manage to make a hole large enough to peer through. Shining a slim flashlight down into the darkness, I am stunned to see a spiral stone staircase, winding its way down and down into the limestone rock on which the villa has been built.

Asking people in the village about the history of the villa, I discover that it has been constructed on the site of an old stone quarry, so that beneath its lower floor there lies a vast chamber. But if this is so, then why did some previous owners, perhaps in an earlier century, seal off the staircase leading down to it? The heavy slabs they used were clearly not intended to be moved – ever. The temptation to move them and explore the villa's hidden underworld is overwhelming.

The problem is the sheer physical power needed to remove the covering slabs. Luckily we have house guests who happen to be young, strong and as curious as I am to find the answer. A shopping trip to buy pickaxes is quickly arranged and we gather in the wine cellar for the ceremonial opening, as excited as Howard Carter and Lord Carnarvon at the opening of Tutankhamun's tomb.

At last the slab is removed and the spiral staircase gapes below us. We take up our flashlights and slowly descend. The steps are carved out of the solid rock and making them must have represented a huge investment of manpower. They seem to go on for ever and I am counting as I go … 31, 32, 33, 34, 35, 36, 37, 38, 39 … and I am on the bottom. So, Thirty-nine Steps – a nice literary touch, which appeals to me. Directly in front there is a long passage. The air is so still and heavy down here that you can feel it pressing against your cheeks. Imagine stale dankness and multiply it by a thousand. Suddenly the pressure changes and a large cavity opens up to my right. It has an arched ceiling of bare stone and at the end there are small carved recesses in the walls, as if made to accommodate idols. It feels like a tiny, underground chapel, stripped naked of all its sacred contents. Perhaps, many years ago, people met down here in secret to pray, or perform some kind of religious ritual.

Returning to the long passageway, we edge our way forward until we come to the base of another spiral stone staircase. We cannot go up it, however, because it is blocked by massive pieces of rock and rubble. And that it is. Nothing more. We feel deflated. No hidden treasures, just this amazingly deep space. Ideal as a shelter if the cold war turns hot, but otherwise useless. As we make our way back, however, we notice that one section of the passage wall is not solid rock, but instead is made up of large stone blocks. There is no mortar between these beautifully crafted blocks – they are so carefully shaped that they fit snugly against one another, leaving absolutely no gaps. Again, an immense amount of labour must have been involved, down here in the depths, to create this wall. Why? We have no idea. So at least an appealing mystery still remains.

Back up in the sunlight, over long drinks, we discuss this sinister 'walled-up section' and what horrors could possibly lie behind it. To us it is just a joke, an idle game to while away a quiet afternoon, but the matter is not allowed to rest there. Our Maltese staff hear about our little mystery and start making enquiries in the village. What they are told has an unexpected impact. Our two maids, who are sisters, suddenly refuse to sleep in the villa and insist on returning to their village home when night falls. For some reason, which they are reluctant to discuss, they are unhappy about using their villa bedroom, which happens to be next to the wine cellar, with its now dark, gaping hole.

Eventually they are persuaded to explain. It seems that, in the village, there is an old legend that, long before the Villa was built, there used to be an older house on the site. Centuries ago, this house was said to be haunted by two donkey-faced girls. These monsters were the daughters of the owners, who were so ashamed of them that they dug a great hole, down into the ancient stone quarry, walled up their donkey-faced girls there and left them to die.

What we have done, inadvertently, is to release the ghosts of these tragic girls back up into the villa. So, after dark, it is *'saha,* goodbye, see you tomorrow' – nothing will keep our maids there. News that we have actually found the walled-up section of the deep passageway is all they need to be convinced that there is a horrible truth behind the village legend – and probably a horrible discovery to be made behind the carefully crafted blocks of stone.

There is nothing for it but to break through the stone barrier and see for ourselves what is hidden there. More pickaxes are bought and a digging party assembled. This time there is slightly less humour and a tinge of apprehension. After all, if we find two hideously deformed skeletons, it is hardly going to add to the Villa's charm. But now we have to know, and so we set to work. Blisters are soon forming on our aching palms and we are panting in the stale, damp air. Each block of stone is about 20 inches long, and it takes ages just to make a dent in one. After toiling away for what seems like several hours, we finally make a small cavity and are able to shine a flashlight into the blackness beyond. What we see astonishes us. Set back a little from the thick wall through which we have just broken is another, *second* wall of equally large, equally heavy and equally well-crafted blocks of limestone. This is too much. It will take days to make a hole big enough to start working on the inner wall. So we abandon our quest. We are able – honestly – to report to the maids that we have found nothing at all behind the walled-up section of the deep passage. They relax and lose their fears of hauntings and ghosts. But it is just as well that they did not overhear one of the house guests muttering, in parody of a popular television commercial: 'If the donkey-faced girls are really in there, they must have been double-wrapped to keep the flavour in.'

## SALVO AND HIS MAGIC CARPET

Ever since falling in love with the jungle paintings of Henri Rousseau, I have dreamt of discovering my very own 'primitive' artist. I know he is out there somewhere, utterly untouched by fashion, totally ignorant of trends, privately painting away to his heart's content in an eccentric, naïve, intensely personal style, just waiting for me to find him and reveal his genius to the world. And it is in a backstreet in a small Maltese village that my dream comes true. Well, almost.

We have brought two cars with us to Malta – a big old Rolls-

Royce Silver Cloud for comfort, and a little red Sunbeam sports car for fun. I am exploring the island in the Sunbeam, driving slowly through the villages, along narrow streets that snake this way and that, forever forking and dividing, creating a complicated, almost organic pattern. In one village in the south of the island, I am looking up at the higher windows when I happen to notice what looks like a first-floor courtyard. There are inner walls surrounding a small, open area and on these walls are dozens of primitive images. I retrace my route and this time stop in the street below. Now I can see more clearly. The walls are all covered in these paintings. There are images of flying birds, caged birds, songbirds, peacocks, parrots, cockerels, chickens, dogs, stags, lions, horses, white rabbits, and monkeys dressed as clowns. There is a depiction of a pond full of fish, a human-headed horse, a winged lion and fighting kangaroos. There are people, too. A little girl sits in a high chair; there are portraits, family groups and cyclists, and a city scene with tall buildings.

My first reaction is one of elation, but then the horrible truth dawns. All these wonderful, naïve images are painted directly onto the stone walls. It will be impossible to move them or exhibit them. The world at large will never see them. There is only one solution. I must buy artist's materials for the painter and persuade him to make new works that are portable.

Back at the villa, I explain all this to our Maltese driver, Domenic, and the plan is put into motion immediately. We buy some boards and brushes and paints and set off in the Royce (as Domenic charmingly calls the big car) to return to the artist's village.

Domenic knocks on the green door and a wizened, white-haired old man appears. His name is Salvo and he is happy to show us his paintings, although slightly puzzled as to why we should be so interested. They are even better at close quarters and Domenic has no trouble in persuading him to make some more for me on the boards I have supplied.

While we are there, Salvo shows us into a tiny bedroom, where he has painted some more pictures on the walls. It is stuffy and the air is stale, as if nobody has used the room for many months. There is an aged carpet on the tiled floor – a carpet that contains a secret, as we will soon discover.

As we leave, and the old Rolls, sorry, Royce, slides gently through the village and out into the countryside, I am full of excited anticipation at the thought of the paintings that will soon be pouring from Salvo's new brushes. France has its Henri Rousseau, America has its Grandma Moses, Scotland has its Scottie Wilson, England has its Alfred Wallace, and now, at last, Malta has its Salvo. And what a wonderful name, like a diminutive of Salvador. I can see it already, boldly spelled out in the window of a smart gallery in London's Bond Street, with the old man himself standing proudly inside at the private view, quietly nodding and smiling, as the art world flocks to marvel at his masterpieces.

Then, as we drive down a country lane towards a small farm, I notice that Domenic is uncomfortable. I am sitting in the back of the car with my elderly mother, and Ramona is up front beside Domenic. Nobody else has spotted Domenic's discomfort. They are looking out of the windows at the Maltese countryside, but my gaze is now fixed firmly on the back of Domenic's neck. As always, he is in the smart grey driver's suit he loves, with a crisp white shirt and dark tie. But to my horror I can now see that, all along the top of his shirt, there are small, dark, moving objects.

Leaning forward, my fears are confirmed. Domenic, who prides himself on always being immaculate, is alive with fleas. In an instant I realize what has happened. The old carpet in Salvo's bedroom must have been a sea of hungry fleas. Our arrival was like a sudden, unexpected banquet for them. If

Domenic has been infested, then what about me? I look down at my wrists and there they are, dozens of them. If they had been bigger I am sure I could have heard their squeals of delight at all this virgin flesh. Now I can feel them scampering around my neck. I have never had fleas before in my entire life and, much as I enjoy novel sensations, this creeping feeling spreading over my skin is one I could cheerfully do without.

I shout to Domenic to stop the car. He pulls up next to a farm outhouse. In a nearby field an aged farmer is toiling away. He looks up and stops in his tracks. His farm is in a remote part of the island. Tourists never come here. And, like many Maltese farmers, he rarely if ever visits the urban districts. So the sequence of actions he is about to witness will leave him puzzled for the rest of his life. This is what he sees:

A Rolls-Royce stops outside his farm and two men leap out. They are not laughing, or even smiling. They ignore him completely, and with a desperate intensity both dash into his little outhouse and start tearing off their clothes. As the shed is open on the side that faces his field, he can see clearly everything that takes places inside it. Now, the near naked men appear to be performing some kind of hideous ritual, leaping about, slapping themselves and pulling at their naked skin. They exchange no words, merely go though this bizarre ceremony and then, without acknowledgement, shake their clothes, dress themselves again, climb back into the large silver car and drive off down the road.

As we pull away, I look back at the farmer. He has not moved. He is rigid, standing staring at his outhouse, his brain cranking away in a slow search for some sane explanation. Back at the Villa, my mother, who has adopted her 'Queen-Mother-after-losing-a-horse-race' smile, disappears and shortly afterwards can be seen dunking herself in stately fashion in the swimming pool. Up and down she rises, time after time, submerging herself completely, then sedately surfacing again.

When Ramona goes into the kitchen to tell Carmen, the cook, what has happened, Carmen rushes to a cupboard and takes out a large spray-can full of a noxious flea-killer. This is vile stuff, and one is meant to avoid all direct skin contact when spraying carpets with it. But Carmen takes no prisoners. She proceeds to spray herself all over, in case Ramona has brought the dreaded pests into her spotless kitchen. Ramona is alarmed at this, but there is no stopping Carmen. She sprays the foul-smelling stuff into her hair and all over her head, as if it were some kind of mild perfume. She is now covered in a cloud of poisonous vapour and we are worried about her health, but she is as strong as a rock and, to our great relief, in the days that follow suffers no ill effects whatever.

When the teeming flea-millions have finally been defeated, I realize that I have a problem. I must visit Salvo again to recover the boards, now boasting wonderful, naïve works of art. A few weeks later, Domenic is hesitantly knocking on the green door of Salvo's little house once more. Like a coward I am standing well back. There is an exchange in Maltese and a painted board is thrust through the half-open door. We shout out our thanks and leave as swiftly as we can. Examining the board I am in for a shock. On it there is a crudely painted bird which totally lacks any charm. I cannot understand it. Did he not try? Later, examining photographs I have taken of his wall-paintings, I notice that one of them bears a date: 1940. Over a quarter of a century has passed since he created his exciting wall-images. Now, Salvo is a frail old man, his painting skills long since departed. I have arrived on the scene too late. There will be no exhibition, no great revelation.

But all is not lost. Even in the rubble of the worst disasters one can find a few gems. I will never forget the look of deep, deep puzzlement on the face of that farmer, and the way he froze like a statue in his field, as we fleetingly invaded his slow, measured, and otherwise essentially predictable world.

The memory of his expression of shocked disbelief has made it all worthwhile.

## WHO IS REMOVING THE GREEN DOTS?

AFTER WRITING *The Naked Ape,* I came to the conclusion that there was something missing from the traditional studies of human behaviour. There are plenty of reports on abnormal behaviour, on tribal rites and rituals, on kinship structures and social institutions, on intelligence tests and learning processes, but there is very little indeed on the central subject of ordinary, everyday, human actions. The way we interact with one another in our homes and streets, in shops and restaurants, on beaches and buses, is rarely honoured with serious, observational analysis. Perhaps, for scientists, it is all too commonplace, too familiar. But by the same token, it is at the very heart of what it is to be human, and I decide to make a stab at investigating it in a systematic way.

In my library there are dozens of dictionaries of words, but no dictionaries of human actions. To a zoologist this is a major omission. The first step one takes when starting to study a new species is to draw up what is called an 'ethogram' – that is, a complete, classified list of every type of action that the animal makes. In each case, the movement is carefully described, along with what causes it and what effect it has. In a moment of boldness bordering on arrogance, I decide to do this for the human species, treating it as though it is a new animal species, encountered for the very first time.

In attempting this I will employ a technique that is the precise opposite of the one employed by Sigmund Freud. When the great man had a patient lying on his famous couch in Vienna, he himself sat facing away, so that he could only hear his patient's voice, but could not set eyes on him. I, by contrast, will only watch my subjects and will not listen to a word they say. I will confine myself entirely to non-verbal 'body language'. As a zoologist, I cannot speak to an antelope or ask questions of a lion, so, treating humans in the same way, I will only observe and record.

One spring day I am sitting at a table in the main square of Malta's capital city, Valletta, sipping coffee and chatting to my publisher, Tom Maschler, who has flown out to discuss my next book. I explain what I am proposing to do, and he is slightly alarmed. An encyclopedia of human actions seems like a massive project, taking years and ending up almost unpublishable. But he encourages me to make a start and see where it goes.

We are watching an old man shrugging his shoulders. I point out to Tom that, unlike the English, the Maltese use a directional shrug. When an Englishman shrugs he directs himself forwards, at his companion, regardless of the subject being discussed. A Maltese, however, aims his hands in the general direction of the subject. If, for instance, he is complaining about something political, he will shrug his hands in the direction of the seat of government. If he is complaining about the lack of work in the docks, he will shrug towards the harbour, and so on. It is a tiny difference, but it makes the body language of the Maltese subtly different from that of the English visitors to the island.

We continue to watch. The old man to whom the shrugger is addressing himself suddenly tosses his head backwards, closing his eyes and pursing his lips as he does so. If an Englishman did this, it would be a sign of irritation or scorn. But if this action is done by a Maltese it simply means 'No!' Again, a subtle difference. By spending hours observing the Maltese population, I have already come to understand a whole range of gestures and small communication actions that differ in some slight way from those of the country where I grew up. I do not use these Maltese actions when I am talking to my Maltese friends – it would seem strange to perform a head toss instead of a head shake. But I understand the actions even though I do not personally employ them. This is rather like the condition a human toddler finds itself in – understanding its parents' words before it uses them itself.

As I keep up a running commentary on the body language around us, Tom remarks: 'You look at people like a birdwatcher looks at birds.' 'Yes,' I reply, 'you could call me a manwatcher.' 'That's it,' says Tom, 'that's the title of your next book. We'll call it "Manwatching".' I am none too happy about this, still having in mind my big 'Encyclopedia of Human Actions'. But I make a mental note of it, all the same.

After Tom leaves I decide to set up a special office where I can start assembling my checklist of human body language. The Villa is big, but throughout the summer months it is always full of house guests – friends taking holidays in the sun – and the atmosphere is wrong. I find a spacious office right on the Sliema sea front, rent it and set to work. I take on an assistant, Trisha Pike, the lively, intelligent daughter of an Army officer who is stationed in Malta. We order a dozen huge boards, eight feet tall by three feet wide, and stand them all around the walls. On these we will pin up hundreds of slips of paper, on each of which will be written one human action. We will then be able to juggle these slips around as we improve our classification system.

At first, it seems a daunting task, but as the days pass, something is beginning to emerge. It turns out that human beings do not make as many different types of action as might be imagined. Because we can combine them in many ways and because we can vary their intensity, this gives a false impression that there are countless ways of using the human body. But if you simply take the basic elements involved, and classify those, the picture does not look so confusing.

For example, we move our eyebrows in only five ways – we raise, lower, knit, flash or cock them. We cross our legs in only four different ways – ankle-on-ankle, ankle-on-knee, knee-on-knee, or tight-twine. And we fold our arms in only four different ways – both-hands-showing; left-hand-showing and right-tucked-in; right-hand-showing and left-tucked-in; both-hands-tucked-in.

And so Trisha and I toil on, pursuing our eccentric task of mapping the human ethogram. Weeks pass, then months. The boards are now covered in hundreds of slips. At the same time, we are compiling files of photographs of all the actions. I am out recording actions on the streets, and every newspaper and magazine we can lay our hands on is being hacked to pieces. Slowly the repertoire of human actions is taking shape. It is amazing the way in which, once you have identified a particular action, it starts coming up again and again, in the same sort of context. Nobody has ever named these actions before, so we have to do it ourselves. And the names must be purely descriptive, never implying a particular function or message.

Although everything is going well, we suffer one bizarre technical setback. Each of the slips, with the name of an action written on it, has a coloured ink spot on it, telling us about its source. There are green, blue, red and yellow spots, depending on the way we have obtained our information about each particular gesture. But one morning, when I come into the office, I find that hundreds of these slips have lost their dots. This is impossible: they are inked on, not stuck on. They cannot just disappear. But they have. Trisha and I investigate and find that all the missing spots are green ones. No other colours have vanished. Could the green ink have faded? No, because many green dots do still survive, as brightly coloured as ever.

I am the least superstitious person in the world, but I can't help feeling that there is something eerie taking place here. Nobody else uses the offices, which are completely empty at night. No prankster could have done it, because the ink is indelible. If we had used small, coloured stickers, I can imagine how somebody, for a lark, could break into the office and peel off hundreds of stickers, but ink marks vanishing like this is beyond the ability of any joker. It is almost as if we are dealing with some dotty – in both senses of the word – poltergeist. Could this old house be haunted?

Rejecting all such nonsense, I decide to make a night-time visit, to see if I can get to the bottom of this minor mystery. I drive up quietly at midnight and enter the office as silently as possible. There is a faint light coming through the window, from the street lamps outside. In the darkness I can hear a strange rustling sound. I am definitely not alone. I edge carefully over towards the light switch, feeling for it with my fingers. Now I have it. I take a deep breath and flick it on. As the light floods the room, I am confronted with an astonishing sight.

All over the boards that line the walls of the large room are literally thousands of huge cockroaches. They are frantically busy eating the green spots on the slips of paper. They are ignoring all the other colours. Their tiny jaws are ripping off the surface layers of paper containing the green ink dye. When they have finished with one spot and scraped the paper clean, they move on to the next one.

I have to absorb all this in an instant, because the bright light sends them scuttling for cover. After a few seconds there is not a cockroach to be seen in the entire office. The rustling has stopped and everything is back to normal, except that, once again, there are many green spots missing.

Unlike most people, I rather admire cockroaches. They are an amazingly successful form of life and they also happen to have a particularly beautiful courtship display, in which the male circles his female, flashing his wing-covers like a showy matador. But even I cannot put up with this level of infestation. The poor old cockroaches will have to go.

It is obvious what has happened. Before we converted the apartment into an office, it had an active kitchen. There were plenty of food scraps for the cockroaches. But now, in a sterile office, they find themselves starved of the usual nourishment and are forced to improvise. Examining our large paper-slip-covered boards, they discover the ink-spots. The red, blue and yellow dyes are inorganic and of no nutritional value, but the green dye must be organic in origin and provides them with hundreds of tiny snacks worth pursuing.

We take a break while the building is treated by infestation experts, and then we return to our task. After several more months it is clear that we are reaching saturation point. It would take a professional contortionist now to perform an action we have not identified and classified. And it looks as though there are about three thousand different actions that the human body performs in ordinary everyday life. I now start to write up my results, describing and discussing each action in detail.

At this point, Tom Maschler contacts me to find out how the new book is coming along. I announce proudly that I have reached the eyebrows. There is a pause. Then he asks: 'Are you going up or down?' When I reply 'Down' I sense that he is not a happy publisher. After much debate it is decided that I should use my encyclopedic records as the information base for some less ambitious books, and this is what I do. When all the records have been transferred into files, the office is closed down and a new phase begins.

**NOTE**

THE FIRST BOOK TO EMERGE FROM THIS STUDY WAS *INTIMATE BEHAVIOUR*. I THEN STARTED WORK ON THE LARGER VOLUME, *MANWATCHING*, BUT IT

SOON BECAME CLEAR THAT I NEEDED TO MAKE FIELD OBSERVATIONS ON A
MUCH WIDER RANGE OF CULTURES. WITH THIS IN MIND, RAMONA AND I
STARTED PLANNING OUR RETURN TO ENGLAND AND TO MY OLD
UNIVERSITY AT OXFORD.

## PUT HIM DOWN, SYLVIA

W HEN THE BRILLIANT Canadian sociologist Erving Goffman
made observations on the behaviour of doctors in operating
theatres, he discovered to his surprise that they often told
risqué jokes and engaged in light-hearted banter while
performing surgery. He came to the conclusion that this was
not, as an outsider might imagine, a crude form of disrespect
for their anaesthetized patients, but a valuable way of defusing
the tension of a life-and-death situation, and that it helped to
reduce the enormity of what they were doing to an acceptable
level.

I have noticed similar tendencies in senior police officers,
High Court judges, airline pilots and ships' captains. Put two
of them together and the irreverence soon surfaces. Put two
from different disciplines together and it even becomes
competitive. Once, at lunch with a senior judge and a senior
surgeon, I eavesdropped on their fantasy of how to stamp out
theft in Britain. The judge would introduce the Middle East
punishment of chopping off the hands of a convicted felon.
The surgeon would freeze the hands and then, if the criminal
managed to get off on appeal, he would stitch them back on –
for a large fee.

This kind of outrageous badinage by powerful men is a
great safety-valve, but it might shock the general public if they
were witness to it. I have to admit that I am rather taken aback

by a particular case of it that happens during a party at the Villa. Among the guests are two local doctors. They are gossiping in the corner of the drawing room at a point farthest from the entrance door. When a new guest arrives he or she can be seen clearly but cannot overhear what the two doctors are saying. As each guest enters the room the medics make a pronouncement: 'Heart, stroke, cancer, stroke, heart, heart' and so on. They explain to me that it is possible to guess at a single glance the most probable cause of death of any adult. I find this rather disturbing, but listen to their comments with morbid fascination.

I am now beginning to see the pattern: heart/stroke/cancer correspond, respectively, to excitable and emotional/ controlled and clever/tense and nice. Of course, any one of these people may be knocked down by a bus or shot by a jealous lover, but if they manage to avoid the exceptional forms of death, they will probably end up succumbing to one of these 'big three'.

The medical emergencies that members of the general public who spend endless hours watching hospital melo-dramas on television knowingly refer to as 'cardiac arrest', 'cerebrovascular accident' and 'malignant carcinoma', and which doctors, with their fancy technical jargon, call 'heart', 'stroke' and 'cancer', account for most of us in the end, and my medical guests are simply playing a macabre game to keep themselves amused. What interests me about their comments is that they are not entirely fanciful. Angry body language does seem to have a clear link to heart attacks. Strokes do seem to chop down the more controlled individuals among us, who may appear calm but beneath the surface are not. And only nice people seem to get cancer. Of course, these are wild exaggerations, but the grains of truth in them start me thinking, yet again, about how rarely we treat human body language as a serious scientific subject.

But my thoughts in this direction are put on hold for the moment by an unusual offer from another of our guests, a young military doctor who is serving with the British Army on Malta. It emerges that he has been treating some of the prostitutes who ply their trade in Valletta's infamous 'Gut', known to all sailors as the most lively red-light district in the Mediterranean. He asks whether our guest of honour (an old friend of ours from London, who is a Harley Street surgeon) and I would like to accompany him on an observational visit to this famous location. If so, he will arrange it with the Provost Marshal – the head of the military police – who will ensure our safety. We are too intrigued to turn him down. The American fleet is in harbour and the Gut will be heaving with life. Also, we will have the luxury of being well chaperoned.

The Gut is a long, very narrow street that runs the full length of Valletta, from top to bottom. Its official name is Strait Street and, appropriately enough, it is a Mecca for straight sex. At its upper end, the girls in the sailors' bars are all very young; here, for instance, one finds the Lolita Bar. Then, as you travel farther and farther down to its lower end, the women get progressively older. At the very bottom of the Gut, the joy has gone. It becomes a very sad scene indeed.

We meet up with the Provost Marshal and start making our way down. There is a great deal of laughter, screaming, singing, loud music and the sound of breaking glass. This is a noisy, bustling, frenetic place, bursting with humanity – hungry, but not for food. As we are strolling down the long slope of the Gut, a hand snakes out and grabs the end of my necktie, pulling it horizontally into a shadowy doorway. The Provost Marshal, who is walking in front of me, senses that I have suddenly stopped walking. He glances over his shoulder and, in a matter-of-fact voice, calls out: 'Put him down, Sylvia.' As if by magic, the tie is released and swings back, like a silk pendulum, to its more usual, vertical position.

Despite its seeming chaos, on closer inspection the Gut is a highly structured, territorially organized microcosm. The Provost Marshal knows where everyone is likely to be, and is pointing out the individual girls as we drift past them, with the explanatory tones of a holiday tour guide. In each case, he describes their particular venereal diseases, for the professional interest of the two doctors. How sad that the Maltese Church forbids these women the use of protective contraceptives. Even the old arch-enemy, syphilis, is present here.

After showing us the sights, the Provost Marshal departs and we decide to sample the atmosphere inside one of the bars. It is a toss-up between the Union Jack Bar, the Splendid Lounge Bar, the Carmen Bar and Ye Old-Vic Music Dancing Hall. We choose the busiest one, on the principle that we will be less conspicuous there. Inside, the noise is deafening. We retreat to a corner and my surgeon friend sets off to buy a round of drinks. We have decided to keep the order simple and I suggest that the local beer, called Hop Leaf, would be a wise choice. He struggles through a swarm of arguing American sailors. One, a lanky white boy, who seems to be at least seven feet tall, is shouting into the face of a muscular black shipmate. Their dispute appears to concern the favours of an unusually attractive Maltese girl. There are many pretty girls, dotted around the room, laughing and flirting with the crowd of sailors. The whole scene is like something out of an old Hollywood musical. At any moment I expect Gene Kelly to leap onto a table and start tap-dancing. But, in the real world, something quite different is about to occur.

Our surgeon has just made it to the bar and, above the din, is shouting his order: 'Three Hot Leaves, please.' At the very moment that he calls out his slightly garbled request, all hell breaks loose. The lanky sailor flings himself headlong across the crowded room, taking bystanders, tables and glasses with him. He and the black sailor are now wrestling, with a level of violence that suggests the imminent death of one of them. There is even the flash of a knife-blade somewhere in the flurry of frantic movement.

For me, this is a golden opportunity to observe human fighting behaviour at first hand. From watching newscasts and reading newspapers, anyone would imagine that the whole world is awash with human violence and that it would be the easiest kind of behaviour to study in the field, but this is not so. In reality, human fighting behaviour is extremely rare. In fact, the most remarkable thing about the human species is that we are capable of living in unnaturally overcrowded populations without suffering from constant brawling and mayhem. It is a remarkable testimony to the innate peacefulness of our species that this is so. Few other animals would behave with such restraint if they were forced to live in our wildly overpopulated condition.

So, for me, the serious fight I am watching is an unexpected bonus. I don't have time to be shocked or frightened because I am trying so hard to follow the exact moves being made by the two men. One feature of their encounter does become immediately clear: it is not even remotely like a John Wayne bar-brawl. In the movies, where every blow has to be carefully choreographed, the fights proceed at a ridiculously slow pace and develop a characteristic kind of rhythm: crash, wallop, crash, wallop. This real fight is performed at lightning speed and with a kind of frantic clumsiness. What makes it so scary for the onlookers is that it can change direction in an instant, flattening people in its wake.

Then the barman presses a hidden warning-bell beneath his counter and, as he does so, I experience a strange sensation. The floor beneath my feet is rising up at an increasing angle. Jumping to one side, I discover that I have been standing on a large trapdoor. As soon as it is fully open, all the little bar-girls run screaming towards it, plunge down the steps beneath it and disappear. The door slams down again and I resume my place in the corner of the room. The bar is now suddenly entirely male, and far less crowded. The fighters have reached a point where they are flat out on the floor, writhing and rolling and twisting as they attempt to destroy one another. There is no ritual here, only all-out physical assault. As they spin about, chairs and tables crash and slide, until at last the door bursts open and the American naval police arrive. The fighters are prised apart and dragged outside to a waiting van. As soon as they have gone, the barman taps on the floor with his heel and the trapdoor beneath my feet rises up again. The little girls troop out from their hiding place and, within minutes, the whole place is back to normal, if one can use such a word in this context.

At sea, the American fleet is 'dry', so when they come ashore for 'R and R' (officially : rest and recreation; unofficially: rage and ravage) they are unpractised at hard drinking. Add to that the temporary release from naval discipline, the presence of bar-girls, and for good measure a racial element, and you have a recipe for sure-fire mayhem. It is clear that what we have witnessed is a commonplace event here and I make a mental note that, for my future studies of human fighting actions, the Gut is a ready-made laboratory.

My surgeon friend appears at last with our three beers and I do my best to convince him that by ordering 'Hot Leaves' instead of 'Hop Leaf Beer', he has unwittingly used an obscene phrase that has triggered the uproar. He doesn't believe me. We pass the rest of the evening observing the various courtship rituals of the human animal, and further desperate knife-fights in the alleyways and doorways. Eventually it is time to depart this, the most notorious of all red-light districts, for the peace of the Villa.

The rest of Malta is fast asleep by now and, as we drive

through the darkly deserted streets, it feels as though we have been attending some strange kind of tribal festival. The whole scene in the bar was so melodramatic, it is hard to absorb the fact that it was for real. We are both tired, and have long since stopped talking, but as we approach the Villa gates, and our waiting wives, my old friend smiles and makes one final comment. 'I suppose we had better perform tonight,' he says.

## NOTE

THE GUT HAS LONG SINCE LOST ITS REPUTATION AS A DEN OF VICE. STRAIT STREET IS STILL THERE, OF COURSE, BUT THE BARS ARE ALL SHUTTERED AND THE SIGNS ABOVE THEM ARE BROKEN AND PEELING. WHEN I RETURNED WITH FILM CREW, THIRTY YEARS AFTER THAT FIRST, MEMORABLE VISIT, WE FOUND IT DERELICT AND DESERTED. ITS GLORY DAYS HAVE FADED INTO HISTORY, REMEMBERED ONLY BY OLD SAILORS AT REUNIONS WHERE THEY RETELL THEIR MEDITERRANEAN ADVENTURES.

MANY YEARS AFTER THAT FIRST VISIT, I HEARD FROM MY SURGEON FRIEND THAT THE GUT HAD COME BACK TO HAUNT HIM IN AN UNEXPECTED WAY. HAVING RISEN TO A LEVEL OF GREAT PROFESSIONAL EMINENCE, HE AND OTHER SENIOR DOCTORS WERE SITTING ON AN APPOINTMENT SELECTION BOARD IN LONDON. A YOUNG DOCTOR WAS USHERED INTO THE FORBIDDING INTERVIEW ROOM AND SAT NERVOUSLY BEFORE THE PANEL. MY FRIEND THOUGHT HE RECOGNIZED HIM BUT COULDN'T PLACE HIM. IN ORDER TO PUT THE YOUNG MAN AT HIS EASE, HE INTRODUCED A PERSONAL NOTE: 'HAVEN'T WE MET SOMEWHERE BEFORE?' TO HIS SURPRISE, THIS SEEMED TO MAKE THE YOUNG DOCTOR EVEN MORE TENSE. MY FRIEND TRIED AGAIN: 'I AM SURE WE HAVE, BUT I CAN'T PLACE IT. WHERE EXACTLY *DID* WE MET?' AT THIS, THE YOUNG MAN COULD ONLY STAMMER OUT THE TRUTH: 'IT WAS IN A BROTHEL, SIR, IN THE GUT, IN MALTA.' MY FRIEND'S DISTINGUISHED COLLEAGUES HAVE BEEN DINING OUT ON THIS FOR YEARS.

## BOATS WITH MOUSTACHES

———◇◇◇———

IT IS WINTER NOW and Malta is quiet. The visitors have gone and the beaches are deserted. The sea-front cafés are empty, but there is a brooding presence here. Large pairs of eyes gaze out to sea. In fishing villages, small inlets and sheltered bays all around the coastline, the extraordinary painted boats unique to the Maltese islands are keeping their unblinking stare fixed on the waves, as if expecting a marine monster to break surface at any moment.

For these are boats with faces. On each side of the prow, centred on a triangular patch of colour called the *mustacc* (moustache) there is a large, carved, wooden eye. The effect of these eyes is to convert each vessel into a huge piece of surreal, multicoloured sculpture – more of a 'being' than a vessel. In fact, to enter a Maltese fishing village is like attending a huge, open-air art exhibition. The exhibits are pieces of decorated wood that also happen to be functional seagoing vessels. Their impact is immediate and inescapable. Few visitors are immune to it, and to walk past a harbour full of local boats without experiencing a strong reaction requires a rare kind of visual censorship.

Why is this? What is it about these small craft that results in their repeatedly being selected as the subjects for travel-book dust-jackets, as centrepieces for coloured postcards and countless watercolours and oil-paintings, and as the reason for special tour-bus visits? It is easy enough, of course, to provide a superficial answer, but much more difficult to find a reply that will stand up to careful scrutiny. It is not enough, for example, to say simply that the boats are gaily coloured; buses are gaily coloured, but no one organizes tourist visits to a bus terminus. Nor is it enough to say that they are appealing merely because they are so unusual, for their appeal lasts long after familiarity has failed to breed contempt. Nor is it their picturesque marine setting, for they appear even more extraordinary when encountered shored-up in a narrow side-street. It has to be admitted, finally, that there is something special about the boats themselves and it is this something that intrigues me.

A check with the Maltese Department of Agriculture and Fisheries reveals that there is a grand total of 948 registered fishing vessels, of which 743 fall into the category of traditional 'moustached boats'. They are located at about thirty sites, scattered around the coasts of Malta and Gozo. There are three kinds – the oldest type being the slender *firillas*, of which thirty-six survive, all over thirty years old. The more heavy-bodied *luzzus* (pronounced 'loot-zoos'), of which there are 336, have largely replaced them. In addition, there are 371 smaller, flat-backed boats called *kajjiks* (pronounced 'ky-icks').

The most noticeable characteristic of these fishing boats is their multicoloured decoration, so I design an outline drawing of one and then get it printed up as a set of black-and-white cards. Armed with a stack of these and a pocketful of coloured pens, I set off for the nearest fishing village. After a little practice I find I can fill in all the colours of a boat in a few minutes, and I soon have a stack of these standardized coloured drawings for analysis.

The pleasure of searching for new fishing-village locations and then sitting in the cool winter sun, filling in my cards, soon becomes addictive and I can't stop. Obsessively, I go on until I have recorded every visible moustached boat I can find. Counting them up, I find that I have 396. I am told that the

missing ones are either on Gozo or shut away in boat-houses
and only brought out when their owners feel like taking them
to sea. In order to make percentages easy to calculate, I am
determined to find four more, to round my total up to 400.
Introducing Gozo into the equation is too complicated, so I
spend some time lurking about Maltese boat-houses, hoping
for glimpses of hidden vessels. With the help of a few friendly
fishermen, who are flattered by the serious interest I am
taking in their boats, I finally manage to complete my set of
400 cards, and set about analysing the results. Every boat has
twenty visible components, each treated as a separate entity
when the boat is painted. This gives me a total of 8,000 colour
patches to analyse.

I solemnly write an eighty-page paper on this analysis. This
is a perverse activity, because I know that it is unpublishable.
There are no journals that deal with quantitative studies of
fishing-boat decoration and, as far as I know, if one did appear
I would be its only subscriber. But I am driven on by a feeling
that art criticism and aesthetic theory has somehow lost its
way. It has developed a foolish attitude that visual art is
something that can only be taken seriously if it has been
exhibited in a gallery or sold at Sotheby's.

To the art world, it would be obvious that my 'pretty little
boats' should not be seriously considered as 'works of art'.
This attitude reflects an unhappy prejudice of modern times.
In an era of growing respect for the fine arts, we are in danger
of overlooking the fact that human art existed for thousands of
years before art galleries were invented. The all too prevalent
idea that 'real' art is confined to non-functional objects, such as
painting and sculpture, is a sad comment on our society. More
and more we are prepared to accept ugliness or, at least,
aesthetic dullness, in our living environments and in the
common objects with which we surround ourselves. In an
effort to counterbalance this trend, we stuff our great galleries

and museums full of the glorious art treasures of the past. Then we excuse the increasing aesthetic indolence of our daily lives by occasional attendance at the insulated splendour of our art 'cathedrals'.

It would be difficult to explain this attitude to the members of earlier, tribal societies, where art and craft were one. For them, all art objects were functional and part of their daily lives. There was no polarization between aesthetics and utility, and their lives were the richer for it. The main reason for the change that has taken place in recent times has been the dramatic population increase to which our societies have been subjected. The inevitable accompaniment to these increases has been the need for the mass production of common objects. Instead of designing, constructing and decorating the objects with which we surround ourselves, we purchase them ready-made and complete. We still have a degree of aesthetic choice, of course, but the selection of a colour or pattern may be severely restricted, or even eliminated, by the manufacturer. In such cases the manufacturer himself is still exercising an aesthetic choice, but his overriding, wide-scale decisions automatically blunt the choices at the level of the individual members of the community.

In the modern world, this 'blunted-choice' trend is growing rapidly, with an inevitable reduction in the aesthetic diversity of everyday objects. However, if the pressure towards aesthetic uniformity is great, it is not yet overwhelming. There are pockets of resistance everywhere. Even the most sombrely conformist of citizens may break loose occasionally and exercise an unblunted aesthetic choice in the selection and arrangement of the colours and shapes of some aspect of his daily life. But not surprisingly, the best examples are to be found in areas where the influences of urbanization are at a minimum, which brings us back to the Maltese fishing villages.

The fishermen responsible for the island-wide 'marine art' exhibition are, of course, unaware of how they are contributing to it. Each one carefully repaints his boat each year (a practical requirement, given the assault of the elements) and has to make a colour choice when applying paint to each section of his vessel. The simplest solution is for him to paint the whole boat a single colour. This happens in some countries, but not here. Here, each of the twenty identifiable parts of the boat is treated as a separate visual entity. Most of the colours employed make no practical difference to the usefulness of the vessel; the decisions are being made for purely visual, non-maintenance reasons. The only exception concerns the bottom of the boat, which is usually covered with a special copper-based anti-fouling paint.

Without going through all the details, my analysis of the 400 moustached boats reveals that there are several principles operating that help to make the vessels visually exciting.

First, it is important for each boat to say 'I am a Maltese boat' and also 'I belong to a particular fisherman'. The authoritarian way to do this would be to have all Maltese boats painted red, and for each one to have its owner's name printed on the side. That is the kind of rigid ruling that would be imposed by a government department. But such rules do not exist here in Malta. The colour pattern of each boat is left entirely up to the individual owner. With this freedom, the two statements are still made, but expressed in a much more interesting way.

It works like this: the bigger a section of the boat happens to be, the more conservative is the choice of colour. The smaller the detail, the more variable the colour. The result of this is that, from a distance, all the boats are clearly labelled as 'Maltese', but when you come closer and the smaller details begin to show up, the individual variations are revealed.

To give just two examples of this: the side of the boat is blue in over eighty per cent of cases. This is a big area and the 'traditional pressure' is great to conform here. By contrast, the little knob that appears on the wash-boards is yellow in only forty per cent of cases, despite the fact that yellow is the favourite colour here. In other words, a big patch of colour is twice as likely to conform with Maltese tradition as a small one.

So the colours send out two messages, one national and one personal. But neither message is fixed; no colour dominates completely on any part of the boat. There are always variations, and these variations themselves vary with the size of the unit. To make matters more complicated, there are also regional variations, with some colours being favoured more in the south (like yellow moustaches, for example) and others more in the north (like red moustaches). Again, this is not a rigid rule, like, say, the colours of local football teams. There are always plenty of exceptions. And it is the presence of these minor exceptions that helps to create the complex visual appeal of the boats clustered in each fishing village.

As a result of the small, personal colour details of the fishing boats, the colour combination on any particular vessel is unique. Well, nearly. To be precise, 398 of the 400 boats display unique combinations. But there are two that are identical to each other in every respect. Puzzled by this, I investigate and find that, unusually, these two boats both belong to the same fisherman.

Other unwritten rules that help to keep the boats visually attractive are: when painting the boat, put one bright hue next to a contrasting one; put a light colour next to a dark one; and make each boat multicoloured, employing at least five or six different colours.

When asked why they paint their boats in particular colours, the fishermen always reply in the same way, saying that it is 'just the way we like them'. Nobody admits to any guidance or instruction from anyone else or from any official authority. Bearing in mind that it takes the fishermen a number of days each year to repaint their boats, it is clear that they have a deep respect for the craft in which they regularly set out to sea. It is almost as if their boats have become members of their family, rather than inanimate objects. When they are first launched, they are 'christened' – being adorned with an olive branch and blessed by a priest. If a close relative dies, the boat is dressed in mourning, like the rest of the family. This is done either by painting the moustache black or by painting a black 'armband' on the vertical stem-post. These black marks will remain in place for the rest of the year, until the annual repainting comes around again.

Also helping to make the boats more human is the pair of specially carved wooden eyes on the moustache. They turn each vessel into a 'person' and give it a much stronger presence. This is an ancient tradition, going right back to early Egypt. Eyes were also painted on the bows of Roman warships and can be seen today in several other countries apart from Malta, including places as far apart as Portugal and Bali.

The superstition underlying these bow-eyes is that their unblinking gaze will be able to 'outstare' the Evil Eye and in this way protect the vessel and its occupants from the powers of darkness. It has always been believed that any form of good luck will attract the Devil and provoke him into causing havoc. So, if fishermen have a good catch, they then fear that something awful will happen to them – but not if their all-powerful bow-eyes are there to defend them.

In Malta's Grand Harbour this superstition has literally been carved in stone. There, a prominent limestone turret, high up on the battlements, displays a huge single eye, staring out over the docks and offering extra protection to the ships sheltering in the creeks below. This island has, in the past, suffered major sieges, from the Turks to the Nazis. It has even seen the decapitated heads of prisoners used as cannon-balls and fired across the harbour. But the attackers have long since vanished and Malta is still here in all its architectural glory. And the fishermen still enjoy good fishing every year, so the reputation of the protective eyes is safe and it is unlikely that they will be discarded for many years to come.

**NOTE**

A QUARTER OF A CENTURY LATER, THE EYES ARE STILL THERE AND APPEAR SET TO CONTINUE THEIR PROTECTIVE GAZE INDEFINITELY.

## THE LATE JIMMY BUNG

I HAVE NO IDEA who Jimmy Bung was, but I have reason to believe that he is dead. I cannot be certain, however, because the sign that has immortalized his name is ambiguous. It reads: *The Fellowship Bar* and then, underneath, it says: *Late Jimmy Bung's Bar.* Now it could simply be that Jimmy Bung retired and the new owner, not wishing to alienate old established customers, retained the earlier name below his new one. Or it could be that, like the Monty Python parrot, Jimmy Bung is deceased, is no more, has departed, has passed on, has been bunged in a hole in the ground.

I will never know the answer because I refuse to enter the bar and ask the barman the truth. This is not because I dislike the local beer – it is excellent – or the local soft drink (called Kinnie, it is deliciously bitter-sweet and unique to the Maltese islands) but because I wish to keep the mystery of Jimmy Bung alive in my imagination. As long as I know nothing more about him, other than that he has relinquished ownership of his famous sea-front bar, he will retain his mystique for me.

The point is that Bung is not a Maltese name. There is no Bung listed in the Malta phone book. And a foreigner would hardly be allowed to run a sailor's bar on Grand Harbour. I am told that there are some Chinese Bungs living in Hong Kong, so perhaps Jimmy was an Oriental Bung who jumped ship in Malta and became a popular local mascot. Alternatively, perhaps Bung is a nickname and is derived from the bung you put in a barrel. There is a Mr Bung's Brewery somewhere in England that may have adopted the name in this way. Perhaps Jimmy Bung was some kind of fictional, legendary nautical figure, well known to every old salt who has ever sailed the Med. I shall never know.

These rambling thoughts are by way of saying that, when in Malta, it is worth looking at the name-plates, signs and titles displayed in public places. They are a delight. You enter a tiny, remote village, little changed since the fifteenth century, and there, at its very heart, next to the church, is the *Elvis Presley Bar*. Even the lorries have names. These are not daubed on, but exquisitely hand-painted onto the bodywork, along with other, ornate decorative devices, as if every one of these exhaust-belching mechanical monsters were really a rare illuminated manuscript. As three lorries trundle past, each named after a Catholic saint, you begin to think this must be an exclusively religious custom, but then the next one arrives and it goes by the name of *Cliff Richard*. (I know he is a saintly lad, but all the same …)

Wander around the yacht marina and again the names are full of intrigue. What can one make of vessels christened *Illi Mani, Cheng-Ho, La Kebekoise, Torgon, Callalloo, Koonawarra* or *Omm Sadina*? Whatever happened to the good old standbys like *Seahorse* and *Lady Luck*?

The names given to some of the shops provide a useful clue as to how many of us must have acquired our modern surnames. One shop will be called something like 'Fred the

Grocer'; another will be 'George the Plumber', but then you see one where the title has been abbreviated by dropping the 'the'. So 'John the Butcher' becomes 'John Butcher'. And 'Joe's Garage' becomes 'Joe Garage'. They are even listed in the Malta phone book in this way. It is easy to see how many English surnames, such as Baker, Carpenter or Barber could have arisen. With us the process has been completed long ago, but here it is still in progress.

## A VISIT FROM ANUBIS

ONE BRIGHT SPRING AFTERNOON an unannounced visitor arrives at the Villa. He is a lean red dog, silent, swift and dignified. He inspects the premises hurriedly, like a commando checking for terrorists. Once he has decided that the building is 'clean', he pauses for a moment and allows himself to be photographed at the top of the stone steps leading down into the garden. He even permits our young son, Jason, still a toddler and not much taller than himself, to rest a friendly hand on his back, despite the fact that he is a complete stranger. There is nothing playful or fawningly friendly about this dog. But neither is there the slightest trace of hostility. Looking at him, we suddenly feel like intruders on his island. He gives the impression of having been here for thousands of years. As we later discover, there is some truth in this.

Our visitor is clearly a canine aristocrat, but he does not belong to any breed we know. However, Carmello, the gardener, who speaks little English, recognizes him immediately. '*Kelb tal-Fenek*,' he explains, 'farmer's dog.' But this is no guard-dog mongrel of the kind we have seen barking from the flat rooftops of farm buildings in the Maltese countryside. Nor is it a shaggy sheepdog. This elegant animal, with the grace of a greyhound and the personality of a wolf, is a noble beast. His short, reddish-brown coat gleams and glistens in the sunlight. His huge, erect ears twist and turn, picking up every tiny sound. His lanky, streamlined body looks as though it has just leapt from an Egyptian wall-painting. This cannot be a farmer's dog – this surely is sacred Anubis himself.

As if to add to his mystical quality, he suddenly vanishes, departing as quickly and as silently as he arrived. Not once during his brief visit did he attempt to ingratiate himself with us. In fact, he barely acknowledged our presence in his domain. He is unlike any dog I have ever encountered before, and my curiosity is aroused. Travelling into the most remote parts of the island, I keep an eye open for him, or one of his kind. And I am not disappointed: there is a whole population of them. But why have we not been aware of this before? They seem to be one of Malta's best-kept secrets – a magnificent, pure breed of dog, unknown to the outside world. I ask what the name *Kelb tal-Fenek* means and am told that, literally translated, it is 'Dog of the Rabbit'. I have once or twice seen a wild rabbit near the clifftops and recall now that they are the same colour – red rabbits, chased by red dogs.

So why is the Maltese Rabbit Dog so little known? The answer comes when we visit a dog show, a rare event on Malta, that is being held at the nearby San Anton Gardens. Looking over the entries, it is clear that imported dogs are the only ones appreciated by these competitive Maltese dog owners. There is only one truly Maltese dog on show – a magnificent Rabbit Dog, brought along by his proud farmer-owner. To our eyes, he is 'Best in Show', as they say, by a million miles. But the judges completely ignore him, giving the top prize to a charming but mediocre German Shepherd

Dog. When we gently ask why the Rabbit Dog has been ignored, we are told that such animals have no pedigree and cannot be taken seriously. How wrong can people be?

On investigation, it turns out that the ancestors of the Maltese Rabbit Dogs were brought to the Maltese islands about three thousand years ago by Phoenician traders, who probably filched them from the ancient Egyptians. The Egyptians were brilliant domesticators and were notoriously possessive about their companion animals, doing their best to keep them strictly for themselves. The same applied to their cats, but the Phoenicians, who have been rudely described as the 'second-hand car dealers' of the ancient world, were ingenious and resourceful traders, and soon managed to spirit a few of these valuable beasts away for sale abroad. They introduced both the precious Egyptian domestic cats ('you are overrun by rats and mice?... we have something here to solve your problem') and the fast Egyptian hounds ('forget your old traps, we have something here to catch your supper for you'). So perhaps the mysterious visitor to the villa really was Anubis, after all.

Ironically, the fact that urban Malta has largely ignored the farmers' Rabbit Dog has protected it from interbreeding and has kept it pure for century after century. Overlooked and isolated in remote corners of the island, this magnificent beast is probably one of the most ancient, pure-bred dogs in the entire world. Malta has a canine treasure, despised by the locals because it is not an exotic import.

Discussing this dog with other British residents on the island, we discover that we are not alone in our admiration for the breed. Indeed, a neighbour has already acquired several with the idea of exporting them to England as a breeding nucleus, to start a pedigree line there. Tragically, she is killed in a car crash shortly afterwards and the project nearly falters, but others step in and, at last, the Maltese Rabbit Dog is to become established in Britain. All that is wrong with it is its name, and this will soon be changed to the much grander-sounding Pharaoh Hound – a title to which it can justly lay claim.

The Pharaoh Hound is not the only canine gem to emerge from these tiny islands. They have also given the world two other fascinating breeds, the first appropriately named the Maltese Dog and the second inappropriately named the Chihuahua. Strangely, I have not set eyes on a Maltese Dog anywhere here, but have seen plenty of tiny Chihuahuas being taken for gentle walks by their (usually very large) owners in the suburbs of Sliema. Because of their respective names these two breeds have wrongly been seen as originating from two widely separated sources. However, early authors made it clear, as long ago as the seventeenth century, that there have always been two distinct types of miniature dog on Malta – the long-haired and the short-haired. The long-haired has managed to keep its name as the Maltese Dog, but for some reason (perhaps the hot climate) it has become less and less favoured here, until it has all but vanished from the island.

The short-haired breed, originally known as the Maltese Pocket Dog, was so popular that, centuries ago, examples were exported to nearby countries such as France, Portugal and Spain. They were later taken to Mexico by the early Spanish explorers. From there they eventually found their way to North America, where they were named after the place in which they had been found in Mexico – namely, the state of Chihuahua. Under this new name they were assumed, incorrectly, to be an ancient Mexican breed. Today there are delightful little 'Chihuahuas' trotting about the streets of Malta, underlining the true, Maltese origin of this, the smallest of all dog breeds in the world.

**NOTE**

BEFORE LONG, THE PHARAOH HOUND OBTAINED INTERNATIONAL RECOGNITION IN THE SHOW RING. WHEN THIS HAPPENED, IT FINALLY CAME

TO BE FULLY APPRECIATED IN ITS NATIVE HOME AND, IN 1974, WAS DECLARED THE 'NATIONAL HOUND OF MALTA'. IN 1977 ITS IMAGE EVEN APPEARED ON ONE OF THE MALTESE COINS. LOCAL EXPERTS THEN STARTED TO VOICE THEIR DISAPPROVAL OF ITS NEW NAME, WHICH LINKED IT TO EGYPT RATHER THAN MALTA, AND INSISTED ON A RETURN TO ITS ORIGINAL MALTESE TITLE OF *KELB TAL-FENEK*. THE INTERNATIONAL DOG WORLD HAS IGNORED THIS REQUEST, HOWEVER, AND IT HAS TO BE SAID THAT, WITHOUT ITS MORE GLAMOROUS TITLE, THE BREED WOULD PROBABLY NEVER HAVE ENJOYED SUCH A WORLDWIDE SUCCESS.

## THE ECLIPSE OF THE BRAIN

F OR A SUN-STARVED Englishman, the Maltese climate is a revelation. Eating at a stone table in the garden on freshly caught fish bought from the morning market, it is possible to reach up, pick a lemon and cut and squeeze it without moving more than a few feet. Bunches of grapes hang down over the table, and a distinction that I have never made before dawns on me: in England I always ate dead fruit. Here I am eating live fruit. The difference in fragrance and texture is such that one never forgets it and never enjoys dead fruit in the old way again.

Another change that surprises me is that I soon stop wearing a wrist-watch. As I am driving an English visitor along a Maltese country lane, he asks me the time. Without thinking, I look up at the sun and say '2.30'. I am not showing off. I am not even aware that I have done anything unusual, but my guest refuses to believe this.

These changes happen gradually, imperceptibly, as you adapt to a foreign climate. Another shift is in the way you expose yourself to the sun's rays. You never see a

Mediterranean resident sunbathing. Nobody who lives under incessantly blue skies treats the sun as if it were a giant sunbed. But as soon as our visitors, freshly arrived from England, have unpacked, the first thing they do is to lie out by the pool and begin soaking up the sun's rays. The only exception to this is David Attenborough, and when I point out to him that he never sunbathes, he replies: 'To the tourist the sun is a friend, but to the traveller it is an enemy.' Then he laughs and says: 'My God, that sounds pompous.' But he is right – if you live in a hot, sunny climate, your skin slowly tans, but doesn't burn. Little Jason, born here and out on the beach every day of his life, now has hair that is bleached blond by the sun. His skin is golden-brown and he has never experienced sunburn, despite spending hours splashing about in the sea, day after day.

Daily exposure to the bright light of the sun also has a strange effect on your state of mind. It calms you and gives you a sense of optimism. It starts me thinking about where the greatest leaps in civilization have occurred. In the ancient world, northern Europe was a barbaric, primitive region. The Middle East and the Mediterranean were the centre for all human progress, from the earliest developments in Mesopotamia, through Egypt, Greece and then Rome. As the centuries sped past, the focus began to move up into cooler regions until northern Europe became the centre for innovation and cultural growth.

If you visit Athens or Cairo today, it is hard to imagine how such places could once have been at the heart of human creativity. The heat is sapping and the sun softens the brain. These are not the places to be beavering away tirelessly at some revolutionary new invention. Yet that is what once occurred there. Was the climate cooler then? The evidence suggests not. Did the inhabitants only become intellectually active in the cool, winter months? That is certainly true for me.

Perhaps the growth of civilization was seasonal, moving forward in short annual bursts. In northern Europe we never have to think of such things. There are no seasons for work – we work all year round. Artificial heating gets us through the winter, and we only have to struggle through the three or four really hot days of summer.

Certainly, for myself, the time will come when I will have to get back into the lousy northern climate, just to reactivate my brain-cells. Down here I am becoming increasingly relaxed, to the point of indolence. It is a sweet life, but I suspect it could easily become sickly sweet.

I am given an unexpected jolt by my young son, Jason. When he is four and a half years old, I take him out into the villa garden to show him an unusual event – an eclipse of the sun. As the moon moves over and darkens the sun, I try to explain to him what is happening, but it is not easy with one so young. He ponders it for a moment and then startles me by saying: 'I am not your son, I am your moon and I will eclipse you.'

Perhaps the time really is coming when I shall have to move on and explore somewhere else, somewhere a little less seductive. An author friend, Hunter Davies, who, like me, has been on the island for some months, tells me that he is going to look for new pastures because, as he says: 'Last Thursday I realized that I had managed to reach a stage where it was possible to take the whole day just to make a cup of tea.'

The trouble is that it is such fun being here on this delightfully rocky little island that it will be hard to break free. But there is so much more to explore – so many more countries to investigate. If I follow my ancestral pattern I will not live past my sixties. I know this because, when I took ten of my male ancestors and averaged their life-spans, it gave me a personal prediction of sixty-one years. That only leaves me about two more decades in which to visit the 180 countries that I have yet to see. So little time, so much to do …

## THE DEVIL ON THE ROOFTOPS

IN THE GROUNDS of the Villa there are some old farm buildings. Inspecting them one day I notice that one of them is adorned with a pair of bull's horns, attached high up on an outside wall. I am told that this was put there to protect the farm animals from the Evil Eye. The animals have long since departed, but the horns remain. Domenic, the driver, asks if I would like to be similarly protected in the studio I have set up above the garage. I may not be as valuable as a pig or a cow, but even so, a little extra protection never goes amiss, so I agree.

Domenic disappears and a few hours later can be heard hammering a nail into my studio door, fixing a fresh pair of horns there, horns that he has just rescued from the local abattoir. I enquire whether this is a local tradition and he tells me that, all over the island, in the rural districts, houses and farm buildings are defended from evil in this way. On my next trip into the Maltese countryside, with a new 'searching image' in my mind, I discover so many protective horns that I am ashamed not to have spotted them before. They are everywhere. Some are sculptured or modelled, but most are the real thing. Some are painted or embellished; others are as nature made them. The vast majority are positioned on the skylines of the buildings, so that the horns jut defiantly outwards like cannon on a ship or a fort. The farther away from the urban areas that you travel, the more of them you see.

I am intrigued to learn more about this tradition, and I

discover that it is thousands of years old. Indeed, the oldest known town in the world – Çatal Hüyük in Anatolia (in what is now Turkey), which flourished eight thousand years ago – had horns displayed on its walls. The bull was important throughout the ancient world. He stood for power because of his immense muscular strength, for animal fertility because of his impressive mating acts, and for crop fertility because of the way the ox-plough opened up the earth for the early farmers. This made him the ideal protector of men, livestock and crops.

It followed from this that, in the minds of the ancient agricultural people, if they were to be successful the great bull had to be honoured. He became a deity, a revered bull-god to be placated and worshipped. His image was everywhere and his horns became his symbol. Later, his horns were also transplanted onto human figures, creating a horned god who eventually became the enemy of early Christians. They then converted this horned god into the devil-figure feared and hated as the great rival of Christianity.

The use of the horn symbol in its original, protective form managed to survive this demonization by the Christian Church and, especially in Italy, developed into a popular hand gesture, the *cornuta,* made with the forefinger and little finger extended. This gesture is also widely used in Malta and can even be seen in painted form on cars and boats. But the bulls' horns on the farm buildings hark back to the original displays of ancient times and reveal local superstitions that have refused to die out. It is amusing to think that these Maltese farmers, now such devout Catholics, should employ a pagan device to defend themselves against evil forces. Indeed, on some farm buildings there is the ultimate irony of a small statue of a Christian saint alongside a pair of satanic horns. But where protection is needed to keep vital crops and animals free from invisible dangers, you take no chances, and accept help from any quarter.

In Malta even the horses have horns. The ones pulling the little *karrozins* – the horse-drawn taxi-carriages of Valletta – often display a small pair of metal horns between their ears. In the centre of these horns is an additional protective device in the form of a long vertical feather, ideally that of a peacock or pheasant. If the feather has an eye-spot on it, this will help to outstare the Evil Eye and will also defend the horse against hostile forces.

The more I look into these matters, the more superstitious the people of Malta turn out to be. One of the strangest examples is built into the religious architecture of the island. The façades of important churches display two large clocks, one on each side above the entrance. One clock-face shows the real time, while the other shows a false time. This is designed to confuse the Devil and prevent him from interfering with special events by fooling him into mistiming his evil visitations.

Old customs that still manage to survive in some regions include putting red ribbons on donkeys to protect them from the Evil Eye; wearing black underwear to ensure pregnancy; fumigating farmhouses with olive leaves that have been blessed in church during Holy Week; and hanging sea-shells around the necks of infants to keep evil spirits away from them.

One of the local beliefs that upsets me personally concerns the Bogeyman. Usually known as the Bo-bo, this hideous creature, an ugly amalgam of a man, an ox, a ram and a donkey, is said to wander the streets of Malta on dark winter's nights, looking for houses with tiny children inside them. Once it finds such a home, it will attack any children it finds who are still awake, terrorizing them with its horrible cries.

This story is told to little children to frighten them into going to bed and I discover that our young son has been told that the 'Bo-bo' will get him one night. I am also beginning to worry that he may soon be indoctrinated into the idea that all people are wicked by nature and will burn for ever in hellfire if they do not behave in certain ways. If we stay in Malta any longer, there is a risk that, despite our best efforts, he will start to believe this nonsense. He has enjoyed every minute of his first few years here, learning to swim like a fish and even to dive from great heights without fear. His tiny body is lithe and strong-limbed from endless hours spent playing on the sandy beaches. It has been an idyllic childhood, but now, approaching the age of five, he must soon start going to school. I hate the idea of him being indoctrinated with a hellfire philosophy which may, in later years, be emotionally difficult to discard.

Much as Ramona and I love the life here, it is time to make a move. Our exploration of the Maltese islands has lasted several years – much longer than we originally intended – and we have learned a great deal. Being part of a culture that is so different from our own has helped to delocalize our thinking. For me, personally, there has been the revelation of the body-language differences. I have started to ask myself difficult questions about why so many human actions are universal, while others vary so markedly. I want to pursue this more thoroughly. I need to study many more cultures and I cannot do that here. Time to move on.

# EXPLORING LANZAROTE

## (1974)

———◇———

BECAUSE OUR EXPLORATION OF THE MALTESE ISLANDS LASTED MUCH LONGER THAN INTENDED, TOWARDS THE END OF OUR TIME THERE, A RESTLESSNESS SET IN AND WE BEGAN TO INVESTIGATE OTHER ISLANDS. CYPRUS WAS THE FIRST, BUT THEN, IN 1974, WE MADE THE FIRST OF THREE VISITS TO THE CANARY ISLANDS. THIS TRIP WAS TO LANZAROTE, AT THE TIME A LITTLE-KNOWN LOCATION. IT HAS SINCE BECOME A POPULAR TOURIST RESORT, BUT IN 1974 IT WAS STILL LARGELY UNTOUCHED BY MODERN INVASIONS.

WHAT LED ME THERE WAS THE EXISTENCE OF A REMARKABLE, CARVED MEGALITH. ALL I KNEW OF IT WAS A DRAWING IN AN OLD BOOK AND I WANTED TO SEE IT IN THE 'FLESH'. SO IN APRIL 1974, RAMONA, A FIVE-YEAR OLD JASON AND I PAID THIS STRANGE ISLAND, SIXTY MILES OFF THE NORTH-WEST COAST OF AFRICA, A SHORT VISIT.

## MAKING TOAST ON AN OPEN VOLCANO

———◇———

ARRIVING IN LANZAROTE you can be forgiven for thinking that you are about to land on the moon. There is no more desolate, pock-marked, crater-strewn landscape on earth. Lanzarote does not have *a* volcano, like some other islands; it is a *mass* of volcanoes. In fact, there are over a hundred of them on an island less than forty miles long and (at most) twelve miles wide. Some are old and grass-covered, but others are raw and rocky, and clearly new – all too new. You get a distinct feeling that the whole place will erupt any moment, like a bad case of geological acne.

Three-quarters of the island is a carpet of lava. Parts of it are covered with such savagely irregular fragments of volcanic ash that no plant can grow and no animal make its home on them. This expanse of jagged, twisted rock has lain there, like a choppy black sea frozen in time, for 240 years, defying any form of life to colonize its surface. When the last great explosion took place, between 1730 and 1736, no fewer than thirty volcanoes became active simultaneously. Molten lava spewed over the land year after year, completely devastating the island. In scenes of unimaginable violence, one volcanic explosion after another submerged what was then a pleasant, fertile land beneath a liquid blanket of fire. Whole towns, villages and farms melted, sank and were gone for ever. Even today, there remains a smouldering heat just below the surface. Dig down a few inches in some areas and the temperature rises to over 200 degrees Fahrenheit. Go down a little deeper, to about 40 feet, and it rises to 1,000 degrees Fahrenheit. Pour cold water on this volcanic ash and, after a few seconds, it hisses back at you as a rising cloud of steam. In global terms, this is an island with a very thin skin.

There are a few hotels here, but the package tours have not discovered Lanzarote yet. For most people, the landscape proves to be too bleak, too harsh, and they seek a softer, lusher world in which to relax. Also, the black volcanic sand lacks the beach-appeal of the white expanses found on the typical coral island. But I am here for a special reason – to track down a megalith that I know only from a drawing in an old book.

Back in the Bronze Age, about four thousand years ago, some extraordinary human beings arrived on Lanzarote, erected a great monolithic stone and carved a pattern of curved lines upon its surface. What drove early men to go to these lengths to leave their mark on the landscape in such a remote, unfriendly place? And what does the pattern of lines mean?

From the drawing it is clear that the great stone has been crudely converted into a primitive Mother Goddess. The pattern of incisions takes the form of a semicircular, multi-lined 'necklace' of a type frequently found on more explicit Mother Goddess figures in other parts of the world. In these other cases, there are usually enough details to see the necklace clearly for what it is, but here, strangely, it is the only image present. It has become the emblem of the Great Mother – her badge of office – and is sufficient, apparently, all by itself, to convert a megalith into a sacred 'being'.

In those very early days, when megalith-builders were sweating away at their self-imposed labours in so many regions of the world, it was clearly important for men to show their devotion to the Great Mother Goddess by erecting huge stone 'embodiments' of her in her honour. The earliest of all the megalithic temples seem to be those on Malta, where the very shape of the sacred buildings echoes the curves of the sacred female. Stonehenge and the other northern megaliths appeared much later. All the megaliths are linked to a form of primitive religion in which agricultural peoples saw the whole planet as the divine 'provider'. The Great Mother Earth became transformed into the Great Earth Mother. And the Great Earth Mother became the Great Mother Goddess. Only much later, when the first cities arose, did God change sex and become God the Father.

I had grown up in the English countryside, in Wiltshire, where Avebury and Stonehenge were my playgrounds. But none of the English megaliths have been honoured with incised decorations; their surfaces are plain. So, for me, the incised stone of Lanzarote has a particular fascination. I know that it is at a place called Zonzamas, so the first goal on arriving on the island is to hire a car and make for that spot. We get there without much trouble but discover that the stone has been removed to the local museum for safe keeping. This is the kind of misguided 'protection' that is occurring all over the world. I say misguided because, unless you can see an ancient monument in its original setting, it is impossible to enjoy its full impact.

Disappointed, we are leaving Zonzamas, when we notice a small fragment of pottery on the ground. Examining it closely I discover that it is covered with primitive incised lines. In a ploughed field nearby we find more of these fragments and we start collecting them. A farmer, who is working in the field with a camel that is pulling an ancient wooden plough, comes over to see what we are doing. At first, I think that perhaps he is cross with us for taking the ancient pottery sherds but, to my surprise, when he sees what we are doing, he thanks us. He explains that he is delighted we are removing these wretched bits of pottery because the field is full of them and his camel finds it difficult to smash them up into small pieces. So much for the protection of ancient artefacts.

At the local museum I finally come face to face with the great megalith, and it is certainly impressive. There is no doubt that this is the Great Mother Goddess, erected here to protect the land from danger. But in the end, even she was no match for the power of the volcanoes. We meet the museum curator, Juan Brito, who has something special to show me, something unique in the island's history. It has been discovered within the last twenty-four hours and he has never seen anything like it.

As so often happens with great discoveries, children were involved. It was a little girl who first spotted the famous cave paintings at Altamira in Spain, and a young boy, looking for his dog, who discovered those near Lascaux in France. Here, in the Canary Islands, it was four schoolboys from the village of Tahiche who had been playing in the crater of an ancient volcano. There, by a lucky accident, they spotted a strange object lying on the surface. It was a stone idol, wedged among some rocks, and it appeared to have come from the remains of a small cave higher up the slope of the crater. The cave was severely eroded and the idol must have been brought down to the lower level by rains that had washed out some of the cave contents.

Near the idol the boys found three other, smaller artefacts. They collected them and took them to their parents in Tahiche. The mother of one of the boys realized the importance of the find and reported it to the mayor of Arrecife, the island capital, and the mayor notified Juan Brito. Brito immediately recognized it as the most important archaeological find in the island's history.

The idol, which is just over five inches high, is complete and undamaged, but consists of only a head and a curiously segmented neck. The base of the neck is flattened, so that the object stands upright when placed on a horizontal surface. It has a refined, sculptural quality with a well-smoothed surface. The only features depicted on the head are two eye sockets and a small, narrow slit of a mouth. The eye concavities are on opposite sides and the mouth is placed high up, giving the head a strange, animal quality.

Despite the degree of abstraction, it is clear that the object is not a human representation, but it is difficult to decide with any certainty what species is depicted. The four rounded, wormlike segments that make up the neck are not of equal size, but taper down in scale from head to base, so that the idol rests on its narrowest segment. It is made of a pale buff, marble-like stone of a kind that can be found on some of the beaches of Lanzarote, scattered among the dark grey volcanic sands. The nearest source for such stone is about four miles from the volcano, which is itself situated roughly four miles north of Arrecife, just to the south-east of Tahiche, in a region known by the ancient name of Tejia.

The idol of Tejia is unique, not only in Lanzarote, but in the whole of the Canary Islands, and I do not know of an artefact closely resembling it from any other part of the world. The small artefacts found with it are linked to the Bronze Age, so it seems likely that this strange, animal-headed idol is also about four thousand years old.

With ancient animal carvings it is usually easy enough to identify the kind of animals involved. To me, this one looks remarkably like a locust, but locusts are extremely rare in ancient art. The only one I have ever seen before came from ancient Egypt. I mention this to Juan Brito, but say that it's a wild idea because I don't think that locusts are ever likely to have been a problem locally. He interrupts me, saying that about twenty years ago the island *had* suffered from a sudden plague of locusts and that, twenty years before that, there had been a locust invasion so severe that even the fishermen's nets were reputed to have been eaten by the vast swarms of insects. To a Bronze Age Lanzarote population, such invasions would undoubtedly have assumed the proportions of terrifying and disastrous events. The locust image could easily have become of major mythological importance to these isolated peoples. So maybe my idea is not so crazy after all – in which case, this strange object is indeed a great rarity in the history of ancient art.

By a democratic family vote it is decided at this point to curb my obsession with ancient art and pay a little more attention to the immediate present. So we set off in search of the world's strangest eating-house – the amazing Timanfaya Restaurant in the heart of the Fire Mountains. This establishment is definitely not for diners of a nervous disposition, since it is built on the tip of a small, frighteningly hot volcano. We have been told that, in the centre of the restaurant there is a large metal grill over a dark, bottomless hole that leads down into the belly of the volcano. Since it is still smouldering angrily away after 240 years, it is supposedly possible to cook your food simply by placing it on this grill. We are sure that this is an exaggeration, but the idea of cooking on an open volcano is so appealing that we aim our somewhat unkempt hire-car up into the black crater-land in the west of the island.

Now we really do feel we are exploring the moon. The entire landscape is deserted and devastated. High above us, in the distance, we can just make out the circular shape of what must be the Timanfaya Restaurant. Then something surreal occurs. We are the only vehicle on the winding road and yet, there ahead of us, is the wheel of a car, overtaking us at speed and racing up the middle of the road, heading towards the restaurant. The car to which it seems to be attached is completely invisible. It has a life of its own and is leaving us further and further behind. It is the ghost-car of the Fire Mountains.

When our own car lurches over and screams to a halt in a shower of sparks, the explanation of the strange apparition is all too clear. It is one of our own wheels that has decided to race us to the top of the volcano. We grind to a juddering halt and reluctantly walk the rest of the way to the restaurant. Calling the car-hire firm to explain our problem, I expect alarm, anger and accusations of dangerous driving. Not at all. There is not the slightest murmur of surprise and a replacement car is on its way.

It turns out that, on Lanzarote at the present time, there are several car-hire firms but no service stations. Filling stations, yes, but proper repair garages, no. So cars frequently break down. What happens to them? They are abandoned – nothing else can be done.

Waiting for our new hire-car to arrive, we settle down to a volcanic lunch. They were not exaggerating. You really can cook your food on the gusts of intense heat that well up from the depths of the volcano. Jason and I take our bread rolls over to the sinister-looking grill, which appears to be guarding the gates of hell, and skewer them on the prongs of long-handled forks. Pushing these out onto the centre of the grill, we wait. After a few moments there is a 'whoooh' noise and we have toast. A few feet outside the window by our table there is what appears to be a metal drainpipe sticking up from the ground. A waiter appears, puts a large funnel in the pipe and pours a bucketful of cold water into it. Then he takes the funnel out and walks away. A few seconds later there is a loud hiss and a screaming jet of steam shoots out of the end of the pipe. Another waiter pushes a branch of wood into a crack in the rocks. It promptly bursts into flames. We are sitting on God's oven.

What puzzles me about this restaurant, which I am told has only recently opened, is how the builders put down their foundations. And why hasn't the whole place caught fire by now and gone up in smoke? Better to concentrate on the food, which happens to be remarkably good, considering how difficult it must be to keep staff up here. Nothing like a little risk-taking to improve the appetite.

After lunch, the replacement car arrives. It is an aged Beetle whose pitted bodywork suggests that the previous occupants were Bonnie and Clyde. The steering-wheel appears to be smeared with glue, so that, once gripped, it is almost impossible to let go. The glue turns out to be a thick layer of coagulated sweat. Why, I wonder, would the previous drivers have been so terrified as to cause their palms to leak this much perspiration? Then, as I drive off, I find the answer – this car hates being steered. It is like one of those airport trolleys that have developed wheel-wobbles and insist on advancing crabwise. We snake and zigzag our way back to the hotel, by which time I have added my own contribution to the adhesive nature of the steering-wheel.

At the other end of the island we pay a visit to the astonishing subterranean nightclub, the Jameos del Agua, where you dine and dance in a vast underground cavern containing a small lake, in which live a colony of blind white crabs. These animals exist nowhere else in the world and must surely be the only species of animal to live solely in one nightclub.

The cave is part of the remains of an underground lava-river. When the volcano now known as the Monte Corona erupted over four thousand years ago, it spewed out a stream of liquid lava that flowed across the island and down into the sea. The outer edges solidified, while the inner part went on running downhill until it left a hollow 'volcanic tube' about four miles long. This is the longest tube-cave in the world and it even runs down into the sea for another mile. Divers who have ventured into its eerie depths can easily see why it is referred to as the 'Entrance to Atlantis'. After the volcanic activity had ceased, the sea water seeped slowly back into the 'tube' and with it, from the depths, came this strange little crab, which then proceeded to develop into a species unique to Lanzarote.

This is clearly a remarkable island, with a brooding sense of danger lurking everywhere. One day, it seems certain, the entire place will be jettisoned into the sky on a vast jet of white-hot, liquid earth. In the meantime, it is a fascinating place to visit, providing another vivid reminder of mankind's ingenuity at colonizing almost every corner of this small planet, no matter how hostile or precarious.

**NOTE**

AT THE TIME OF OUR VISIT TO LANZAROTE, IN THE EARLY SEVENTIES, ONLY 2,500 BRITONS WERE VISITING THE ISLAND ANNUALLY. A QUARTER OF A CENTURY LATER, THAT FIGURE HAS RISEN DRAMATICALLY TO 569,000. SO I WAS WRONG — LIKE ME, PEOPLE DO FIND THE STARKLY HOSTILE LANDSCAPE FASCINATING.

THERE IS AN INTERESTING POSTSCRIPT TO THE STRANGE 'LOCUST IDOL'. I MENTIONED THAT THE ONLY OTHER EXAMPLES OF LOCUST CARVINGS KNOWN TO ME CAME FROM ANCIENT EGYPT. RECENT STUDIES OF THE GUANCHES, THE EARLY OCCUPANTS OF THE CANARY ISLANDS, HAVE SHOWN THAT THEY MUMMIFIED THEIR DEAD IN THE EGYPTIAN MANNER, SUGGESTING THAT PERHAPS MY LINKING OF THE TWO CULTURES WAS NOT AS FANCIFUL AS I THOUGHT.

# AROUND EUROPE IN SEARCH OF GESTURES

## (1975–1976)

DURING OUR SOJOURN IN MALTA I WAS VISITED BY MY OLD PROFESSOR, NIKO TINBERGEN, WHO PERSUADED ME THAT ONE DAY SOON I SHOULD RETURN TO OXFORD TO JOIN HIM IN THE DEPARTMENT OF ZOOLOGY, WHERE HE WAS STILL LEADING A TEAM STUDYING ANIMAL BEHAVIOUR. WITH HIS POWERFUL 'WORK ETHIC' HE FELT IT WAS HIGH TIME THAT I STOPPED LUXURIATING IN THE SUNSHINE AND WENT BACK TO UNDERTAKE SOME SERIOUS RESEARCH. THE TRUTH WAS THAT I HAD ALREADY BEGUN TO TIRE OF THE SOFT LIFE, AND MY 'HUMAN BODY LANGUAGE' PROJECT WAS REACHING A STAGE WHERE IT NEEDED A NEW IMPETUS OF THE KIND THAT CAN ONLY BE FOUND IN A UNIVERSITY DEPARTMENT. SO, IN 1974, WE BOUGHT A HOUSE IN THE BANBURY ROAD, CLOSE TO THE CITY CENTRE OF OXFORD, AND I BEGAN A NEW PHASE OF MY INVESTIGATIONS INTO HUMAN BEHAVIOUR.

MY TIME IN MALTA HAD CONVINCED ME THAT TOO LITTLE WAS KNOWN ABOUT THE WAY GESTURES, EXPRESSIONS AND GENERAL BODY LANGUAGE VARY IN DIFFERENT CULTURES. WHAT WAS NEEDED WAS A WIDESPREAD SURVEY OF AS MANY COUNTRIES AS POSSIBLE, MAPPING THE BODY LANGUAGE IN PLACE AFTER PLACE AND THEN FITTING IT ALL TOGETHER TO CREATE A COMPREHENSIVE HUMAN 'BODY-LANGUAGE ATLAS'. IT WOULD BE TOO AMBITIOUS TO ATTEMPT TO COVER THE WHOLE GLOBE ALL AT ONCE, BUT A START COULD BE MADE IN EUROPE AND THE MEDITERRANEAN.

WITH A RESEARCH FELLOWSHIP AT WOLFSON COLLEGE AND A RESEARCH GRANT FROM THE HARRY FRANK GUGGENHEIM FOUNDATION IN NEW YORK, THE SCENE WAS SET, AND IN 1975 THE 'GESTURE-MAPS' PROJECT BEGAN IN EARNEST. I WAS JOINED IN THIS ENDEAVOUR BY SOCIAL PSYCHOLOGISTS PETER COLLETT AND PETER MARSH AND LINGUIST MARIE O'SHAUGHNESSY. WE DECIDED TO VISIT FORTY LOCATIONS IN A TOTAL OF TWENTY-FIVE DIFFERENT COUNTRIES, RECORDING THE LOCAL GESTURES AS WE WENT. IT TOOK A LONG TIME TO COMPLETE THE WORK AND OUR JOURNEYS WERE NOT WITHOUT INCIDENT, BUT WE DID IN THE END MANAGE TO PRODUCE A REPORT THAT WAS THE FIRST OF ITS KIND, SHOWING THAT EACH HUMAN GESTURE HAS ITS OWN SPECIAL GEOGRAPHICAL DISTRIBUTION AND THAT IGNORANCE OF LOCAL DIFFERENCES CAN OFTEN LEAD TO DISASTROUS MISUNDERSTANDINGS.

## LOUDER THAN WORDS

SOME PEOPLE SAY that body language is a trivial subject. What does it matter if someone gestures this way rather than that? The answer is that it can sometimes matter a great deal. Indeed, it can even mean the difference between life and death. Consider this incident:

Two young male Scandinavians are taking a vacation in a Mediterranean country. They are both strong swimmers and they soon tire of splashing up and down in front of the crowded tourist beach. They strike out for a serious long-distance swim and eventually, coming around a headland, find themselves confronted by a coastal military installation.

Standing on the rocks is an armed guard. He spots the two swimmers and, thinking they might be spying, beckons to them to come ashore for questioning. When they observe his beckoning gesture they misunderstand it. They think he is telling them to turn back and swim away, which they promptly do. They believe that they are obeying his order. He believes that they are trying to escape. If they are trying to escape they must, as he suspected, be spies. So he shoots at them. And they are both killed.

How could this be? How could they have misunderstood such a simple request? The answer lies in the precise form of the beckoning gesture. In northern Europe, where the swimmers came from, a beckon is performed by scooping a hand upwards towards the body with the palm *up*. In southern Europe, where the armed guard comes from, a beckon is performed by scooping a hand downwards towards the body with the palm *down*. If a northerner sees the 'southern beckon', it looks to him like a 'go away' gesture. And this very small difference in body language cost these two innocent people their lives. For them, body language was certainly not a trivial matter.

This is just one example of the small, but important ways in which people can make unfortunate and unnecessary mistakes when meeting foreigners face to face. As our 'gesture-maps' research team begins to work its way across Europe, recording the details of local body language, we are surprised at just how many variations we encounter. So, too, are many of the people we meet. Everyone seems to believe that their own personal repertoire of gestures must be widely understood.

We encounter a classic example of this in central France where two local anglers are sitting side by side on a riverbank. The fish are not biting and the anglers are happy to answer our questions. When asked the meaning of the 'ring-sign', in which a hand is raised with the tips of the thumb and forefinger touching to make a circle, both fishermen reply without hesitation. Simultaneously, one says 'OK' and the other says 'Zero'. They are old friends and they look at one another in complete astonishment. How can they have given different answers? They start a heated debate and it is clear that neither is going to give way.

Their difference is not a subtle one. As an OK sign, the ring-gesture means that something is good. As a zero sign, it means that something is bad. Without realizing it, the two French fishermen are living in an 'overlap' zone, where a single gesture has two different meanings. We find it as surprising as they do that such a contradictory situation should exist. But this is not an isolated case. Most of the gestures we are studying turn out to have several meanings. As you move from one part of the world to another, the meaning changes and, wherever this happens, there may be a region where both meanings exist side by side.

Alternatively, there may be a sharply defined 'gesture frontier'. For instance, in Portugal, holding your ear lobe is a well-known gesture that says something is very good. Just across the border, in southern Spain, it has a completely different meaning. There, the same action is a strong criticism of people who do not pay their share. But it would be wrong to describe these meanings as 'national differences', because this ear-touching gesture is unknown in central and northern Spain.

Remarkably few gestures follow precisely the borders of modern nations. Most have their own, ancient distribution – being either restricted to one region within a country or spread out across several neighbouring countries. This is because most of the symbolic gestures we use today are more ancient than our contemporary political boundaries. Indeed, some of our European 'gesture frontiers' are more than two thousand years old. Human body language is amazingly conservative and long-lasting. Our unspoken loyalty to our gestures is much greater than our much flaunted allegiance to our flags.

As a field research team setting out to uncover these gestural differences we find that acquiring our information is not always easy. It is true that in most of the countries on our itinerary the local people are extremely helpful, but in one or two places they seem to resent our probing into their personal habits. Instead of being flattered by our interest, they are deeply suspicious of our motives, as though we are some kind of undercover governmental team investigating local skulduggery.

In Bulgaria, for example, we are sent packing and have to cross the country off our list. The Bulgarians apparently feel we are up to some sort of mischief. When our researchers stop at a bar for a much-needed drink, the barman is happy to serve them and take their money, but as soon as they have left he phones the police. A police car quickly catches up with them and insists that in Bulgaria it is an offence to drive a vehicle after having consumed even a single alcoholic drink. We are forced to abandon our research there.

In another country, Tunisia, we encounter other difficulties. We cannot all get rooms in the same hotel. I have already arrived and settled in. My stiflingly hot cell of a room has no air-conditioning or ventilation, and the management makes a brave attempt to placate me by offering me an elaborate pink drink in a tall glass full of fruit and flowers. The hotel has clearly overbooked and there is no hope of improving my accommodation, so I give in and try to sleep. In the morning I start worrying about the nearby hotel into which the others are booked. They are due later in the day and I decide to confirm that they have three good rooms ready and waiting for them.

The desk-clerk at their hotel assures me that all is well, but his body language is rather stiff and inhibited, one of the telltale signs that someone is not telling the whole truth. I insist on knowing the kind of rooms they have been given. I point out that the three of them have been travelling for weeks, working in other countries, and will not be in the mood for hot, stuffy cells and placatory pink drinks. What they will need is a good night's sleep. Watching the young assistant manager's tight smile, I have my doubts about whether they will get it.

I insist on knowing their room numbers, but I am told they have not been allocated yet. When I persist he finally admits that there is a problem. This hotel has also overbooked and there is only one room available for my three colleagues. But not to worry, it is a big room. I explain gently that one of them is a young woman and two of them are men. 'So what is problem?' he asks. 'They are not married,' I explain. 'Don't worry,' he replies, with a virtuoso shrug of his hands, 'when they get here, we will marry them.'

Despite all my protestations, there is no escaping the fact that they simply do not have any more rooms, so I give up the struggle and await the arrival of my friends. To kill time I drive to a local camel market to study Arab bartering behaviour. There are more than just camels on sale here. Among an amazing variety of goods laid out on the ground, there is a great pile of second-hand underclothes, another mountain of second-hand spectacles and – I tell no lie – a heap of second-hand dentures.

I have a small ciné camera with me and start filming the Arab greeting rituals as new arrivals at the market meet up with old friends. It is beginning to dawn on me that Arab body language is even more distinct from European than I had realized. Then, through my lens, I see an extraordinary incident. Someone is getting stoned. I am not talking about drugs: this is stoning in the biblical sense. An angry man is throwing rocks at a screaming woman. Nobody is going to her aid. She is dodging the missiles as best she can. I keep filming and become completely absorbed in recording this ancient custom. With my eye pressed firmly to the eyepiece of my camera, it is as if I were at the movies. My brain somehow refuses to believe that what is happening in front of me is real. This is an exciting scene and, as I try to follow the action, I am thinking to myself that I am really lucky because now the young man is turning to face the camera and is going to throw his next stone right at me. What a good picture that will make – very dramatic. I am so engrossed that I feel no danger. Then suddenly it dawns on me that I am not, after all, sitting in a cinema, but standing in a North African camel market, and I make a hurried exit. Now I understand why it is that cameramen in war zones are sometimes killed because they refuse to stop filming when the bullets begin to fly. It's because, like me, they think they are at the movies.

I pick up my friends at the airport and take them to their hotel. I have explained that there may be difficulties, but they are in no mood to listen. They are exhausted, and all they want is a bath and a good sleep. Oh dear. Inevitably, explosions erupt when they discover that they only have a single room between the three of them. Enormous pink drinks arrive, to no avail. They are justifiably furious. The management say they will solve the problem and will provide them with separate accommodation. I am greatly relieved and depart for my own hotel.

The next morning, when we meet up again, I enquire how things worked out. It seems that the hotel's solution was to put cords across the room and hang blankets from them. This improvised version of 'separate accommodation' left a great deal to be desired, but they were all too tired to complain further and collapsed into their beds in what one could only describe as a three-star doss-house. This morning things look brighter. North Africa is fascinating and we are off to interview the Bedouin tribes-people about their body language, which promises to be an intriguing experience.

Unfortunately, we have not allowed for the extreme sexism

of this desert culture. The men agree to answer our queries, but not if female members of the tribe are present. As soon as we settle down and put the first question to them, they bark instructions at their women who all promptly disappear and do not return. It seems that, as some of the gestures are of a sexual nature, we will be discussing matters fit only for male ears. So be it.

Now all the tribeswomen have vanished and are out of earshot, but our local interpreter sadly informs us that there is still a problem. The men will not talk to us just yet. What is wrong? Have we offended them in some way? No, it is not that. It is that one of *our* party is a woman.

By this stage of our investigation, our female team-member, Marie O'Shaughnessy, must be familiar with almost every obscene gesture known to the human race, but when we explain that she does not mind if some of the matters we discuss are rather rude, it has no effect. There is a blunt refusal by the Bedouin males to talk about *any* gestures until she has left us. Marie accepts defeat and disappears behind some bushes, where she cannot be seen but does her best to hear what is going on. Now at last we can talk.

The body language of the Bedouin is richly rewarding. They seem to have more ways of insulting one another than any other culture we have studied. My favourite Arab insult consists of tapping the forefinger of one hand against the bunched fingertips of the other hand. This can get you into serious trouble. This can get you killed. The symbolism is simple – the forefinger is your mother and the five fingertips she is pressed against are five men. The gesture means 'you had five fathers' – in other words, your mother was a whore.

After this first Bedouin encounter, we develop an efficient pattern. At each Bedouin camp, (1) we arrive, (2) their women leave, (3) we settle down, (4) Marie gets up without a word and hides behind a bush, (5) we complete the interview, (6) she rejoins us and (7) we move on to the next interview. I am sure that feminists would frown on this procedure but we have no choice. It is either Marie-in-the-bushes, or no research.

In other regions we hit different problems. The most unexpected is that people are sometimes *too* helpful. If someone we are interviewing does not know a particular gesture, they will somehow find an answer, rather than disappointing us. The horned hand (with the little finger and forefinger stiffly erect like a pair of bull's horns, and the other two fingers held bent down by the thumb) is popular in southern Europe but is unknown in the far north. One helpful northerner, not liking to let us down, explains that, to him, this horned hand means 'Pills for the Mills'. We faithfully record this in case it has some special, local significance. Further investigation reveals that it is a joke gesture. The 'Pills' is really 'Piltz', short for Piltzner, a brand of beer. And 'Mills' is short for 'the Sawmills'. The two-fingered gesture, he explains, is a man from the sawmills ordering four beers.

The ring-gesture I mentioned earlier has several meanings – OK, zero, orifice, threat, and so on – as one moves across Europe. In one place, to our great surprise, it acquires yet another: we are told that it stands for 'Thursday'. We are nonplussed by this until the man we are interviewing holds up his hand and starts counting off his fingertips, starting from his little finger – Monday, Tuesday, Wednesday, Thursday. Mystery solved.

Of all the strange encounters we experience in our travels around Europe and the Mediterranean in search of gestures, my favourite moment occurs on the stone doorstep of a little village house high in the Italian mountains. A wizened, white-haired old man is sitting there puffing philosophically on his pipe. We approach him and ask if he would mind talking to us about his gestures. He looks up at us and sighs. 'Not again,' he says. 'Last week it was Germans wanting to measure the shape of our skulls.' He rises, turns, and disappears inside his house. And who can blame him? If we are not careful, there will soon be five research scientists to every surviving peasant.

Our task is finally completed and we return to our Oxford base to analyse all our results. For the first time, we will have some accurate maps of a number of important, symbolic gestures. If the knowledge we gain from these maps can help to reduce international misunderstandings, then it seems to me that our brief intrusions into other people's lives will have been justified.

## NOTE

THE 'GESTURE-MAPS' PROJECT WAS COMPLETED IN 1976. AFTER SOME DELAYS, IT EVENTUALLY APPEARED IN PRINT IN 1978, IN A BOOK CALLED *GESTURES; THEIR ORIGINS AND DISTRIBUTION*. IT WAS THE FIRST STUDY OF ITS KIND TO BE PUBLISHED.

# MANWATCHING IN ITALY

## (1977)

In 1977 THE BBC ASKED ME TO MAKE A TELEVISION PROGRAMME ABOUT MY STUDIES OF HUMAN BODY LANGUAGE. THE BUDGET FOR THE ONE-HOUR PROGRAMME WAS LIMITED, SO WE HAD TO MAKE DO WITH ONLY TWO FOREIGN LOCATIONS. OF ALL THE MANY PLACES WE HAD VISITED IN THE PAST TWO YEARS, DURING OUR GESTURE-MAPPING OF EUROPE AND THE MEDITERRANEAN, I CHOSE MALTA AND ITALY. I PICKED MALTA BECAUSE I KNEW IT SO WELL AND ITALY BECAUSE IT IS SO WONDERFULLY RICH IN BODY LANGUAGE AND ESPECIALLY IN GESTURE. THE MALTESE TRIP WAS REWARDING BUT UNEVENTFUL. IT WAS NOT UNTIL WE REACHED ITALY THAT SOME INTRIGUING PROBLEMS BEGAN TO ARISE.

## GEORGE RAFT STRIKES AGAIN

If THERE WAS a Nobel Prize for gesticulation, a Neapolitan would win it every time. In the north of Italy they snootily claim, 'We never gesticulate', emphasizing this fact with bold hand flourishes. In the south they make no bones about it. They wear their gestures with pride. With centuries of practice they have refined the movements of their hands into a wonderfully expressive art form.

This is why I am here, with a BBC film crew, to capture the

most poetic body language in the world. Each morning, Neapolitan males gather in coffee-houses and on street corners, ostensibly to drink and talk, but in reality to conduct invisible orchestras with their hands. There are special centres, like the magnificent Galeria Umberto, a great, glass-covered walkway, where gesticulating reaches a crescendo of manual elegance. So intent are they on their rippling, dipping, waving, undulating fingers that they appear to be completely oblivious of our wandering camera. I walk among them, watching and studying, followed by a camera team. Although we are conspicuous, we are ignored. We might as well be waiters, weaving our way through the crowd with yet another tray of espressos, so engrossed are they in their performances.

I sit down at a table, order a cup of coffee and proceed to talk to the camera, explaining the meanings of some of the gestures we have been recording. Still nobody bothers me. If only it were always this simple. It is nearly lunchtime and we have all the pictures we want, so we start to pack away our camera gear. This acts like a secret signal. Suddenly everything changes. The whole population of the Galeria seems to be converging on us, all talking at once. My producer, Barry Paine, like me, speaks no Italian. Happily, Marie O'Shaughnessy, who is now acting as our production manager, is fluent, so we all point helpfully at her. The moment she starts talking to them in their own language, they surround her.

As we watch, something even stranger happens. They are all putting their hands in their pockets and pulling out some kind of card. Barry and I crane our necks to see what these cards say. They appear to be identity documents of some kind. Is this some sort of political protest? Are they a notorious rebel group, trying to use the unsuspecting BBC as a mouthpiece for their grievances? What on earth is going on?

Marie is clearly becoming agitated. They are pressing close

all around her and some of them are shouting at her. I beckon to her to come across and explain the problem. She asks them to wait and pushes her way through the crush of bodies. Her explanation is worthy of a Fellini film. It goes like this:

When we started filming here this morning, word went round Naples that a professional film crew were in the Galeria Umberto making a movie. The assumption was that it was a big-budget feature film and, as a result, every out-of-work actor in Naples made a beeline for the Galeria, with his actor's union card snugly tucked into his pocket. Not wanting to risk being rejected as unsuitable for the crowd scenes, each of the actors refrained from contacting us, and instead simply stood around talking and gesticulating in their usual manner, providing the colourful background atmosphere that they were sure we wanted. No wonder they had so expertly avoiding looking at our camera or waving at it. They were pros. They knew their job and they were doing it – rent-a-Neapolitan was in full swing. All the most experienced ones made sure that they were caught by the camera as it was weaving in among them and, once they knew for sure that they had been included in the scene, they were certain that, as union members, they would get a full day's pay.

And that, Marie explains breathlessly to us, is what they are now demanding. About a hundred of them, and all insisting on the standard union rate. Barry Paine is aghast. 'Tell them this is not a feature film. This is a low-budget documentary and we have nothing to spare. We can pay them nothing.' He is right, of course, but Marie's expression makes it clear that translating his remarks is going to get her into serious trouble. She is no wilting flower, however, and bravely throws herself back into the excited crowd. I am fascinated by her performance. What a woman. It is brilliant. She is now gesticulating like a true Neapolitan and for one fleeting moment the idea flashes through my mind that we should now be filming her own body language. But that would only help to escalate our crisis. She is giving them hell, as best she can with one lone female voice, and they are now becoming visibly angry. There are no police in sight and no sign of any helpful bystanders. We have got to find a solution ourselves, and quickly.

I start studying the protesters more closely, looking for some clue. Because Barry and I do not speak Italian we are being left alone and, standing at the side of the crowd, can watch the action very clearly. A pattern is beginning to emerge. This is not an amorphous crowd – there are ringleaders present. They are trying to look like all the others, but as I watch I can see that there are three of them who are making all the running. I call Marie over again. 'Tell that big, muscle-bound one, who is always closest to you, that we cannot deal with this unruly mob. Tell him he must pick three representatives to come away with us for serious discussions, to be conducted in a proper manner. And tell him to announce that he will be negotiating on behalf of everyone.'

Grateful for any suggestion, Marie plunges back in and puts my idea to Muscleman. He agrees, a little too quickly I think, and selects the other two ringleaders without any hesitation. Speaking to the crowd, he manages to quell their mood and gets them to disperse. We then make our way, with much relief, to our TV van. This roomy vehicle can easily take a few extra bodies and we are soon lurching away in search of a suitably relaxed restaurant to give our new-found friends a good lunch and, more importantly, a surfeit of Italian wine.

Our driver, on loan from RAI, the Italian equivalent of the BBC, is a man of few words, but it is abundantly clear that he is not too impressed by what we are doing. He happens to look remarkably like the old Hollywood gangster George Raft and has probably been told that so many times that he has started to adopt the tight-lipped persona of his famous lookalike. He drives us in silence to a square with an ideal restaurant – the

kind where people spend three hours passing the time of day
while eating several plates of spaghetti. The lunch goes well.
Marie entertains our three new friends who, now that they are
certain of being paid something, have conveniently forgotten
about their absent colleagues. We explain that we cannot pay
them for what they have been doing in the Galeria, but that we
will now pay them for some new filming, in which they will sit
in the square and discuss Italian politics. It turns out that one
is a Royalist and one a Communist, so the gestures will come
thick and fast and be completely genuine.

We move them out onto a bench in the middle of the square
and set up our camera. The wine has relaxed them and the
political debate that follows is gesturally spectacular. We are
certainly getting our money's worth and the day is a success
after all.

Then it happens. The cameraman shouts out: 'It's gone all
tweed!' I thought this must be some technical term for picture
break-up, but it is not. A very broad-shouldered man, wearing
an incongruously expensive tweed jacket, has slowly walked
into the middle of the square and placed himself firmly in front
of our camera lens. 'Marie, ask him to move, please,' says the
cameraman. She does so, but he ignores her. Instead of
looking at her or replying, his sole response is to take a long,
pointed flick-knife out of his elegant jacket pocket. He opens it
and begins cleaning his nails with slow, deliberate actions. His
deeply tanned face is expressionless.

I look at our three friends on the bench. A few moments ago
they were big, tough and muscular, laughing and shouting as
they argued for our filming. Now, with the arrival of Big
Tweed they appear to be shrinking before our eyes, as though
they are inflatables with the stoppers pulled out. They fall
silent and then stare into the distance, clearly wishing they
were somewhere else.

Marie asks our driver what is going on. All George Raft says is 'Capo'. But it is enough to explain our little difficulty. The man is obviously a member of the local Mafia and we have strayed into his little patch of Naples without asking his permission. There are Mafia taxes to be paid and we have ignored this unwritten rule. So he is going to stand there, preventing all filming until we pay up.

'Ask George Raft what we should do. Should we pay the man? Or do we call the police, or get RAI on the phone, or what? How serious is this?' Barry is suddenly, and with good reason, back in the role of worried producer again.

Marie goes into a huddle with George Raft, who by now is looking as darkly threatening as Big Tweed. His ego is being assailed by this unwelcome intruder and his inner identification with the renowned Hollywood gangster is beginning to assert itself. Glowering at Tweed, George allows the corner of his mouth to open sufficiently to emit the Italian equivalent of 'leave it to me'.

We are impressed, as we are supposed to be, and are only too happy to leave it to him. But at the same time we decide to pack up our gear and abandon any further attempt to film in this city, where clearly nothing is for free.

George takes Tweed down an alleyway and out of sight. About five minutes later he returns alone and gestures to us to climb in the van. As we drive away from the square we notice that George's face is looking slightly shinier than is appropriate for a top Hollywood gangster. Marie asks him what has happened in the alleyway. When George tells her, all she says is 'Mother of God'.

Her reaction does not bode well for tomorrow's filming in Naples. We look at her, questioningly. She explains: 'He said, "That was a silly man, so I took him down the alleyway and hit him." Honestly, that's what he told me. So I asked him what we do now and all he said was, "Leave town." And I think he meant it.'

'Ask him if we could leave tomorrow after doing some more filming,' suggests Barry, without much hope. She does. His reply is that we should leave first thing in the morning, before it gets light.

Back at our hotel the seriousness of our situation is brought home to us. We have prudently decided to have dinner there instead of going out on the town. During the meal, Marie overhears one of the waiters say to another member of the hotel staff: 'These are the ones.' We are on the other side of Naples, but word of our escapade seems to have spread fast. We decide then and there that dawn will be a really good time for a drive to Rome, and turn in for an early night.

In the first light of morning, Naples is mercifully quiet. This is not an early-morning city and we are soon safely on the main road north to Rome. 'What are we filming in Rome?' asks the cameraman. A reasonable-enough question. The truth is that I haven't the faintest idea. Rome is not in the script. But when you are on location with a film crew, you must always have a decisive plan. To dither or admit that you haven't a clue destroys the momentum. So I make a snap decision. 'We will film the Pope,' I reply airily. 'I would like to get shots of the subordination kneeling behaviour of people in St Peter's Square when the Pope comes out on the balcony. And I want shots of the Pope's special wave. He holds his hands palms-up and then slowly, rhythmically, raises and lowers his arms. It's his trademark papal wave. Should be easy. I doubt if the Mafia control that particular patch. It is not even in Italy – the Vatican is a separate State. So we should be OK.'

'What about permissions?' asks the cameraman, who would like a little unfettered filming for once. 'No problem,' says Barry. 'I told RAI last night that we are changing our plans and they have arranged for us to have the best man in Rome on the job. He's said to be the world's greatest fixer. His name is Furio.'

## FURIO THE FIXER

THE THICK-SET, muscular, black-haired figure of Furio is there to meet us, bursting with helpful energy. He has found us a sinister hotel, full of antique statues, that is reputed to have had a chequered history about which it is best not to enquire. We hold a meeting to plan our strategy. Barry explains that we would like to film the Pope at the Vatican and, if possible, he would like to take some shots of me walking around the Colosseum. 'Very difficult, takes long time to get Pope Permit, but don't worry, I fix it. See you later,' says Furio and disappears before we can give him any more details.

We unpack and Furio reappears to take us out to dinner. 'Looking good, but we must apply Vatican in morning,' he says breezily. 'Let's go.' Some of us squeeze into his car and the others follow in our own. He takes off with the kind of acceleration that would have thrust us into orbit if his car had been pointing upwards. He clearly knows every short cut in Rome and soon so do we. Suddenly, turning a corner, he comes face to face with an ugly-looking protest parade. Angry men carrying large placards are marching down the centre of the street. Had I been driving, I would have taken immediate avoiding action and turned off down the first available side-road. Not Furio. He hurtles straight at them and then, to add insult to possible mass injury, he opens his window and bellows abuse at them. At the very last moment, before we are engulfed, he swings his car down a small alleyway and accelerates with even greater abandon than before. Screaming around a tight corner, he narrowly misses a stunning, long-haired blonde who is standing talking to someone at the side of the alley. 'Hey, Ursula!' he shouts happily from his window at the startled figure of the James Bond screen goddess Ursula Andress.

Eventually we arrive, shaken and stirred, at a strange-looking restaurant. Furio is well known here and the food is good, but the atmosphere is oddly 'clubbish', and I cannot put my finger on what sort of affiliation the restaurant might have. Marie says it is 'very political'. I enquire what sort of politics and she replies: 'Don't ask.' Since I have an intense dislike of all extreme forms of politics, there is nothing to be gained from learning which particular form of human idiocy is entrenched here, so I take her advice and focus myself on the food.

The next morning we set off for the Vatican. According to Marie, Furio has explained to her that it normally takes several years to obtain official permission to film the Pope, but like all good fixers he has a contact on the inside who may be able to speed things up for us. It will have to be a very special sort of contact if they can speed the process up from a few years to a few hours.

Frankly I am puzzled by all this fuss. All I want to do is to point a distant camera at the Pope high up on his balcony, and at the faithful in the square below. There will be dozens of tourist cameras doing precisely the same thing, so why should our BBC request be such a big deal? Marie thinks it is because we are professionals and I suppose that must be the explanation.

We have penetrated deep inside the Vatican complex now, and Furio is leaping into action. We are all ushered into an impressive suite of offices and asked to wait. A door opens and a solemn lady dressed entirely in black stands before us. She proceeds to grill us at length about our project and our motives. She has a strong American accent and there is a strange feeling that we have somehow strayed into the Pentagon.

This is getting out of hand. The Pope is not even in my script. But we eventually manage to convince her that we are engaged in making a serious documentary about human behaviour and that it is not a Monty Python sketch in disguise. At last she is satisfied and we are issued with our Pope Permits. These are numbered badges that we have to wear on our clothing. Sporting our precious badges we are ushered across a courtyard and into a side door. I assume that this will lead us back through into St Peter's Square with all the tourists. But I am in for a shock.

As we walk though the door we find ourselves standing on a huge marble stage in the centre of which is an imposing marble throne. As we peer at it we realize we are not alone. A glance to our left reveals several thousand pairs of eyes staring at us in hushed disbelief. Silently, we gaze at them and they gaze at us. It is not clear who is the more perplexed by what they see. We were expecting tourists in the square. They were expecting the Pope. But instead of His Holiness, what they see, strolling casually up to the papal throne, is a somewhat bedraggled group of strangers dressed largely in scruffy jeans and T-shirts.

The truth dawns on us. Furio has certainly fixed it. Not appreciating our modest needs, he has majestically pulled enough strings to obtain permission for us to film nothing less than a papal audience. I take a closer look at my badge and, sure enough, there are the words *per udienza*. Even my poor Italian can understand that. No wonder there was such a careful screening. Seven years earlier, when visiting Manila, this particular Pope was attacked by a knife-wielding would-be assassin dressed as a priest. Since then, they are clearly taking no risks. Our seemingly truculent attire hints at some sort of rebel feeling. It is hardly surprising that they were so suspicious. But despite everything they have accepted us and here we are.

The hushed crowd in front of us has been waiting eagerly – probably for years – for this special moment, and all they get is us. What a let-down. Some of them are probably rationalizing the situation by imagining that we must be the dirty poor who will have their feet ceremonially washed by His Holiness. Others may have spotted the camera equipment and realized that we are a film crew who, with typical media arrogance, have failed to dress with appropriate respect for the occasion.

Looking at our sound man, I am horrified to see that he has large Mickey Mouse stickers on his headphones. This must look like a deliberate insult, but there is no way we can explain the mix-up to the audience, or apologize, so we sidle down to the bottom of the marble steps in front of the stage and crouch in a corner, awaiting the Pope's arrival. A huge tree-trunk of a man in a dark blue suit with an ominous bulge under one arm approaches us and hisses: 'No closer to His Holiness than ten paces.' Presumably this is considered to be safely beyond knife-lunging range. We nod gravely. There is no point in telling him that a hundred paces would be fine.

A loudspeaker announces that the Holy Father will soon be with us. He will be borne down the central aisle on his portable throne, the *Sedia Gestatoria*. It is carefully explained that this elevation is not to emphasize his high status but simply to make him visible to all the pilgrims who have made the long journey to be with him today.

There is an eruption at the back of the vast hall. The Pope's procession is entering and all solemnity vanishes. People are on their feet, cheering, clapping, waving and taking flash pictures. 'Holy Mother of God, here he comes,' whispers Marie, whose Catholic childhood is beginning to seep through her tough adult professionalism.

The smiling Pope, in his traditional white robes, is indiscriminately blessing everyone in sight. He is clearly a very old man and visibly frail, but gamely continues making the sign of the cross, time after time after time. His ornate throne is carried aloft on two long, heavy poles that rest on the shoulders of huge Pope-bearers. These men are progressing very slowly down the aisle towards us. We are so stunned by this unexpected event that we can only stand and stare, but then Barry snaps out of it and realizes that we should be doing something to justify our presence. So, under his guidance, we advance in a little cluster, with camera and sound cables strung between us, up the aisle to meet him. Then we begin to retreat in front of him, keeping pace with his bearers, so that we can capture his triumphal progression on film.

He has nearly reached the front of the aisle when we realize that we have been backed up against the steps in front of the stage and cannot go any farther. Now his bearers are lowering his portable throne and de-poling him. To allow him to dismount, the poles have to be slid forward and laid to one side. We are dangerously close to the operation but there is nothing we can do about it. One of the poles shoots forward and goes between the cameraman's legs. He lets out a respectfully muffled scream and falls backwards onto the sound man, who, connected by cables, also collapses. Barry, Marie and I are crouching behind them to make ourselves as inconspicuous as possible and it is at this moment that the Pope, having dismounted, comes face to face with us.

At close quarters it is clear that he is so elderly that, were he not the Pontiff, he would probably be in a home for the confused. Seeing us prostrated before him, he assumes we are paying him some kind of extreme, medieval homage and, with a beaming smile, approaches us, bends over and bestows on each one of us a personal sign of the cross. All I wanted was a long-distance shot of him and here I am receiving an intimate papal blessing. As a non-believer I feel extremely uncomfortable. It has all been a horrible misunderstanding. I have not tricked my way in here and yet I feel guilty of deception. I suppose I should have left the moment I realized the truth, but like the others I have been carried along by the pomp of it all.

When the Pope is finally ensconced on his marble throne on the great stage, we manage quietly to make our escape and, with a sigh of relief, head for the Colosseum. Whenever I have visited this towering building before it has always been full of crowds of wandering tourists but today it is starkly empty. I point this out to Furio, who says, yes, it has cost him a great deal of money to get the place cleared for me. This man is dangerously good at his job. What other wonders can he perform?

As it happens, there is one last favour. When we arrive at Rome airport, Marie discovers that, in all the excitement, she has left her passport behind at the hotel. She will miss the plane. Furio tells her not to worry and disappears. There is an announcement to say that our flight will be delayed because the aircraft has developed a technical fault. By a strange coincidence Furio arrives triumphantly back with the missing passport just before it is announced that our flight is now ready to leave. It must have been a coincidence, surely. But RAI did say that Furio was the best fixer in Rome, so who knows?

**NOTE**

THE DATE OF OUR VISIT TO ROME WAS 1977 AND THE POPE IN QUESTION WAS THE EIGHTY-YEAR-OLD POPE PAUL VI, WHO DIED THE FOLLOWING YEAR. WHAT I DID NOT KNOW AT THE TIME WAS THAT THIS WAS THE POPE WHO, AGAINST THE STRONG URGING OF HIS SPECIALIST ADVISERS, HAD ISSUED AN ENCYCLICAL CONDEMNING ALL FORMS OF CONTRACEPTION. AS A BIOLOGIST WHO HAS STUDIED THE TRAGIC RESULTS OF OVERPOPULATION, I AM FORCED TO SAY THAT I CONSIDER THAT ACT OF HIS TO BE A CRIME

AGAINST HUMANITY, BASED ON HIS TOTAL MISUNDERSTANDING OF HUMAN EVOLUTION. BUT I DON'T THINK THAT WOULD HAVE STOPPED ME FILMING HIM. IT IS MY JOB, AS AN OBSERVER OF THE HUMAN SPECIES, TO STUDY ALL ASPECTS OF OUR BEHAVIOUR AND TO KEEP MY STUDIES COMPLETELY OBJECTIVE. IT WOULD BE LUDICROUS TO STUDY ONLY THE BEHAVIOUR OF PEOPLE OF WHOM I APPROVE. EQUALLY IT WOULD BE LUDICROUS FOR ME TO PRETEND THAT I DO NOT HAVE STRONG PERSONAL FEELINGS.

# THE GREAT PACIFIC CRUISE

## (1978)

---

IN 1978, I WAS INVITED TO GIVE A SERIES OF LECTURES ON BODY LANGUAGE. HAVING SPENT THE PREVIOUS YEAR TALKING ENDLESSLY ON THIS SUBJECT, I POLITELY DECLINED. ENOUGH IS ENOUGH. BUT, THEY SAID, THE TALKS WOULD BE GIVEN ON BOARD THE WORLD'S MOST EXCLUSIVE LINER, THE *QUEEN ELIZABETH 2*. NO, I SAID. BUT THE *QE2* WOULD BE CRUISING AROUND THE PACIFIC OCEAN AT THE TIME. NO, I SAID, LESS FIRMLY. BUT YOU COULD BRING YOUR FAMILY WITH YOU, ALL AT OUR EXPENSE. THAT DID IT. WE STARTED PACKING AND WERE SOON WINGING OUR WAY TO JOIN THE GREAT SHIP ON THE OTHER SIDE OF THE WORLD.

## THE MYSTERY OF THE TEN TALL TRUNKS

---

WHAT ARE ALL THESE London double-deckers doing in the streets of Manhattan? I remember now, this is not New York, we are in Hong Kong. The nineteen-hour flight leaves you strangely vague and woozy. There is no way your biorhythms can cope, so you just sleep and peer through the blinds whenever some confused, internal alarm-clock stirs you. And what a sight it is, what an explosion of street-signs, what a forest of skyscrapers. Six million human beings scuttle and shuffle around in this swarming colony. At least a million of them must be shopkeepers, selling everything that has ever been sold by one human being to another.

The *QE2* is docked at the newly completed Ocean Terminal, a unique structure that looks as if someone decided to build a new Harrods right in the middle of Southampton docks. Hundreds of glamorous shops are packed together in the endless arcades, right next to the giant ship. Everywhere else in the world you step off the ritzy carpets of the great cruise liners and onto the harsh smelly shell of the cavernous docking sheds, with customs officials, police, workmen and whistles, barriers and officialdom. But the cunning Hong Kongers are shopkeepers right up to the water's edge. Within twenty paces of the gangway you are surrounded by exquisite displays of carved ivory (pity the poor elephants ... there are 174 ivory dealers in Hong Kong), beauty parlours, tailors (I have a fine suit made to measure in forty-eight hours, and they thank me for giving them so much more time than usual) and shops crammed with gifts of every conceivable kind.

The variety is shattering: alongside a window stuffed with Nikon and Pentax cameras, there is a display of local food delicacies, including things that look like mummified genitals, witch's roots and flattened, dried lizards. In the hills above the city the scrub shelters porcupines, muntjac, rhesus monkeys and a whole host of other wild species, but none ventures down into this vast human zoo – if they did they would promptly be eaten. Everything seems to be devoured here. There are, by the way, no fewer than thirty-one snake dealers in Hong Kong, all selling killed-to-order snakes for the housewife with a discerning palate. The snakes sit in little wooden boxes, row above row, awaiting their fate with silent immobility.

Children in wire cages play on the decks of the boats of the floating town, while the tallest skyscrapers in South-east Asia look down unfeelingly on the rickshaw poverty. I could spend weeks here, exploring the maze of Hong Kong, but our ship-joining instructions demand that we stop our wandering and report to the main gangplank for boarding.

Staring up at the side of the ship, at very close quarters, is overwhelming. It looks more like a skyscraper that fell over and floated. The moment you step inside, the image changes. The mood is strangely familiar from television. This is not a vessel, it is a spaceship. As we move out of harbour the feeling is confirmed. There is a whole world here – silent elevators, uniformed crew, long corridors, dark colours, bright colours, quiet voices over the intercom, the gentle hum of the air-conditioning. We are not sailing, we are gliding off to take up our orbit in space again and, in three days, we will beam down in Japan. The sea is miles below us; there is no engine noise. Everyone is relaxed. The passengers give the impression of having nothing to prove. There are just over a thousand of them (and about as many crew), and this unique little village community is already beginning to reorganize itself – to absorb the changes that the Hong Kong stop has wrought on its structure.

At each major port a few get off and a few get on. New faces appear at the next table in the restaurant, new greeting ceremonies are performed, new bridge partners discovered, fellow countrymen identified. There are small shoals of Japanese exploring with their cameras. They photograph everything. One Frenchman complains mildly that they photographed his wife leaving the ladies' lavatory. They photograph my son and me playing shuffleboard ('Hold pliss, zanku') – what on earth do they *do* with all these pictures? At a reception to meet the captain, they pose in teams clinging closely to his vast 6 foot 3 inch frame while their relatives crackle their little flash bulbs, and then they all swap around to do it again. It goes on so long that an aide has to arrange an urgent call from the bridge, to protect the captain's valiantly persistent smile from collapsing with muscle-fatigue.

The captain is a splendid man – a benign, holiday version of Jack Hawkins in *The Cruel Sea*. The rest of the crew have also clearly been chosen by central casting. They are exactly as the movies would have you imagine them. The waiters in the restaurants are perfect – slightly familiar and jokey in a Michael Caine way, but more efficient than seems possible. Our young son is brought a glass of milk at our first meal, just *before* we were about to ask whether he could have one. And the food arrives so swiftly. 'The caviar,' Magnus Pike had informed me a few weeks earlier, 'is e*nor*mously good. You'll like that.' I did indeed. It was the best I had tasted outside Moscow. At night the image of the ship changes and it becomes a Las Vegas hotel, complete with casino, nightclubs, cabarets, dancing, outrageous cocktails, and star entertainers. There is a different show every night and a different film as well, screened in a cinema almost as good as the Curzon. I must confess that watching *Star Wars* in a luxury cinema, in evening dress, gliding across the Pacific at thirty knots, has a certain appeal. It is foolish to be impressed, I keep telling myself, but ...

———

It must be the breeding season for Japanese choppers; there is a vast swarm of tiny helicopters hovering over the ship. What are they doing in such huge numbers, as we edge into Kobe for our first look at Japan? A pair of binoculars quickly tells us what we should have guessed – yes, they are full of men festooned with Nikons and Pentaxes, all clicking away in an orgy of exposed celluloid. Now we are touching the dock and a band in red tunics is playing oompah, oompah and Kobe Queens in doll costumes and doll cosmetics are distributing flowers and traditional prints of Japanese mountains to everyone within reach. Now we are beaming down into inscrutable Japanese smog to take a fiendish bus ride through an impenetrable Japanese traffic jam, while our guide gives us a lecture about Japanese pollution (yes, they really do wear surgeon's white masks in the street) and Japanese inflation.

For a guide, he is seriously overqualified and is determined to convert a simple sightseeing tour into a university linguistics seminar. We pass a filling station and learn that the Japanese symbol for gasoline means, literally, 'stone water'. We come to some roadworks and discover that the sign for 'danger', which consists of a little sloping roof with two identical squiggles underneath it, means, literally, 'two women under one roof'. I am beginning to warm to the Japanese language. There is clearly more poetry and humour in it than an ignorant foreigner might imagine. Our slender-bodied guide then explains that, in English, his name means 'big belly', the incongruity of which delights young Jason. It causes slight offence, however, when we try to be friendly by calling him that, since in reality his name is the difficult-to-pronounce 'big valley'.

The bus grinds on, past those ancient Japanese shrines known as the Baseball Arena and the McDonald's Hamburger Restaurant, up into the mountains behind Kobe to look at the view and our ship lying in harbour. But there is too much smog to see it. Time for refreshment.

The bus stops outside an undistinguished building and we are ushered inside. We are in for a shock, because there, behind the boring, modern façade lies a scene of totally unexpected beauty. A magical garden has been built here, with so much attention to detail that it literally makes one gasp. The exquisitely textured rocks, the little clear pools of water filled with giant fish, the cascades and tiny waterfalls and the small, meticulously positioned shrubs and plants are nothing short of a major work of art. Each of the huge fish –

ornamental Koi Carp that have been selectively bred for centuries to perfect their brightly coloured patterns – seems to be aware of our presence and is eyeing us inquisitively to see whether we have brought food with us. The combination of the dullness of the façade and the brilliance of the garden somehow sums up the condition of modern Japan. It is a nation of delicately refined and highly disciplined traditions that has allowed itself to become thickly coated, almost smothered, in the ugly, competitive industrial thinking of the West. You even start wondering whether those magnificent Koi Carp come with batteries included.

Time is up. So down we come again in our soullessly efficient bus, just in time to catch the rush of traffic converging on the harbour to see us off. I have heard of gridlock in New York, but this is something new – this is Kobe docklock. None of the tour buses can get back to the ship because of the massive congestion. So the ship cannot sail and the crowds will not disperse until they have seen her sail. Stalemate. Our resourceful guide attempts to appease us by distributing local delicacies – dried squib strips. These are not appreciated. An elderly lady enquires, incongruously, whether the Kobe Sex Store is still open. It is the best laugh in town, she assures us. Several hours later, or so it seems to those of us who fear we may be left behind, we finally edge our way back to the docks and to safety.

Perhaps Yokohama will be better? But this time we dock in the rain and mist, through which we can see 200,000 Japanese umbrellas, held by the faithful Yokohamans who have come to see us arrive and who must by now be having trouble with 200,000 light meters. More beautiful girls in traditional costumes trip puppet-like through the public rooms dispensing gifts – for each passenger there is a posy of silk flowers and three packets of local cigarettes (to help keep up the smog-count?).

Tonight it is off to glamorous Tokyo clubland. We speed by the exotic Japanese neon signs, McDonald's again, and there is Hon'able Kentucky Fried Chicken and, of course, beloved Coca-Cola, and – my God, it can't be true – a Berni Inn. Travel certainly broadens the expletives. Our guide tells us that in the most expensive part of Tokyo we would have to pay twelve million dollars for eleven square feet of land. This even impresses the Texan millionaires in our group. As we pass the Imperial Palace we are informed that in earlier days the moats were filled with poisonous snakes. That's one way of dealing with nosy neighbours.

The elaborate Tea Ceremony is intriguing, and makes the typical English tea break seem horribly coarse and clumsy by comparison. The geisha dancing following the traditional meal, eaten squatting on the floor, is also absorbing. Sadly, at least half of our party are too old to get down to floor-level. Since tradition demands that there shall be no chairs present, the more elderly visitors have to be provided with beer crates on which to sit. This slightly damages the refined atmosphere of the geisha performance but, even so, the comparison between the delicate grace of the geisha dancing and the clip-clop of English folk-dancing is not a happy one.

Then on to the climax of the evening – a Tokyo 'nitespot'. Most of the *QE2* shore-party are eminently respectable American matrons, and at least three of them could be Barry Humphries. What they see in the show that follows leaves them poleaxed and almost speechless. It is the sudden unexpectedness of it that causes the whalebone to snap and crackle. After an attractive group of high-kickers have finished, the Oriental-plush, Disney-rococo interior dims and a spotlight picks up a young couple identified as George and Monika who are going to do something 'stylish and elegant'. The fact that she is only wearing a piece of string and he is clad in nothing more than a small leather pouch has me worried, and when he unstrings her and begins stroking her with his tongue I realize we are in for a difficult ride back to the ship.

Our guide senses that all is not well and tries to lighten the atmosphere. 'I am too young to see that cabaret,' he laughs. (He is twenty-five.) 'Well,' snaps a white-haired Texan, 'we are too old.' The guide decides not to push his luck any further and stares intently out of the window. The silence roars, as we speed past an illuminated street sign reading '86' (the number of people killed or injured at that corner during the past three months). Overhead are other special signs that indicate the length in kilometres of the traffic jam ahead; these flash into use every morning and evening, and much of the rest of the day, too. The roadside trees are bound and propped up with stakes to protect them against pollution. More face-masks. And there is Tokyo Tower, an exact replica of the Eiffel Tower in Paris, but naturally the Japanese version is bigger – by just three feet. Our guide says farewell. Again he is overqualified. In this case he is a clinical psychologist, but with inflation as it is …

It is comforting to be back in the womb of the great ship again and heading out to sea. Japan gives us one last, vivid memory – a bloody great earthquake under the sea, offshore, which produces a howling gale and a roll that even this vast piece of metal cannot subdue. But the ship's doctor is ready even for this. There is a magic injection, a quick jab of the needle and a half-hour snooze, and all seasickness feelings vanish. We don't believe it, but it's true.

It is as well that the injection works, because this afternoon I am due to give the first of my four talks on the subject of body language. The ship is still heaving from side to side as I make my way to the ship's concert hall, which doubles up as the lecture theatre. I am thrown from wall to wall of the long corridor, as if repeatedly punched by an invisible man, first with a left hook, then with a right. As I arrive at the stage door, it occurs to me that nobody will be there. The giant auditorium will be deserted. Everyone will be lying on their cabin beds, clinging to the bed-frames. This is not a storm. This is not a hurricane. This is a major seismic event, reducing the world's greatest liner to a bobbing cork. Nobody will be there and I will be able to crawl back to the security of my little bunk. But I have reckoned without the 'seasoned travellers'.

As I walk out onto the lurching stage and grab the lectern for support, I survey the auditorium. There they are, the tough ones. These are the ones who would rather risk concussion than admit that the sea has beaten them. They are all very old and have clearly each crossed many oceans in their time. They are sitting rigidly in their seats, clasping their armrests as firmly as they can without appearing to be alarmed. There is only a handful of them, scattered about the theatre in ones and twos, but I am determined to reward them for their gritty determination. So I launch into my talk with as much gusto as I can muster.

As mustered gusto goes, it is not bad, considering the fact that, as I speak, I keep listing to the left and then to the right, and can only read my notes during the brief vertical moments between these two extremes. In fact, all goes remarkably well until the ship makes an even greater effort to dip its funnel in the boiling waves. As this happens, and forces me to hang onto the lectern (which mercifully is bolted down) with both hands, I hear an ominous creaking noise. It is the sort of coarse groaning sound one associates with heavy ropes pulling on tortured woodwork on antique sailing vessels, just before the captain shouts 'abandon ship'. It is not conducive to verbal fluency, but by this time I doubt if my valiant audience is paying much attention anyway. There it is again, and again, a sinister, rhythmic creaking coming from my left. Glancing across, I see the cause. It is indeed a case of thick ropes pulling on tortured woodwork. The woodwork in question belongs to the legs of a grand piano that has been tied down at the far side of the stage. With each lurch of the ship, the piano lunges a few inches towards me and then, with the next lurch, it lunges away from me. Each tug seems to loosen the ropes slightly and each lunge is that little bit longer than the previous one. I am due to speak for an hour, and I am now convinced that the ropes will not last that long and I will die in mid-sentence, flattened by a catapulted grand piano. At least it will be quick and will liven up my obituary but, in the immortal words of W C Fields: 'On the whole, I would rather be in Philadelphia.'

Somehow, the ropes hold out and I keep on delivering my speech, although I suspect that my own body language is by now far more interesting than my words. At last the talk is over and, duty done, I struggle back to my cabin. On the way I notice staff patrolling the decks and corridors carrying buckets filled with sawdust. Presumably there are those on board who have yet to discover the secret of the magic injection.

My subsequent lectures are a stroll after that, and with the sea growing calmer with every mile, life on board soon returns to its luxurious norm. Now we are off for a long spell, real cruising this time, halfway across the huge Pacific to Hawaii. The ocean-village settles down to the important matters at hand, like what to wear for dinner. No, not the women – they have automatically brought enough to display a new costume every night – I mean the men. What has happened to the austere black of the male dinner jacket? It has almost vanished. Even the tropical white tuxedo is scarce. In their place parades a fashion show of gaudy male colours – dinner jackets in beige with brown piping, or green silk with black patterns, or black with silver flowers, or orange and blue tartan, or you name it.

The 'black tie' of the dinner invitation has exploded into

colours to match or contrast with this new trend, and there is even a first glimpse of what will undoubtedly be tomorrow's male formal wear – the open-necked dinner suit. To get past head waiters in future, this will have to copy the device I observed on the *QE2*. The fashion rule-breaker ensures success by making his open-necked formal wear twice as opulent as the necktied equivalent. The shirt is specially designed in pink with a black-edged, velvet trimmed frill, to match the pink and black velvet of the jacket. The tielessness becomes deliberate rather than casual, and another of society's little costume barriers falls. The man at the next table, Ramona points out to me, has not worn the same dinner suit twice since we set sail … and he keeps this up for two weeks, always in colour harmony with his wife.

After dinner, decisions, decisions … should it be the latest Al Pacino movie, a game of chess, dancing in one nightclub, listening to the orchestra in another, playing roulette in the casino, attending a violin recital in the Queen's Room, or playing millionaire bingo for prizes up to $1,685? Bingo is usually played by the world's losers, but here it is being played by nature's winners, and they get angry when they fail to win a prize. 'Shake the bag,' they snarl, 'shake the bag!'

There are so many millionaires on board that they do not make a good audience for the professional entertainers. The performers describe them to me as 'totally unresponsive' and assume that they do not enjoy the acts. But this is not true. Watching them closely, I realize that they do indeed enjoy themselves, but they do so without fuss. They do it quietly, not feeling the need to demonstrate their pleasure simply to satisfy the performers. They have paid huge sums of money to be on this trip, so they are not surprised to be entertained – they expect to be. This is no comfort to the entertainers, and some cannot help expressing their feelings. An Irish comedian ends his act by saying: 'Thank you for making me realize that money isn't everything.' But this is water off a duck's back and is mild compared with the way the passengers treat one another. Rich wife to rich husband, who refuses to dance: 'You were full of life a few moments ago. Now you're dee-ad. You bare-stirred!' Rich woman to rich man who is complaining about waiting for a porter: 'Get in line, you loudmouth. He's mine, mine!'

I am enjoying making notes on 'millionaire behaviour' because it is rare to be able to see it at such close quarters. One of the first things people do with big money is to throw up a wall around themselves. But here, on board ship, they are unusually exposed and it is possible to see how, with the security of wealth, many of the anxious courtesies of life – pleasantries the rest of us exchange every day because we share a sense of vulnerability – are often completely missing from the repertoire of the seriously well-to-do. And humour, so much of which is born of fear, is rare in their world.

There is a difference here between Old Money and New Money. Old Money has learned through long experience that you need to reward servants to gain the best service. Old Money people may not smile as much as the rest of us, but they do generally avoid rudeness. New Money has yet to learn this trick. Watching them mixed together, late at night in this bizarre marine 'village' community, it is fascinating to see the many subtle ways in which reserved Old Money looks down its nose at flashy New Money. Their disdain is even greater than New Money's is for the rest of us. What a feast of social nuances! For me, as an observer of the human scene, this is almost as good as being jettisoned back into the social snobbery of Victorian England at the height of the Industrial Revolution.

One small lesson I learn is that Old Money people have the courage of their convictions. They also have the courage of their misconceptions. If they hold a particular belief, that idea is grasped so tightly that they never let go, regardless of the evidence. For example, an elderly English lady is bewailing the way in which US troops brought American slang to Europe during World War II. 'Before the war our young people were well spoken but after it they became slovenly. Instead of talking properly, it was OK this and OK that. Terrible!'

Normally I would let such a statement go, but as an Englishman I am embarrassed that she has said this in the hearing of some Americans who are too polite to challenge her. Personally I have always enjoyed the way the Yanks have played with and embellished the English language. Apart from Webster's irritating spelling revisions, their influence has been largely imaginative and colourful. So I rise to the occasion and hear myself say: 'You are wrong about the OK, it was popular in England long before World War II.' She swivels her head around as though it were on a stick and stares at me. 'Nonsense!' she says emphatically. Undeterred, I continue: 'As a matter of fact, it was well known in England even in Victorian times, back in the nineteenth century.' 'Rubbish!' she says. I persist: 'Over a hundred years ago, in the 1860s, there was a famous music-hall performer on the Victorian stage. Known as the Great Vance, he sang a song called "Walking in the Zoo is the OK Thing to Do". I happen to know about it because it was the first time that the word "Zoo" was ever used.' She blinks at me with a look of mild distaste. 'I don't believe you,' she says, enunciating her words very carefully, and with that she stalks off. I give up. Old Money is so impervious to new facts that it is simply not worth the effort. New Money is more flexible in this respect. After all, you never know when a new fact might come along that could lead to, say, a revolutionary form of coat-hanger that could be supplied to every wardrobe in the world. So New Money, despite its brashness, tends to keep its options open.

ABOVE: *The Villa Apap Bologna in Attard, our Maltese base from which we explored the Mediterranean.*

BELOW: *A Naked Eye carved in stone, watching over Grand Harbour in Malta.*

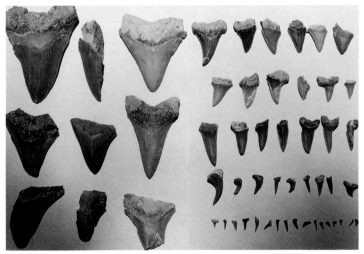

ABOVE AND BELOW: *The wall paintings at the village house of the Maltese artist, Salvo.*

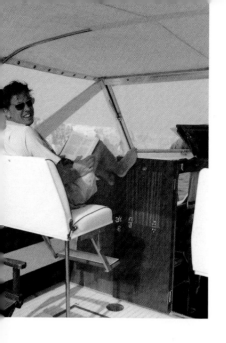

ABOVE LEFT: *David Attenborough relaxing on the* Argo *on the way to Filfla Island.*
ABOVE RIGHT: *The author swimming from the* Argo *to the boulder-strewn beach of Filfla.*
BELOW: *An aerial view of the miniature 'lost world' of the island of Filfla, a few miles off the coast of Malta.*

*The vivid decorations of typical Maltese fishing boats. The black 'moustache' indicates a death in the fisherman's family. The red 'moustache' is favoured in the north of the island, the yellow one in the south. The bow-eyes are there to outstare the 'Evil Eye'.*

ABOVE: *The delightful bar-signs of Malta.*

LEFT: *The unexpected visit of the aloof 'Anubis' dog to the Villa Apap Bologna.*

ABOVE: *Protective horns placed high up on Maltese farm buildings to protect the occupants from attacks by the Evil Eye.*

RIGHT: *After a childhood spent near the sea, five-year-old Jason has no fear of water.*

ABOVE: *The bleak, moonlike landscape of Lanzarote. The white spot in the distance is the abandoned hire-car, one of whose wheels had preceded it up the mountain road.*

ABOVE: *The great megalith of Lanzarote, before it was removed to the local museum. The inscribed 'necklace' suggests that this was a Mother Goddess stone.*
LEFT: *The unique, locust-headed Idol of Tejía found on the slopes of an extinct volcano on the island of Lanzarote.*

ABOVE: *In our gesture-survey of European countries, multilingual Marie O'Shaughnessy proved to be an indispensable member of the team, always ready to deal with local problems.*

LEFT: *One of the famous Barbary Apes living on the Rock of Gibraltar – the only wild monkeys in the whole of Europe.*

THIS PAGE: *Professional footballers from Oxford United enjoying a summer break in Tenerife.*

OPPOSITE PAGE, BELOW: *The balls needed to play Shrovetide Football are displayed in the local bar at Ashbourne in Derbyshire. One is the Tuesday ball and the other the Wednesday ball.*

ABOVE: *An 1880 print of the Ashbourne football riot that gave rise to the term 'local derby'.*

RIGHT: *Shrovetide Football in progress - there are no rules and no limit to the number of players.*

OPPOSITE PAGE, ABOVE: *Travelling in Africa, between one isolated tribe and another, calls for many rough landings in small aircraft.*

OPPOSITE PAGE, BELOW: *By a remote waterfall in Kenya's Rift Valley, a circle of young boys prepares to leap into the water to catch Tilapia. They use no equipment , resurfacing with the live fish held between their teeth.*

RIGHT: *One of the Kenyan fishing boys with his catch in his mouth.*

BELOW: *For some Turkana tribespeople in Kenya, home is a small round hut in an almost unbearably hot, desolate landscape.*

ABOVE LEFT: *Young Samburu warriors used to spend many hours meticulously decorating one another with body-paint. The male-bonding aspects of this process have suffered since they acquired small hand-mirrors that enable them to apply make-up to their own faces.* ABOVE RIGHT: *In the Samburu tribe the girls decorate themselves by smearing red ochre on one another's breasts.* BELOW: *The young warriors of the Samburu tribe, called the 'Moran', performing a war dance with a serious purpose.*

Later, while we sleep, the ship's presses produce the *QE2 Express,* the liner's own newspaper, delivered under the door of each cabin every morning, in case we want to keep in touch with the ordinary world out there. No thanks. In the morning air we surface to count the number of albatrosses following the stern. I marvel at the fact that they have been with us now for literally thousands of miles. Another six hundred miles have slipped by since yesterday, and I am tugged relentlessly from table tennis to swimming to mini-golf to shuffleboard by a stubbornly active young son who views relaxation as some kind of terminal illness.

Each game is approached as though our very lives depend on the outcome. Is there anything more devoutly competitive than a nine-year-old boy? Rules have to be obeyed to the letter. Precise scores have to be kept and there is no place for levity or interruption once a contest is under way. Imagine his glowering disbelief, then, when a flamboyant American, dressed in black, flowing clothes and looking rather like a long-haired Robert Mitchum playing the role of a renegade priest, invades our territory. We are poised at the climax of a sharply contested table-tennis game when this intimidating figure has the nerve to sit down on the edge of our table-tennis table and casually engage me in conversation. I reply to his questions with the sort of clipped, exaggerated brevity that pushes politeness to the edge of collapse and would make it quite clear to any normal social being that I am keen to resume my game. But this is no normal being, this is a tele-evangelist on holiday, and he refuses to budge. With his Deep South drawl he continues to make small talk, explaining airily how he has cured the blind, the lame and the deaf on TV, while we continue to hold our 'about to play' postures in frozen silence.

After a while, the usual courtesies demand that I should say something, so I ask him what he is doing on this cruise.

'Spending God's money,' he replies, with a cynical smile. At these words I get a flash-picture in my mind of all those poor, gullible souls who have been smiling their soft-boiled smiles, swaying their trusting bodies in unison, and 'praising the Lord' at his odious prayer meetings. I see them digging their hands into their cheap, Sunday-best suits to pull out dollar bills they can ill afford to spare, and giving them to this grinning charlatan, and my long-standing opinion of organized religion plumbs new depths. He must see something in my eyes because he saunters off and leaves us to our game. In religion, as in politics, it is all too often the case that the scum rises to the top. The real nourishment is to be found near the bottom of the jar.

The days merge into one another, and just as I am about to feel guiltily hedonistic, there are the hills of Hawaii in the far distance and a new bustle and excitement. We will be there in a couple of hours and I decide to pass the time in the ship's cinema where they are thoughtfully screening the epic *Hawaii*. We have just reached the point in the plot where the sailing-ship has dropped anchor and beautiful young Hawaiian girls are swimming out to greet the sailors with warm smiles that promise untold delights on the tropical beaches, when we realize that the *QE2* has reached the real Hawaii outside and is about to dock.

Abandoning the fictional Hawaii, we move quickly outside to compare it with the factual one. The *QE2* is easing her way into the harbour of the main island in the group, Oahu. This is something of a let-down. There are no girls swimming out to the ship with garlands of flowers. Instead we are faced with a large building just beyond the dock, capped with the giant initials IBM. It is all much more like *Hawaii Five-0* than a paradise isle.

The staff of the *QE2* have been especially looking forward to their time on shore here, but a shock wave goes through the ship when they learn that all leave has been cancelled. The passengers are unaware of this, but we have made friends with the ship's doctor and, since my lecture duties make me 'half-staff', he tells us in confidence that there is an emergency. An elderly lady has gone missing, and the entire crew has been enlisted to search every inch of the ship, from stem to distant stern. On a ship of this size, this is no mean task, and it will probably take them the whole of the time we have in Hawaii to quietly carry out this arduous duty.

This ban on going ashore does not apply to Ramona, Jason and myself, so we hire a taxi for a ride around the island's wilder places. We have soon left IBM behind and are heading into the centre of Oahu. Now we are back in the tropical island of the imagination. I ask the driver to stop the car on a forest road. He is puzzled, as there is no tourist attraction here. No shopping mall in sight, no shops selling trinkets proclaiming 'Aloha' or 'Hang Loose Hawaii', no postcards of girls with half-coconuts on their breasts and grass skirts over their American panties. Nothing but tangled undergrowth – but this is precisely what I want.

While he waits patiently at the roadside, we plunge into the dense vegetation and then pause to absorb the atmosphere. There is a strong fragrance of hot, damp volcanic earth. Every plant here is alien to us. Every insect belongs to a species we have never seen before. As with most small islands, there are no big wild animals, but the place is alive with brightly coloured birds and impossibly large butterflies. It is a moment that will lie sharp in the memory.

Despite the way these islands have been wrenched into the twentieth century, the beauty and the atmosphere remain, just so long as you take the trouble to escape from the hula-dancing, nightclubland of Waikiki Beach. And the waters are so warm, the beaches so soft and inviting … I feel sure that I will be back one day, to explore the dozens of smaller islands, to lie in the sea and watch the fish rush past – some of the most exotic in the world. Later I buy a local marine guidebook and discover that, amazingly, there are no fewer than 420 species of reef fish around these islands and that 120 of them are found nowhere else in the world.

Back on the ship, we are dying to know whether the missing passenger has been found. No, she has not. She must have gone overboard. As she was too old and too frail to climb over the stout railings that line the ship's decks, this suggests that she must have been thrown overboard. Murder on the *QE2*! Where is Monsieur Poirot when you need him?

I ask whether we will see the Hawaiian police coming on board, but am told that, since the *QE2* is registered at the English port of Southampton, it will be up to the Southampton police to investigate. I can see the scene now, back home in the local police station: 'Perkins, I want you to nip over to Oahu to investigate a missing person. Foul play is suspected.' 'Right, sir. I'll just phone the wife and tell her I'll be late for supper. Anyone here heard of a village called Oahu? It's where? Aloha, aloha, aloha? No, be serious.'

We are intrigued to discover that the missing passenger has occupied a cabin close to ours. We have seen her every night, getting ready for dinner. This does not mean we have been spying on her – her preparations have been rather public. The fact is that she has not been travelling light. She has so many 'hanging-wardrobe trunks' full of clothes that they will not fit into her cabin. The surplus ones have spilled over into the public space just outside the elevator we use, where ten of them have been stacked in a neat row. Each night she appears there with her trusty steward and gets him to open one trunk after another, while she chooses a dress for dinner from the literally hundreds hanging neatly inside.

From what we see of her, she is a lively, cheerful lady and as happy as anyone on board. Nicknamed 'the Duchess' by the crew, because she is so finicky with her appearance, she has defiantly dyed her white hair red and, in temperament, is about as far from suicidal as it is possible to be. So, not only is it impossible for us to imagine her clambering up and over a railing, but it is also impossible for us to imagine her wishing to do so. We are convinced that someone must have wanted her dead. But who and why?

Further questioning reveals that she is an eccentric Swiss multi-millionairess, whose family are waiting in Hawaii to meet her and see her safely home to Europe. As outlandish rumours spread around the crew like wildfire, people can be heard asking the inevitable question: 'Who might benefit from her sudden demise?' Fantasy scenarios proliferate. Who was the mysterious Australian man who was seen with her shortly before her disappearance? Has someone hired a hitman to fling her overboard? In the meantime, her ten tall trunks are formally sealed with metal bands and I can't resist the temptation to take a photograph of them to remind me of this bizarre incident.

Whatever the truth of her case (and, as far as we know, it never came to court), it occurs to me that, if you do want to get rid of somebody, suggesting a long sea voyage has a lot going for it. With a thousand passengers, some embarking and disembarking at every port, with no professional police force on board, and with the deep ocean all around, the possibilities for an untraceable disappearance are endless. I will never again accuse Agatha Christie and her colleagues of being contrived and artificial in their plots.

We all hate leaving Hawaii and wish the ship's engines would break down. But it's over two thousand miles to our next stop, San Francisco, where a special welcome is awaiting us, it being the *QE2*'s maiden visit to that delightful city, and we cannot delay. The *QE2* is more punctual than any airliner. After another blissfully unreal, orbital spell at sea, we wake early to gaze up at the broad span of the Golden Gate Bridge as it passes majestically overhead. Around us is a spectacular armada of small ships, including a fully rigged pirate galleon, an old paddle-steamer and the usual jet-happy fire-boats, squirting a multi-hose spray of welcome alongside us. Thousands of small speed-boats, cabin cruisers, and sailing-boats criss-cross our path and, as we pull into the dockside, a Dixieland jazz band strikes up a uniquely American salute.

Soon, it is cable-car rides, and strolls through Fisherman's Wharf, and once again I fall in love with this most appealing of all American cities. Everywhere there seems to be music – a rock band playing in a city square, a group of strolling players in an arcade, a clown on a unicycle fooling around in the middle of a crossroads, a quartet of bongo drummers thumping away for themselves on a small beach. Unbelievably delicious shellfish is on sale at every corner. There is also my favourite sideshow, the Automatic Human Jukebox, with twenty selections; simply drop in a coin and press the button: down comes a flap and up pops a small bearded man who plays – live – on a trumpet, the tune of your choice. One of the new skyscrapers has been built in the shape of a tall, sharp-pointed pyramid – even the architects seem to feel the need to have fun here.

On board, there is a whole new crowd of younger Americans, and tonight, as we sail, it is an American cabaret with comedian Bill Cosby, who mystifies the British as much as Dickie Henderson puzzled the Yanks earlier on. Humour, most humour anyway, travels badly. Singers and dancers fare much better.

Time is running out now. It is such a short run to Los Angeles and our last breakfast before disembarking. Somehow, the planet has shrunk a little. I notice that several rich American ladies are kissing their waiters on the cheek as they say their final farewells. The ties are so much stronger at sea, even after only a few weeks. Suddenly we are back in an airport again, worrying about our seat numbers. What a crass way to travel. How boring, how impersonal. It is hard to leave that wonderful floating village. As we overheard the elderly Swiss lady remark, as she stood in front of her ten tall trunks, trying to choose something stunning to wear for her last dinner on board: 'You're never the same, after you've been on a cruise.'

# EXPLORING GIBRALTAR

(1978)

---

IN 1978, I WAS ASKED TO WRITE AN ARTICLE ABOUT GIBRALTAR. IT WAS THE GENTLE NUDGE I NEEDED TO EXPLORE A LOCATION SO SMALL THAT IN THE PAST IT HAD NEVER REGISTERED ON MY FOREIGN ITINERARIES. LACKING THE USUAL SANDY BEACHES AND WITH A STRONG MILITARY FLAVOUR, IT HAS NEVER BEEN A MAJOR TOURIST RESORT. BUT GIBRALTAR HAS A FASCINATING HISTORY AND ITS CURIOUSLY TENSE RELATIONSHIP WITH SPAIN HAS GIVEN IT THE UNWELCOME BUT INTRIGUING CHARACTER OF A BESIEGED CITY-STATE. AND IT HAS SOME UNIQUE INHABITANTS THAT I HAD ALWAYS WANTED TO MEET ...

## APES ON THE ROCK

---

HOW MANY WILD MONKEYS do you think there are on the continent of Europe? The answer is forty-three, and they are all to be found in an area of less than one square mile, on the jagged crest of the Rock of Gibraltar. I have read about them many times, but now I have come to see them for myself.

Although Gibraltar is firmly attached to the southern tip of Spain, its cultural isolation makes it feel much more like a tiny island. In fact, it is so small that, as you come in to land, you are grateful to feel the plane coming to a halt, just before it slips into the sea. From above, the airstrip resembles a beached aircraft-carrier. The ends of the short runway reach out into the sea on both sides of the neck of flat land that connects the Rock to the Spanish mainland. The main road to Spain crosses the very centre of the runway, at right angles to it, and when a plane is coming in to land the road traffic is held up for fifteen minutes, like vehicles waiting at a railway level-crossing.

But despite its modest size, this is a fascinating place – a location that was witness to one of the most dramatic events ever to occur on earth. If only it were possible to sit on top of this proud rock with a time machine and turn the clock back five million years – what a spectacle you would see. For it was then that the Atlantic Ocean broke through to form the Mediterranean Sea. At this very spot there must have been the greatest waterfall in the history of the planet. What a sight!

The famous Rock apes have been clambering about the steep slopes here for centuries and nobody knows for certain how they first arrived. The most romantic notion is that they came through an underground passage beneath the Straits of Gibraltar and emerged from one of the 144 caves that honeycomb the Rock. The natural home of the animal (the Barbary Macaque, to give it its correct name) is in the Atlas Mountains of Morocco, but although the North African coast is only fourteen miles away across the sea, this explanation, sadly, is pure fantasy.

Another idea, that the Gibraltar monkeys represent a remnant population dating from the ancient period when Europe was joined to Africa, before the Atlantic broke through, is also improbable, because no fossil Rock apes have ever been found on Gibraltar. The most likely answer seems to be that Moorish invaders, who settled on the Rock about a thousand years ago, brought pet monkeys with them and that enough of them escaped to climb up to the inaccessible summit and establish a small breeding colony there.

As the centuries passed, their numbers rose and at one stage there were 160 of them. In modern times, with more and more people living on Gibraltar, the wild apes became a pest, descending in raiding parties to steal fruits and vegetables from the houses and gardens below. To protect human possessions, the army started sniping at the monkeys until, by 1924, there were only three left alive. They could easily have become extinct at that point, but the wily trio managed to survive and continued to breed.

By 1927 there were eight of them and the numbers rose again in the thirties, but with the outbreak of war in 1939 they suffered once more. Winston Churchill, knowing of the legend that when the apes vanish from the Rock, the British will lose Gibraltar, became concerned about their plight. Learning that their numbers had dwindled again to a mere seven animals, he issued an order that henceforth their colony was never to be allowed to fall below the figure of twenty-four. A collecting party was sent into the Atlas Mountains and new apes were imported to swell the ranks of the Gibraltar originals. By 1947 the success of this Churchillian inter-vention had been so great that the ape pack had grown and split into two colonies – the Middle Hill pack and the Queen's Gate pack – which still exist to this day.

The Middle Hill pack, consisting of eight males and ten females, are the really wild ones, scampering about near a military installation and unseen by ordinary visitors. It is the Queen's Gate colony of eight males and seventeen females that are the tourists' delight – friendly, relaxed animals who face the clicking cameras with the patient dignity of local celebrities. They tolerate even the closest approaches of their human admirers, disrupting the harmony only occasionally with a sharp grab at an unprotected hat or handbag. It is the fact that they are living in complete freedom that elevates these apes above the usual zoo monkeys, and gives them their special appeal. It makes one feel privileged to be able to enjoy their company in such intimacy.

The success of the present arrangement is due almost entirely to the ceaseless efforts of one man – Alfred Holmes. Sergeant Holmes, of the Gibraltar Battalion, is the only soldier in the world with the official title of 'NCO i/c Apes'. This unique military ape-keeper has been looking after Gibraltar's greatest tourist asset for twenty years. It is thanks to him that there are no more raids on the gardens below, that the animals are well fed and in excellent health, and that their relations with tourists are so amicable and trouble-free. It is he who is the true pack-leader, scolding delinquents, protecting the persecuted, treating the sick and generally keeping a skilful eye on the well-being of every one of his forty-three strange 'troopers'.

The apes are all listed on official army records and there is an allowance of 15 pence per head per day for fruits, nuts and vegetables to supplement their wild diet of seeds, berries, roots and insects. Sergeant Holmes knows each one by name, and if he shouts out for Alfred or Joshua, it is only Alfred or Joshua who looks up to see what he wants.

Thinking of their large canine teeth, I ask him how he catches them for examination or medical treatment. 'With my bare hands,' he replies. 'What else can I do? They are too cunning to be trapped.' Rather him than me – and rather him than any zoo keeper I know.

'Watch this,' he whispers. A tiny, black-furred baby ape has wandered a short distance from the protective arms of its sleeping mother. Sergeant Holmes moves towards it. Before he had taken three paces the huge male, Jimmy, the second-in-command of the pack, leaps to his feet and swiftly crosses in front of Holmes to block his approach. A moment before, Jimmy was a slumped lump of dozing fur, apparently oblivious of all around him. But such poses can be deceptive, as his sudden transformation into a defensive barrier of swinging muscle reveals.

I enquire what Jimmy would have done if Sergeant Holmes had been quicker off the mark and had managed to snatch up the playful baby. 'He would have been very angry with the baby's mother and would have scolded her for being so careless,' is the unexpected reply.

'But don't you ever get savaged yourself?' I ask. 'No, no, they scream and shout at me, but over twenty years I have only a few small scars to show for it.' And off he goes with an armful of melons, apples and grapes to ensure that his hairy friends will be ready to face their multinational public with contentedly full bellies.

As the morning sun rises over the ridge of the Rock, I glance up at the sky and catch sight of a swarm of tiny black specks. Binoculars reveal that they are birds of prey soaring at aeroplane height in the warm thermal currents. I count fifty-one in a few seconds. Then more and more come into view, gliding off towards the African coast to the south. They are Honey Buzzards, gathering here from all over Europe on their annual migration to their winter quarters. A local ornithologist tells me that, the day before, no fewer than four thousand passed over – an extraordinary sight unparalleled anywhere else in the world, and just one of the unique occurrences that make Gibraltar a bird-watcher's paradise. Vultures, eagles, kites, storks and flamingos all pass over, and a Gibraltarian with a pair of field-glasses is seldom bored.

This fact leads to a strange coincidence. The local television station, hearing of my visit to inspect the apes, has asked me to call in at the studio to give a short interview for their local news magazine. It must be the smallest TV station in the world and with one of the smallest viewing figures. The studio is in the basement of an old house, and after I have completed my interview I am told there is someone on the phone for me. 'Is there no escape?' asks a familiar voice. 'I turn on the television set in my hotel, tune into Gibraltar TV, and what do I get? You!'

It is my old chum David Attenborough, who is whizzing around the world making his new natural-history series, *Life on Earth*, and who, on seeing my face on his screen, has momentarily had to double-check to see which country he is in. Neither of us knew the other was in Gibraltar, and we meet up briefly to compare notes. He is not, like me, here to study the apes, but is instead filming the massive bird migrations. (We have met like this before. Once, in London, I went to a tribal art gallery to pay for a Dogon Granary Door – no home is complete without one – that I had recently purchased there. I found David in the gallery and asked what he was looking for. 'I am just buying a Dogon Granary Door,' he replied, 'before flying off to New York.' 'What a pity,' I replied. 'I was there yesterday.') We both travel so much that it is a wonder that we ever manage to have dinner together. But if my travel rate is impressive, David's is in a different class. I have a large map of the world at home, covered with little coloured pins to show my young son where I have been. If David had such a map, it would be easier for him to put pins in places where he had *not* yet been.

The next morning I turn my attention to the Bay of Gibraltar and my eye is caught by another animal spectacle – a huge school of almost a hundred dolphins, flinging themselves out of the water in playful, curved leaps, their pale, silvery bellies glinting momentarily in the sun before they disappear, to leap again a few moments later.

I have come for the apes, but Gibraltar has more to offer, it seems, and a tour of the Rock brings further surprises. In addition to the 144 caves, there are thirty-four miles of man-made tunnels. The biggest of the natural caverns, St Michael's

Cave, is festooned with some of the most impressive stalactites and stalagmites I have ever seen – some as tall as eighty feet and as thick as giant forest trees. In the main hall of the cave there is a thousand-seat theatre with acoustics so perfect that no man-made space has ever equalled them. People are sitting quietly listening to recorded music, unable to believe their ears. The live concerts here must be memorable indeed.

The following day I cruise around the Rock in a sleek 80-footer, *Conquest III*, enjoying the sight of a flying fish skimming above the surface like a huge locust. Seen from a distance, the image of Gibraltar keeps changing. From one angle it reminds me of a drowning mountain with only the peak still visible; from another it looks like the scarred ruin of a gigantic sphinx guarding the Iberian Peninsula; from yet another it becomes a vast fossilized cathedral; from farther away it changes into a great molar tooth gleaming in the mouth of the warm Mediterranean Sea.

Talking of teeth, it was here on Gibraltar that the very first Neanderthal skull was found, back in 1848. It was, in fact, discovered eight years before the one in the Neanderthal Valley in Germany that gave our primitive, heavy-browed relatives their name. So, to be correct, we should really speak, not of Neanderthal Man, but of Gibraltar Man, and give him the precedence he is due.

Gibraltar's other claim to fame, of course, is its magnificent harbour, sadly almost empty today, and the cause of much bickering between Britain and Spain. Most people in Britain are pleased to think that the Union Jack still flies over the Rock and that the vast majority of the twenty thousand Gibraltarians still wish to see it. But Spain feels differently. It is almost as if their political leaders are unable to forgive us for being beastly to the Spanish Armada. For years now they have kept up a blockade of the tiny frontier that crosses the narrow isthmus joining the Rock to the Spanish mainland. At the border post the black Gibraltar gates stand symbolically open wide. Next to them the green Spanish gates are securely locked. (Gibraltarians refer to this scornfully as the 'Garlic Wall'.)

The bottom rung of the green gates gleams silver, scuffed bare by a thousand frustrated shoes, as Gibraltarians with Spanish relatives shout to them across the hundred yards of no-man's-land beyond. There, plainly in sight, but held back by a further Spanish barricade, their mainland friends and relations gather each Sunday morning for an exchange of news and greetings. Victims of ancient historical disputes, perpetuated by status-conscious politicians, they have no option – other than a long and costly trip via some other country such as Morocco. But to travel a hundred miles to cover a hundred yards seems so ludicrous that few can face it.

Instead, Gibraltarians have largely accepted their isolation and have turned in on themselves. The benign siege of the Rock has effectively changed Gibraltar into a lone city-state and, with its internal trading, its 1,600 tourist beds in ten hotels, its five beaches, its casino and its great harbour, it has been surprised by how little it needs the umbilical tie with Spain. But just as the Rock has started to strengthen its delightfully unique identity, it looks as though the pressures may be easing. With post-Franco Spain heading for the Common Market, the signs are that soon the barricades may come down and the Spanish people will at last be able to treat the Rock as a fascinatingly different and unusual holiday resort on their doorstep, rather than as a thorn in their foot.

But whatever happens, the jutting jagged outline of the Rock will continue to cast its shadow and its spell over all who come here ... with the added attraction of a quick fifteen-minute flip over to Tangiers for a sharp Arab contrast, and the beguiling presence of the friendly, now almost sacred apes, on the towering peak above, to add a little spice to the visit.

**NOTE**

TODAY THERE ARE ABOUT 250 ROCK APES ON GIBRALTAR, AND THEIR FOOD
IS BEING LACED WITH ORAL CONTRACEPTIVES TO KEEP THEIR NUMBERS FROM
INCREASING FURTHER.

# TRAVELS FOR *THE SOCCER TRIBE*

## (1979–1980)

———◦◦◦◦———

AFTER COMPLETING A GENERAL STUDY OF BODY LANGUAGE IN *MANWATCHING*, I WANTED TO FOCUS ON ONE PARTICULAR HUMAN EVENT THAT COULD BE ANALYSED IN MORE DETAIL. THE EVENT I CHOSE WAS THAT WELL-KNOWN ARENA DISPLAY, THE FOOTBALL MATCH. THE FACT THAT I STARTED OUT KNOWING VERY LITTLE ABOUT THE GAME WAS AN ADVANTAGE BECAUSE IT ENABLED ME TO APPROACH THE SUBJECT WITH A FRESH EYE. EVERYONE ELSE WRITING ABOUT THE SPORT WAS SO KNOWLEDGEABLE AND SO DEEPLY ENTRENCHED IN ITS FINER POINTS THAT THEY WERE UNABLE TO STAND BACK AND VIEW IT FOR WHAT IT IS: A STYLIZED HUNTING RITUAL IN WHICH THE PRIMEVAL HUNTING PARTY HAS BECOME TRANSFORMED INTO THE MODERN TEAM OF PLAYERS. ROBBED OF THEIR PREY-HUNTING ACTIVITIES BY EFFICIENT AGRICULTURE, THE YOUNG MEN OF THE TRIBE — THE TRIBAL HEROES — NOW FIND AN OUTLET FOR THEIR INBORN HUNTING URGES IN THE SYMBOLIC PURSUIT OF GOALS. THIS EXPLAINS THE INTENSE PASSIONS THAT ARE AROUSED BY THE GAME AND ITS GLOBAL SUCCESS AS A MAJOR SPORT.

IN 1977 I BECAME A DIRECTOR OF MY LOCAL FOOTBALL CLUB, OXFORD UNITED, AND IN THIS WAY WAS ABLE TO OBSERVE EVERY ASPECT OF THE SPORT. THREE YEARS LATER I HAD SEEN ENOUGH TO BE ABLE TO START WORK ON A BOOK ON THE SUBJECT, CALLED *THE SOCCER TRIBE*. IN ORDER TO GATHER INFORMATION AT FIRST HAND I NOT ONLY ATTENDED ALL THE HOME MATCHES BUT TRAVELLED TO

THE AWAY MATCHES ON THE TEAM COACH AND, ON TWO MEMORABLE OCCASIONS, EVEN WENT ABROAD WITH THE TEAM. I ALSO VISITED FOOTBALL MATCHES IN OTHER COUNTRIES — IN EUROPE, NORTH AMERICA, ASIA AND AUSTRALIA.

TO CAPTURE THE FLAVOUR OF THESE TRAVELS, I HAVE SELECTED TWO SPECIFIC OCCASIONS. THE FIRST WAS A TRIP TO TENERIFE, IN THE CANARY ISLANDS, IN 1979, WHEN THE OXFORD UNITED TEAM WAS BEING GIVEN AN END-OF-SEASON BREAK IN THE SUN. THE SECOND WAS A TRIP TO THE NORTH OF ENGLAND IN 1980 TO WITNESS THE NEARLY EXTINCT SHROVETIDE FOOTBALL, THE LAST REMNANT OF THE MEDIEVAL GAME FROM WHICH ALL THE SIX MODERN FORMS OF FOOTBALL HAVE DESCENDED.

## PRESS-UPS AND PELVIC THRUSTS

I AM SOARING THROUGH the air and landing with a majestic splash in a Tenerife swimming pool. Nothing unusual about this, except that I am fully clothed. The four young footballers who have hurled me into the water are now turning their attentions to an attractive young girl they have just met, and she too is tossed, screaming, high in the air and disappears in the deep end. Now it is the turn of their team captain, followed by eight of the other players, culminating with the joker who started it all.

It is the end of a long, hard season of professional football, one in which most of these young men will have suffered painful injuries of one sort or another. But today they are relaxing, taking a week's holiday together at their club's expense, before breaking up for the summer recess. They are here in the Canary Islands with their manager and his assistants as a reward for their loyalty to the club and to ensure that they return next season in the right frame of mind. Football matches are won as much by the collective mood of the team as by individual skill, and this trip is intended to be a mood-enhancer.

Officially I am here to represent the board of directors, but the reason I have volunteered for this role is that I want to take the opportunity to observe the behaviour of professional footballers at close quarters, for the book I am writing about the sport. The public has a very clear picture of what they consider to be the typical footballer: he is physically fit, fast on his feet, mentally thick and verbally inarticulate. I have already discovered that this is only a partial truth. He may be fit and fast, but he is certainly not thick.

This mistake about the mental aptitude of footballers is made because human intelligence is usually tested verbally, as if word skills were the only kind known to man. But they are not. One can be skilful with one's eyes (like an artist), with one's ears (like a composer) or with one's muscles (like a sportsman). Given a typical intelligence test, the artist, composer or sportsman may appear to be well below the level of someone who lives by the written or spoken word. But if a verbal genius were tested for visual, auditory or muscular skills, he might find himself suddenly at the bottom of the scale. A poet cannot perform a brilliant free-kick in a football match, any more than a footballer can give a poetic response to the question, 'How do you feel now that you have won this important match?' His answer will be one of the following: it's a dream come true; I can't put it into words; it hasn't sunk in yet; it's unbelievable; or, it's a great feeling. His range is very limited because he is exhausted after running around for ninety minutes; because the emotional state of great elation is not easy to put into words; because he has never been trained to verbalize his feelings; and because he would become the victim of interminable ridicule by his team-mates if he replied:

'I am suffused with a protean glow that dances over my limbs like the embrace of an unseen lover …'

The first thing you notice when footballers talk among themselves is the speed of their wit. Their humour is often cruel and is used to deflate any team-mate who shows the slightest signs of egotism. They are always ready with a quick-fire put-down, and any player who fails to join in this ongoing game of friendly banter soon finds himself in trouble.

One famous player, who failed to wear the required ego-mask of the professional footballer, suffered badly as a result. To give a single example: when his team was staying at a hotel in a foreign city, he received a message that a local magazine wanted to interview him and photograph him wearing full playing kit. He was to wait for the journalist and his photographer at the hotel reception desk at 7 pm. As the rest of the team left the hotel, they waved goodbye to him and then spent a riotous evening together out on the town. Needless to say the message was a false one, sent by them, and the hapless 'star' was left stranded, waiting for ages for the non-existent journalist to appear.

The reason for this mocking, anti-ego behaviour is that, to succeed, footballers must work as a team. They can never know the ego-luxury of the solo performer. But although they are constantly teasing one another, they will be fiercely protective if anyone from outside their close-knit group offers the slightest opposition or hostility.

It is impossible to enter their group without being a player. You can only gain membership by running out onto the pitch, watched by thousands of pairs of critical eyes, to engage in a professional game of football. In my role as a director of the club I am looked upon as a complete outsider, but I confuse players because I do not behave like a typical director.

When there are drinking games, for instance, I agree to take part in contests than even the assistant manager (for fear of ridicule) refuses to enter. If I want to get close enough to their world to be able to write about *The Soccer Tribe,* I have no choice. And I don't even like beer. One game, for some unknown reason, is called 'Captain Bluff'. It starts out with a full pint glass of beer and the contestant intoning: 'Captain Bluff drinks for the first time with one finger one thumb.' There then follows a sequence of small 'single actions', as follows: he picks up his drink with one finger and one thumb, takes one mouthful of beer, puts the glass down, taps once on the table, taps his right shoulder with one finger of his left hand and taps his left shoulder with one finger of his right hand. Then the whole sequence is repeated with two of everything, then three of everything, and so on, until the glass of beer is empty.

If any action is accidentally omitted or done the wrong number of times, the victim's glass is promptly refilled and he must start again. If there are too many accidents, he becomes steadily more drunk and therefore less capable of completing the sequence of small actions. The inability to complete the sequence is considered a hopeless failure, and all the players dread losing face, so the whole contest becomes quite a serious matter. I notice that the team's 'hard man' is over in the far corner of the bar secretly rehearsing the sequence over and over again, getting ready for his turn.

After I have been on holiday with the team for several days, they realize that, although I am officially here to represent the club's board of directors and, in theory, could attempt to impose some sort of restraint on their wilder activities, I am, in reality, not going to raise a finger to stop them. When they hurl me in the swimming pool it is not an insult, it is a compliment. They are throwing one another in and, by adding me to their ritual are allowing me closer than usual to their group. Having sensed that I am neutral and offer them no threat, they allow me to witness even their most unconventional activities and trust me not to report them. So I won't break faith with them, except to say that they could have taught marauding Vikings a thing or two.

The banter never ceases. Group-levelling activities occur time after time. This even applies to girls. The unmarried players have found several appealing young women who are attracted to their physically exceptional bodies. If one of them scores (sexually), he is not possessive, but is only too happy to see his team-mates succeed with the same girl. This 'passing around' of girlfriends may seem callous, but it is simply a measure of the extent to which selfishness is suppressed between team-mates, both on the field and off it.

One particularly attractive young girl is working her way steadily through the single members of the team. Despite her obvious pleasure in these private encounters, her demeanor is anything but brash. In fact, in public she is appealingly demure. She is also kind-hearted. When some of the players tell her that one of the team is hopeless with women and has never 'been with a girl', she agrees to help. That night she goes to his room and befriends him. The players who have set this up cannot resist sneaking a look at the action. They climb on one another's shoulders, with great acrobatic dexterity, to peer through his first-floor bedroom window. After a few moments they collapse in a heap, nearly suffocating with suppressed laughter. Recovering, with some drinks at a nearby bar, one of them explains: 'You see, doc, he was going up and down.' More laughter. 'But not what you think, doc. He was doing press-ups.'

On the last day of the holiday, when we are waiting for the luggage to be placed in the airport bus, the girl who has been so generous with her favours appears with a small camera. She arranges a number of the players into rows, as though she is taking a formal team group photograph and is about to take a snap of them when she spots that one of the married players has joined the group. 'No, no,' she says, 'not you, I didn't sleep with you,' and shoos him away. Her group photograph is to be made up solely of her holiday conquests. And there they sit, a cheerfully male-bonded group, without the slightest sign of embarrassment.

In tribal studies, anthropologists have discovered that polyandry (the sharing of one female by several males) is extremely rare and that when it does occur it involves men who are full brothers. This says something about the way team-mates see one another. It is almost as if they were one person, rather than a group of separate individuals. On the pitch the team has been described as 'a super-being, a twenty-two-legged monster with a single ego'. And this is what I have found, even here in Tenerife, a thousand miles away from their pitches. It is something they cannot switch off and its persistence convinces me that my analogy with the primeval hunting party is fully justified.

Without this potential for intense male cooperation, our species could never have flourished, back in those prehistoric days when we needed to kill large prey animals to enrich our diet. Today, with a food surplus at our disposal, our societies have found a satisfying substitute for the ancient hunt, and these young footballers that I am putting under the microscope will be there every Saturday to act out the drama for us. Only this interpretation can explain the almost unbearably intense emotions that are repeatedly aroused in vast crowds by such a childishly simple ball game.

## WHY ARE THEY BOARDING UP THE WINDOWS?

———≈∞∞≈———

Two LARGE BALLS are hanging, side by side, from a beam above the bar of the Green Man Hotel at Ashbourne in Derbyshire. They are cork-filled, leather-covered and painted a glossy white. On this white background careful decorations have been added along with the words 'God Save the Queen'. Each ball also carries a date. The one on the left is for Shrove Tuesday and the one on the right for Ash Wednesday.

Catching my first glimpse of them, I am struck by their accidental symbolism. Indulging in a flight of fantasy, I see this small town in the north of England as the home of a legendary hero who has castrated a giant and, in triumph, has hung his trophy up in the local inn for all to see. Look, everyone, the monster is impotent!

The reality is almost as extraordinary, for these two decorated balls are the last survivors of an ancient and now almost extinct game – the sport of Shrovetide Football. And it is this antique pastime that is the parent of all today's great professional games of football, games that have become a massive, worldwide industry. Rugger, soccer, American football, Canadian football, Gaelic football and Australian Rules – all are the modern descendants of what is happening here.

For over a thousand years the young lads of the British Isles have amused themselves by playing 'at ball'. It was called 'football', not, as most people imagine, because the ball was kicked by the feet, but because those who played it could not afford horses and had to play on foot. It was 'on-foot-ball', not 'with-foot-ball'. The posh sports, enjoyed by the rich, were played on horseback. Football was the game of the ordinary people and it was as rough and tough as they were.

There were few rules for the playing of medieval football and the ball could be handled as well as kicked. The game frequently became so riotous that it had to be outlawed by the King. English monarchs issued proclamation after proclamation expressly forbidding it, on pain of imprisonment. It was first banned by Edward II in 1314, then by Edward III in 1365, Richard II in 1388, Henry IV in 1410,

Henry V in 1414 and Edward IV in 1477. By the sixteenth century it was referred to as: 'a devilish pastime ... wicked and to be forbiden ... a bloody and murthering practise ... [in which] sometimes their necks are broken, sometimes their backs, sometimes their legs, sometimes their arms ... sometimes their noses gush out with blood, sometimes their eyes start out ...' And so on.

The truth was that football had become a widespread outlet for informal violence and was threatening to distract young men from the more formal, state-approved violence of warfare. Ye gods, it was even beginning to interfere with archery practice! It had to go. But it steadfastly refused to go and, despite every effort by the courts and governments of the day, it kept on resurfacing. In later centuries it even became popular in exclusive boarding schools, where it was employed to enrich the ordeals of the sons of the gentry (and perhaps assist in turning them into the vengeful adults who could discipline distant colonies). It spread from there to universities and was soon being exported around the globe. At these educational establishments some kind of order was introduced. Each seat of learning developed its own special rules to reduce the chaos typical of the lawless peasant game. Unfortunately, each place had its own set of rules, so that when they played one another there were interminable arguments about whose style was to be followed. Many of these differences were ironed out but one remained: some schools allowed the old custom of handling the ball to continue, while others outlawed it and insisted that the ball be touched only with the feet. This difference was never settled and so the old game split into two – rugger and soccer.

In North America this split caused havoc because the British had, more or less by accident, exported rugger to Canada and soccer to the United States. When a team of Canadian students from McGill University decided to play an

international match in the United States against Harvard
students, there was an impasse. Once the astonished
Americans had seen the Canadians handling the ball during
their warm-up practice, they were outraged. They declined to
play the game unless contact was restricted to the feet. The
Canadians felt this would put them at a disadvantage, so they
refused. After much heated discussion it was decided to
compromise and play soccer for the first half of the game and
then switch to rugger for the second half. And that is what
they did. The date was May 1874 and after this historic match
the Americans decided that the handling game was much
more satisfying and soon abandoned their original soccer
tradition. Their new style of play developed into what is now
known as American football and, to this day, it still retains a
few technical differences from the Canadian version.

In Australia they stuck to the old handling game, but played
it at cricket grounds, which explains the large oval pitches still
employed there today for 'Australian Rules football'. In Ireland
they also kept the old handling game, but the Gaelic version
remained even more traditional, retaining the old spherical ball
of the medieval game. And that is how the six modern versions
of football evolved from the ancient British ball game.

Everyone knows these modern games. They are performed
in front of millions in packed stadia, watched on countless
television screens and endlessly discussed on the sports
pages of every newspaper, all over the world. Their immense
success overshadowed and eventually all but eliminated their
founding father, the rowdy medieval game. In fact, most
people assume that the old game has completely vanished,
along with many other popular early British pastimes such as
bull-baiting, witch-burning and public hanging. So had I, until
I started to probe the origins of football, as part of my study of
its customs and rituals. Then I found that the true, lawless,
medieval game was still managing to cling on in one or two

corners. This discovery is what has brought me here, to Ashbourne, on the day before Shrove Tuesday, to witness 'real' football played in the ancient fashion.

In order to absorb the full flavour of the game, my friend Peter Collett and I have booked rooms in the local hotel and it is here, on the Monday evening before the annual event, that we have encountered the first sign of the contest to come, namely this pair of beautifully decorated balls hanging over the bar. Peter, a psychologist who has always been fascinated by social rituals, is keen to take photographs of tomorrow's event. Like me, he has never seen any reference to this ancient survival and his curiosity is aroused. We start asking questions and the barman explains the sequence of events.

The most striking rule of play is that there aren't any rules of play. Once the game has begun, anything goes. In earlier centuries this led to much maiming and murdering. Old scores were settled under the cloak of playing at ball. The situation became so outrageously brutal that in the year 1880 the Derby police were called in to quell what had become a full-scale riot. This notorious incident gave rise to the expression 'a local derby', which is still used today whenever two neighbouring football teams meet one another, and when above-average tension is expected as a result.

Today, we are told, the violence is far less extreme and, as observers, we will be in no danger. (This proves to be untrue.) As he says this, there is a loud hammering noise outside. Looking out onto the street, we can see that the local shop-keepers are boarding up their windows. Yes, well, it can still get a bit rough, we are told. One year the pressure of the crowd was so great that they burst through a large shop-window, and now people take precautions.

We ask for a simple description of the game we will see tomorrow. In summary, it goes like this:

First things first – the pubs and bars in the town are open

all day and until 4 am the following morning. Why? Because nobody sober would be stupid enough to take the risks involved in playing the game. The action begins at 2 pm, when the ball is thrown into the crowd in the centre of the town, and it ends when someone manages to touch the ball three times on one of the two goals. The goals are three miles apart. They used to be two mill-wheels, but one of the mills disappeared, so now one goal is a standing stone on the site of the old building. The players have eight hours in which to achieve this feat. The game is called off at 10 pm, if nobody has managed it.

There are two teams, the Uppards and the Downards. The place where you were born determines to which team you belong. If you were born north of the little river, the Henmore, which runs through the middle of the town, you are an Uppard; if you were born south of it, you are a Downard. This distinction applies, not just to the inhabitants of Ashbourne, but to the entire human race. All Icelanders, for instance, would be Uppards, and all Australians would be Downards. This may seem irrelevant, but it is not, because anybody in the entire world is eligible to play. In reality there are usually only a few thousand players, mostly from the town itself, and, of those, perhaps only a few hundred serious contestants at the very centre of the action.

The mass of people surrounding the ball and trying to get hold of it, like some bloated rugger scrum, is called 'the hug'. This swarm of humanity moves like a whirlwind through the town, crushing everything in its path, until someone, called a 'breaker', manages to tear free with the ball and make a run for it, followed by a baying mob.

This is not an easy game to win and those who have achieved it are proud men indeed, with their photographs displayed in the town as local champions. Were it not for increasing drunkenness and exhaustion as the hours pass, the game would probably never be won; but eight hours is a long time, and in the end somebody usually manages to gain possession of the ball and make a run for it. If he is an Uppard he has a final ordeal to face because, in order to touch the ball on the surviving Sturston mill-wheel, he has to crawl through a small hole in the wall of the building and then clamber along a spindle above deep water, to tap the mill-wheel three times with the ball. Often this has to be done in the dark and with a pack of opponents attacking him, so it is considered to be extremely dangerous. The Downards have an easier time, because the standing stone that is now their goal is in an open field.

With this extraordinary scenario in our minds, Peter and I are looking forward to the drama of the following day. In the morning we drive to the two goals to convince ourselves that they really do exist. And they do, exactly as described. At lunchtime there is a great feast and speeches by the mayor of Ashbourne and by the celebrity whose honoured task it is to 'throw up' the ball. At 1.45 pm this celebrity (a local notable with the good English name of Sir John FitzHerbert) takes up the Tuesday Ball and, supported and protected by three large bodyguards, sets off on the traditional processional route to the start of the game. There, in an open space called the Shaw Croft, holding the ball above his head, he mounts a flight of steps to a special platform, high above the huge crowd that has gathered. He then leads the crowd in singing 'Auld Lang Syne' and 'God Save the Queen'. At 2 pm sharp, he hurls the ball high into the air, above the crowd, which lets out a great cheer.

Peter is annoyed to see that the ball has instantly disappeared into the dense sea of bodies and shows no sign of reappearing, so he plunges into the 'hug' to try and get some close-up shots of it. This brave action proves to be the last I will see of him for some time. In fact, I will not find him again until much later in the day, after he has been released by the local hospital.

I try to follow the course of the action as it surges this way and that. The hug slowly moves across the open space until it reaches a main road. A middle-aged lady in her small car is stranded in the midst of this turmoil and sits sobbing behind her steering wheel as her car is crumpled under the weight of bodies. Such is the crush that I can now see the car is moving slowly sideways as if it were being carried away by a flood. This is definitely a day to be avoided for local shopping trips.

Now the hug has crossed the road and, twenty minutes into the game, is flattening trees and fences as it swirls towards the River Henmore. In it plunges, going Uppards. This is all happening in the dead of winter and the water is freezing, but the action, involving literally hundreds of players, remains stubbornly waterlogged for over an hour as the knot of bodies thrashes around in the river, before a breaker manages to switch the focus to a nearby field. Half an hour later a serious fight erupts and another breaker manages to grab the ball and swim across a fishpond with it. He is clearly a Downard, because he is heading back towards the place where the game began. From there the action moves into the centre of the town and by 5.30, for the first time, it is nearer to the Downard goal than the Uppard one.

I am surprised by the intensity of the ritual. There is no laughter or fooling about. The whole event is characterized by a serious, stubborn determination to win at all costs. Folklore societies tend to transform ancient customs into politely sanitized replicas that are 'fun for all the family'. This is certainly not fun and it is definitely not for all the family. It is the real thing – one of the few ancient customs that have not deteriorated into Disneyfied tourist attractions. This is partly because it takes place on a weekday in the dead of winter and partly because it is still so dangerous. The only concession to modern times is the ambulance standing by on the fringe of the town, to carry the injured to the nearby hospital.

As the light starts to fade, the streets of Ashbourne are awash with vomit and blood. Some of the blood, I now discover, belongs to Peter Collett, who reappears with surgical stitches hanging from his face. His sliced chin, acquired as he disappeared beneath the hug, needed five stitches and his gashed hand is also in a bad way. We decide it is time to call it a day. The game is only four hours old and has another four to go, but we have seen enough and make our escape.

I feel guilty that my fascination with the roots of football has caused Peter so much discomfort, but I notice he is wearing his minor damage with some pride, like a badge that says 'I was there'. (Later, when he sent me his photographs of the event, he added a note saying: 'Thanks for taking me up north. Wouldn't have missed it for all the stitches in the world.') I suspect that the many bruised and battered Uppards and Downards, as they gather in the Ashbourne pubs late at night to swap stories, will feel much the same way. Therein, no doubt, lies the secret of this bizarre event, the last remnant of a thousand-year-old sporting tradition.

The serious thought that I take away with me from Ashbourne is that today's soccer hooligans can be explained as ancient players newly relegated to the role of spectators, a role that ill suits the intensity of their feelings. Take away the medieval 'hug' and they create one of their own. Set them outside the field of play and they start their own 'game', but this time played without a ball. For me, attending Ashbourne's Shrovetide Football has provided a much clearer understanding of the strength of feeling that accompanies modern football. At heart it is not a game at all, but a primeval test of manhood, and the famous old soccer saying: 'Football is not a matter of life and death, it is much more important than that', seems entirely appropriate.

**NOTE**

FOR THOSE WHO LIKE TO CHECK RESULTS: THE SHROVETIDE FOOTBALL GAME WE WERE WATCHING (ON FEBRUARY 19TH, 1980) FINISHED GOALLESS AT 10 PM.

MY BOOK ON FOOTBALL, *THE SOCCER TRIBE*, APPEARED IN 1981. IT HAD MIXED FORTUNES. THE FOREIGN EDITIONS WERE WELL RECEIVED, BUT AT HOME THE PROFESSIONAL FOOTBALL-WRITERS RESENTED MY INTRUSION INTO THEIR TERRITORY, AND THE BOOK WAS ROUNDLY ATTACKED. DESPITE THIS, THE EFFORT HAD BEEN WELL WORTHWHILE BECAUSE IT HAD TAKEN ME INTO A NEW WORLD — THE WORLD OF PROFESSIONAL SPORT — THAT HAD PREVIOUSLY BEEN A CLOSED BOOK TO ME. I DECIDED TO MOVE ON TO ANOTHER ARENA, THE RACETRACK, AND STUDY THE WORLD OF HORSE-RACING.

I AGREED TO MAKE A FILM ON THE WORLD OF RACING ANIMALS FOR THE BBC'S NATURAL HISTORY UNIT IN BRISTOL. THIS TIME, THE DEVICE I USED TO PROJECT MYSELF HEADLONG INTO THE SPORT WAS THE PURCHASE OF A RACEHORSE. BY A LUCKY CHANCE THE HORSE WE ACQUIRED TURNED OUT TO BE A WINNER AND WE RAPIDLY BECAME RACING ADDICTS. THE WHOLE FAMILY ADORED THAT HORSE, WHICH WAS AS BEAUTIFUL AS IT WAS FAST. THEN TRAGEDY STRUCK. IT WAS OUT ON A SIMPLE TRAINING RUN WHEN A FREAK ACCIDENT OCCURRED AND IT BROKE A LEG. AS IS THE CUSTOM WITH RACEHORSES, IT WAS SHOT ON THE SPOT. WHEN WE WERE LATER TOLD WHAT HAD HAPPENED, WE WERE SO DEVASTATED THAT FOR YEARS WE NEVER VISITED ANOTHER RACETRACK. I ABANDONED MY FILM PROJECT AND TURNED MY ATTENTION TO AN ANALYSIS OF BRONZE AGE ART. I FELT SAFER THERE. IF AN ANCIENT CERAMIC FIGURE BREAKS ITS LEG, IT CAN BE RESTORED.

# IN AFRICA FOR *THE HUMAN RACE*

(1981)

———————

IN 1981, I STARTED WORK ON A TELEVISION SERIES ABOUT HUMAN
BEHAVIOUR FOR THAMES TV, CALLED, RATHER GRANDLY, *THE HUMAN
RACE*. AFTER MY RETURN TO OXFORD IN 1973, IT HAD NOT BEEN MY
INTENTION TO UNDERTAKE PROLONGED TELEVISION WORK AGAIN.
BETWEEN 1956 AND 1967 I HAD MADE ABOUT 500 PROGRAMMES —
ENOUGH FOR A LIFETIME, I THOUGHT. IT WAS NOW MY INTENTION
TO DEVOTE MY REMAINING YEARS TO RESEARCH, WRITING BOOKS
AND PAINTING PICTURES. I HAD MADE SINGLE TV PROGRAMMES,
USUALLY CONNECTED WITH ONE BOOK OR ANOTHER, BUT A WHOLE
SERIES WAS DEFINITELY NOT ON MY AGENDA. THEN PRODUCER TERRY
DIXON PAID ME A VISIT AND EXPLAINED THAT HE HAD A WAY OF
PUTTING HUMAN BEHAVIOUR ON THE SCREEN THAT MIGHT APPEAL
TO ME. IT WOULD INVOLVE A GREAT DEAL OF FOREIGN TRAVEL,
OFTEN TO REMOTE AND USUALLY INACCESSIBLE PLACES. MY
CURIOSITY WAS AROUSED. IT SEEMED LIKE A DAUNTING TASK, TO
PORTRAY THE WONDERFULLY COMPLEX 'HUMAN RACE' IN JUST A FEW
HOURS OF TELEVISION, BUT THE NOVELTY OF FILMING ABROAD,
ESPECIALLY IN AFRICA, HAD HUGE APPEAL. I WAS SOON HOOKED AND
BEFORE LONG WAS WINGING MY WAY TO KENYA TO JOIN PRODUCER
MARTIN LUCAS AND HIS CREW, WHO HAD GONE ON AHEAD OF ME.

## SYNCHRONIZED NOSE-BLEEDING

———⊰⊷⊰———

I OPEN THE WOODEN SHUTTERS of my thatched hut and there it is: the orange glow of an African dawn, the chatter of unknown species of birds, the scurrying sound of small, brown-furred mammals, the smell of animal-stained earth. My senses are buzzing with new information. The landscape before me is machine-free and man-less as far as the eye can see.

But what am I saying? I hate the dawn. I am a night person. At home I take two hours each morning to evolve from hibernating slug to active human being. So what the hell am I doing here gazing out of my window at sunrise, like Julie Andrews about to burst into some nauseatingly uplifting song? The answer is that Africa changes the rules. It moves the goalposts. It takes urbanized Western Man and, with a single shutter-opening, transforms him into a romantic Victorian naturalist.

As I watch, a herd of zebras stroll into view. The animals move with the slow, casual superiority of bargain-hunters browsing in a street-market. Nothing much here for them – better move on, but slowly does it, no need to rush. Suddenly a stallion takes offence and twists around to face a rival. Together they rear up on their hind legs and attack one another with their front legs, at the same time trying to bite one another's neck. For a moment they look as though they are auditioning for a heraldic crest, but now they are fighting in earnest, spinning round, kicking out backwards, spinning back again, chasing, biting, screaming. Running a harem has never been easy, as any sultan will tell you.

When the zebras move off, a pack of baboons arrives and strides through the landscape, watchful and alert, like advancing troops. They pause and rest. While they have the chance, the infant baboons jump down from their mothers' backs and start play-fighting in the dirt. Why do the playful activities of animals nearly always take an aggressive form? One of the big males comes across to have himself groomed by one of his females. As he does so, he passes close to his playing infants who break off and stare at him in panic. His reaction is to give them a submissive, lip-smacking gesture, reassuring them. It is fascinating that a dominant male will momentarily put on a subordinate face to make himself less frightening and in this way to lower tension in the group. A bit like politicians kissing babies.

As the baboons stir themselves and move away, a hornbill flies down to inspect an interesting-looking object on a low branch. And a ground squirrel runs across the open space in front of my hut, stops, sits up and devours a small nut. Nocturnal Africa has bedded down, daytime Africa is stirring, taking its turn.

For the next few weeks there will be no newspapers, no radio, no television, no correspondence, no telephones, no appointments, no shops, no cinemas, no car parks, no towns. Why don't I live here? Why do I put up with the hassle of urban life when I could look out of my window each morning and simply bask in the unfenced, uncontrolled world that has been existing like this for a million years? When I am in England, curiosity makes me watch the news, listen to the reports, scan the headlines, keep up with gossip, follow developments. And what do I get for my trouble? Usually, a long list of other people's troubles that I can vicariously make my own. The very latest assortment of major anxieties and minor worries that I can feed into my all-too-receptive brain cells. Somewhere in the world there will always be a screaming atrocity to accompany the gentle crunching sound of morning toast. We can always rely on the news-gatherers to track down the latest human folly or natural disaster to make us feel happy it is not hitting us personally, while at the same time leaving us with a lurking fear that perhaps tomorrow it will.

To hell with civilization, that overblown traffic jam of impatient humanity, that gridlock of frustrated improvers and deal-makers. For a while I am going to turn my back on all that and record the lives of those who have kept faith with the ancient cycle of tribal existence. We will be filming the courtship and dancing rituals of the Samburu and the primitive architecture of the Turkana. We will be watching the young warriors applying their make-up, the girls smearing their breasts with red ochre, the women feeding their babies, the small boys catching fish in a steam, the elders gathering under a special tree to discuss the issues of the day. The noble savage rides again. But I do wish that our Samburu contact, when asked what gifts he would like us to bring him, had not requested T-shirts with slogans on them. The trick with good documentary film-making is to get there before coca-colonization has set in. We may only just be in time.

I am collected from my little hut and taken to a landing-strip. When I say a 'landing-strip', you can forget control towers and runways. What I mean by a landing-strip here is a more or less even patch of grassland with an oil drum to mark the spot. A tiny aeroplane comes in to land, bumping to a halt right in front of me. The door opens and out jumps a Jack Russell Terrier. I know they are the most intelligent breed of dog in the world, but I always assumed that landing a light aircraft would be beyond them. This one manages it by having the most experienced co-pilot in Africa, a wonderfully bush-wise man by the name of Dave Allen.

Dave's colourful wife, Petal, met me yesterday at Nairobi International Airport. She had created something of a stir by marching through into the customs hall to greet me. Her helpfulness nearly caused an incident because, when she then went to leave with me, they demanded to see her papers, assuming that she had just arrived in the country from abroad. She gave them an earful of cheerful abuse, and they eventually relented.

I can think of some airports where we would have ended up with prolonged interrogation and strip-search, but Nairobi International still manages to retain a human face. This had helped me earlier, before Petal arrived on the scene, when I was going through the health check. A uniformed official demanded to see my obligatory medical certificates but I had none. I have always hated inoculations and vaccinations and usually don't bother with them. It is rare to be asked to show proof of them, but this time I was caught out. All I had in my briefcase were some very old certificates that were hopelessly out of date. As a long shot I dug these out and handed them over. The airport official opened them and studied them closely. I knew I was in trouble. There would be a lengthy delay and I might even be sent back home on the next flight. I really must get over this irrational fear of foreign bodies entering my bloodstream. The uniformed official looked at me for a moment, nodded, handed me back my certificates and waved me through. When I asked Petal how I had managed to get away with this she replied: 'Oh, I expect he couldn't read.'

Now I am meeting up with her legendary husband and his famous flying dog. We clamber into the small plane and the Jack Russell leaps up onto Dave's lap as he fiddles with the controls. The dog's eager face peers out of the windscreen, his short, docked tail brushing Dave's chest as it wags with excitement. We are off to meet up with the film crew in some remote spot and I am about to enjoy some of the most bravura flying I will ever encounter.

Dave's little plane has become an extension of his body. If

he can think of a manoeuvre, he can make his plane do it. His landings are especially impressive. We are looking for a particular Turkana tribe, a very small, isolated group of no more than about thirty or forty people, who are living near a settlement appropriately named Porr. The small round huts in which the people live are of such stark simplicity that they will be ideal to represent the beginnings of human architecture.

Dave knows of a landing-strip in the vicinity and we are on the lookout for it. We have made contact with the rest of the team who are in another small aircraft, flown by a young assistant of Dave's, and together we are homing in on what I fondly imagine will be a long, smooth strip of land. Silly me – it turns out to be a short, bare patch of earth strewn with small rocks and boulders, more reminiscent of the surface of the moon than a friendly airfield. We descend gracefully like a falling leaf and grind to a halt almost immediately. How does he do that? The flying dog, as always, is first out, flinging himself fearlessly from the open door. It's one small step for a man, but one giant leap for a Jack Russell.

Dave calls up the other plane that is circling above us. His young assistant has seen the rock-strewn patch and bluntly refuses to land. Sensible man. As we clear the 'runway' of rocks, to assist our take-off, I am still mystified as to how Dave managed to miss them when we came in. They are scattered everywhere – a whole carpet of them. It was a miracle that we did not hit one and topple over. Dave goes off in search of the Turkana, but soon decides that they have moved on. Being pastoral herders, they are not truly nomadic, but are likely to shift from place to place in search of better grazing. And it is clear that this dry-as-dust, desolate place could not support domestic livestock. So we are piling back into the plane again and, before I have had time to make a will, are airborne once more.

After a great deal of searching we spot the tribe and, to my great relief, there is a real landing-strip near their new home-base. It will be an easy landing this time. Silly me – on closer inspection it emerges that somebody has built a pile of stones right in the centre of the strip, halfway down its already modest length. Even Dave seems a trifle perturbed by this, but it is more a case of his irritation at someone's stupidity than of any fears that he cannot land.

We come to a halt next to the pile of stones and open the door of the plane. Instantly we are hit by a sickening stench. It has to be the worst smell my nostrils have ever encountered. Dave explains: 'One of the tribe must have died and they have decided to bury the body in the middle of the runway. Only they don't dig a hole, they just cover the corpse with small rocks.' So that is what rotting human flesh smells like. I know the scene well from horror movies. The police enter a shuttered room where the victim's body has been lying for days. The senior detective curses and claps a handkerchief to his mouth as he throws open the windows. The junior detective rushes from the room and we hear him vomiting somewhere outside. It is a cinematic cliché, but now I am experiencing it for real and it is seriously unpleasant.

The other plane manages to land and we all depart as quickly as we can to film this tiny tribe. I ask how we are paying them and am told that money is meaningless, so we have brought sacks of food. They are pleased with this and are wonderfully cooperative. Apart from the fact that they have domestic animals – cattle and goats – their way of life is much as it must have been for thousands of years. I say this with confidence because I cannot imagine any ways in which it could be more primitive. The huts are tiny wooden domes just big enough to hold one or two people. I take a closer look at one. Inside, placed together on the ground but clearly visible from the outside, are the few personal belongings of the hut's owner. Some wooden tools, sticks, a few coloured feathers.

And that's it. We are in the second half of the twentieth century, but standing here I could be in the year 2000 BC.

The strangest aspect of our visit to this tiny tribe is that they do not show any marked reaction to our sudden invasion. They are not hostile, nor are they friendly. They do not wave to say hello or to say goodbye. They do not stop what they are doing while we are here, and they are perfectly happy to let us film them doing it. It is as though we have so little meaning in their lives that they have no relevant reactions to offer us. And they are so close to the edge of survival that they have nothing to spare for any passing pleasantries. For some reason, their indifference towards us is haunting. If they are not pleased to see us, I would rather they complained about us. This dumb acceptance is scary, as though they have lost their human energy and become some other kind of being.

The next day we descend on a remote mission, where the next stage of human architecture is awaiting us. A major advance in technology – little round huts again, but this time on stilts, offering night-time protection from wandering predators. Conditions here are so appalling that the missionary is astonished that I am being asked to stand, bareheaded, in a patch of sunlight and talk to the camera. The temperature is so high that ordinary thermometers cannot register it, and he is concerned that I will suffer from heatstroke. He disappears to fetch me some water.

To avoid overheating I crouch in a patch of shade like the rest of the crew and then, on cue, walk out into the open patch of sunlight. As I start to speak, I see a galaxy of tiny white stars and my words dry up in my mouth. The agitated missionary appears, carrying a bucket of water. Apparently it is not for me to drink. He wants to throw it over me to stop me from burning up. Martin Lucas, my director, is horrified as this will ruin the continuity.

The missionary is stopped and looks deeply concerned.

Personally I feel fine and I am not sure what all the fuss is about. So I try again. Once more I start to black out as soon as I hit the patch of sun. I go through this abortive routine several times until Martin, a tough, bearded, Hemingway type, strides out to remonstrate with me: 'What's the matter? Why can't you say the words? All you have to ...' And, as he exposes himself to the blast of the sun, his voice trails off, he becomes dizzy and his legs start to buckle. They get him back into the shade. Now he understands.

Giving the sun a little more respect, we do our best in the shadows and get our shots. Then we climb back into our plane. Today we are in a single, slightly larger aircraft that will seat all of us. Dave and his dog have departed to other duties and left the young assistant pilot in charge of us. We take off and, as we climb higher and higher, feel gloriously cool for the first time today. I am surprised to discover that my nose is running, as if I have a cold. Wiping it, I see that my handkerchief is bright red. My nose is bleeding. How strange. I am at the front of the aircraft and I swivel round to look at the others. What an extraordinary sight. They are all sitting there with their noses bleeding. Like me, they are barely aware of it. I point at my nose and then at the bloodstains and they get the message. If there were a prize for synchronized nose-bleeding, we would be in with a chance.

The explanation is simple enough. We have been working in temperatures of about 130 degrees Fahrenheit in the shade. In full sunlight, this must have risen to about 150 degrees. What happens at these abnormally high temperatures is that any moisture on the skin vanishes. Sweat is actually sucked out of your sweat glands before it has time to spread. The result is that, instead of feeling hot and sticky, you are deceptively, comfortably dry. Your most exposed patch of moist skin is that inside your nostrils. The heat starts to suck at that as well, bursting the tiny capillary blood vessels inside your nose as it does so. But your nose doesn't bleed because your blood, too, is being dried out and vaporized away into the air. Only when you cool down – which we are doing as our plane rapidly gains height – do your burst capillaries start to bleed again. And there you have it, synchronized nose-bleeding.

Our next port of call is a small mission south of Lake Turkana near a huge waterfall. There we will be filming little African boys catching fish in their mouths, like human otters. This water-rich environment will, we feel sure, be cooler. Wrong. The sound of the cascading water may make it feel cooler, psychologically, but in reality the heat is as intense as before. And this time our production assistant passes out completely. More missionaries to the rescue. They take her to a small room in the mission to recover. On the shelves in this spartan building are some strange, three-lobed nuts decorated with bands of coloured beads. They are fertility charms: local women carry them in their clothing in order to ensure that they will conceive. We are told that even to touch one is enough to cause a pregnancy.

I am not surprised that a woman living here would find it difficult to become pregnant. Anything as energetic as making love in this intense heat seems out of the question. And even if she managed it, the burning air would probably already have sucked the sperm straight out of her man's body and up into the stratosphere. So magic charms are at a premium. When asked if we have similar amulets back home, I explain that there, if a woman did wear a pregnancy charm, it would probably be to prevent that condition rather than to encourage it. If she wore an amulet, a gold replica of a contraceptive pill would be more appropriate.

Outside at the waterfall there is a scene of primeval splendour. Dozens of small, shiny, naked, jet black boys are standing in a circle in the water that spreads out into a little lake below the falls. Someone gives a shout and, on this signal, they all fling themselves beneath the surface. There is a brief thrashing of limbs in the water and then, one by one, they begin to surface. Almost every boy now has the flapping body of a live Tilapia fish held firmly between his brilliant white teeth. The tails continue to flip up and down as the boys wade ashore. Once on land they string their catch onto long cords and quickly leap back into the water for another plunge. This is fishing without equipment, fishing of a kind that could have taken place thousands of years ago, even before the invention of spears, sticks, hooks, knives, clubs, nets or any other man-made device. Our most ancient ancestors could have added valuable protein to their diet in this way, possibly even at this very spot. There has been a great deal of argument recently about whether mankind went through an aquatic phase before emerging onto the plains and savannahs of Africa to hunt down large prey. If man the fisher did precede man the hunter, this is how it must have looked. These little boys are the living proof that it could have happened before any technical advances had been made by our evolving forebears.

As we take off again from this location, I have two unanswered questions at the back of my mind. First, how do fish manage to survive in water that must be almost as hot as a hot bath? Second, in that primeval landscape, why did we not see Johnny Weissmuller diving from the top of that amazing waterfall, after giving vent to his wonderfully evocative ape-call? I mention to the cameraman that this would make a wonderful movie location and he agrees. (Later we discover that we are both wrong. The heat is so intense here that, sadly, it has turned all our film stock a golden yellow.)

Tonight we are staying at a game lodge to the east of Lake Turkana. For once there is a decent landing-strip. The huts are pleasantly clean and, heaven be praised, there is even a swimming pool. To be more precise, it is a natural pool fed by a hot spring. We dine well, drink far, far too much, and then all leap into the pool together – a moment of pure abandon following an exceptionally tough day. It is dark and late at night and we are the only ones using the pool at this hour, so someone decides that we should take off all our clothes and throw them onto the side of the pool. Then we can lie in the steaming water (a mere 95 degrees Fahrenheit) in a state of complete, unencumbered relaxation: a sort of alcoholic Zen. It is all very innocent and we are splashing happily about like a group of overgrown children, when two sinister, swarthy white men in black suits emerge from the lodge building, walk all the way around the pool and sit down in two lounge chairs near the water's edge. Their presence has in an instant destroyed the fantasy world we have created for ourselves. It is obvious that they have been watching us from the bar inside the building and have decided to place themselves in a position that will force us, once we have finished swimming, to walk past them naked to reach our clothes. The female members of our team are reasonably angry about this and there are whispered debates in corners of the pool as to how we can drive these unpleasant intruders away.

We know who they are from earlier in the evening. We have been told by our waiter that they are the armed bodyguards of Mussolini's daughter, who happens to be staying at the lodge while on a safari holiday. The reason they are so conspicuously and incongruously dressed in smart suits, out here in the back of beyond, is that they have to hide the handguns they are carrying. Their boss having retired for the night, they are bored and at a loose end. Our childish escapade is the only cabaret they have.

Recalling my 'primate threat-stare' strategy that worked so effectively when applied by David Attenborough to an Italian millionaire in Malta some years earlier, I explain to the team that all we have to do is to swim over to the spot where the two men are sitting and line up tight against the tall side of the pool. The water level is well below the top edge there, so we will be completely invisible to them. Then, when they are wondering where we have gone, we will all pull ourselves up so that we suddenly appear as a row of solemn heads staring straight at them. We will say nothing, will make no expressions and will not move until they have become so uncomfortable and disconcerted that they get up and leave.

Everyone agrees drunkenly that this is an exceedingly good plan and we proceed to put it into action. We swim over and line up along the side of the pool, with our hands stretched above our heads and our fingers clasping the top edge of the pool surround. Then on a signal we all heave ourselves up until we can rest our chins on the stonework. We all gaze up at the two scowling faces above us and then, thanks to the booze, collapse in helpless laughter and have to sink back into the water again. Sober, we know we could do it, but sobriety is not, at this moment, our strong suit. We calm ourselves down and try again. This time the scowls of our gun-toting victims have been replaced by sneers. For some reason, these sneers reduce us to further helpless collapse and we sink once more from view. The third time that we rise up to confront them, the two men are in the act of getting up and stalking off. One of them pauses and turns back to snarl at us: 'You scramble your brains, you know?' We are not sure how to interpret this statement. They are so depressingly grown-up and boringly buttoned-down that we assume they are offended by our childish behaviour, which they probably ascribe to heavy drug use rather than typical film-crew high jinks. But who cares, the 'primate threat-stare' strategy has worked once more and we have scored a pleasing if microscopic victory in the battle of life.

Next morning the men in black are back, this time attending their mistress who, we discover, always takes her breakfast with her stuffed cat (a late pet) sitting on her table. I must confess that I find this a sad sight, but it does have one point in its favour. As a travelling companion, this taxidermized feline may fall short on interactive rewards, but it does at least avoid quarantine problems.

Today we are off to meet the Moran. This is the name given to the young warriors of the Samburu tribe. They have promised to perform a war dance for us, in full warpaint. It all sounds a bit contrived and artificial to me, but we will see.

The Samburu are an elite branch of the Masai. The Masai look down on all other tribes of Africa and the Samburu look down on the Masai. So these are seriously noble tribespeople and we will have to be on our best behaviour. The Moran, who used to have to kill a lion with a spear to gain manhood, are renowned for their bravery. They have run short of lions lately and we are hoping that, in their search for a suitable substitute, they have not set their sights on wandering employees of Thames Television.

Their appearance is certainly impressive. For their special ritual occasions they go to great lengths with their body decoration. Their make-up is astonishingly elaborate. It takes the young warriors several days to apply it and each night during this time they have to rest their heads on special wooden pillows. These carved supports keep their hairstyles from becoming crushed while they sleep. In the old days each young male had to make up the face of one of his companions. This was a useful male bonding device, but then some of them managed to beg small hand-mirrors from visitors and now most of them make up their own faces.

The Moran are wonderfully, uninhibitedly vain, but to them this vanity is a virtue. A young warrior must not only have the best spear, he must also look the best. It is a crucial matter of status. Each one competes with his companions to display the most beautiful adornments, the most exquisite patterns of painted lines on the skin, the most elegant headgear. There is no mock modesty here. This is in marked contrast to the behaviour of the young pseudo-warriors of Western society. The young sportsman, novelist, pop star or film actor, who is famous for his brilliant professional achievements, can afford to go to a party or visit a restaurant wearing deadly dull clothing and, if interviewed, can risk being self-critical, because his fame in society will have preceded him. He may look unshaven, scruffy or dowdy, but it doesn't matter because we all know who he is and that he is rich and famous. Among tribespeople this does not apply. Having no media, no hype and no publicity, they are what they are. How they display themselves is all they have. So they pull out all the stops and shamelessly compete with one another.

As observers, we are the winners, because the sight of a whole group of Moran dancing together is hard to forget. Their war dance is wonderfully rhythmic. They advance in a tightly clustered group, stamping with their feet and uttering a loud exhalation – Hoowah! Hoowah! Hoowah! – as if they were a single huge organism. Each man holds a spear aloft. The sharp tips of the spears are usually protected by a leather covering, but when they mean business, they remove these little sheaths and expose the sharp metal points. I notice that they have done this and that it makes them look much fiercer than usual.

It is explained to me that we are lucky because this is not a 'party-piece' put on for the benefit of our camera, as we imagined. It seems that during the night there was a Turkana raid resulting in the loss of some Samburu cattle, and the war dance we are filming is for real. For the sake of their honour as young warriors, they will have to go and kill some Turkana, and the extra effort they are putting into this synchronized panting is a way of working themselves up to risk their lives. This is not folk-dancing for tourists. One can feel the aggression building. At one point they have to cluster around me for the camera and as they do so, one of them leans over towards me and hisses an English obscenity into my ear. Glancing quickly sideways I see a strangely hardened smile on his face. The two words he has uttered are probably the only English expression he knows. The chances are that he overheard them one day, used in some angry exchange between two white men, and has cleverly memorized them for later use.

The message is clear enough – we have outstayed our welcome. There is, however, the little matter of the carcass of a cow that they have been promised as payment for allowing us to film them. It was supposed to be here by now and it has not arrived. Our Masai fixer was seen earlier in the day smoking 'funny cigarettes' and we are not sure whether he became too spaced out to set off for the distant market, load up the jeep with the meat and set off again for our Samburu location. There is no sign of him and the Moran are, as they say, growing restless. They are sitting on the ground now in a tight group. Each man holds his unsheathed spear vertically like a flagless flagpole. Their synchronized panting has given way to synchronized spear-shaft waggling. Each man holds his vertical spear near to its base and then jiggles his hand, sending a vibration through the whole length of the shaft. The result is an ominous forest of upright, wobbling spears.

One of the Morans now stands up and starts declaiming to the rest of the group, pacing up and down and talking, talking. We have no idea what he is saying but our contact man suggests that, while we wait for the meat to arrive, we sit in our Land Rovers and keep the engines running. I assume he is joking, but apparently he is not. So it is with great relief that, after what seems like an interminable wait, we notice a tiny moving speck that is the meat-wagon appearing on the horizon. When it arrives, all is sweetness and light once more.

But despite this more relaxed mood, there remains a steely strength beneath the delicate body-painting and I have a feeling that the cattle-thieving Turkana will be in for a tough time in the hours ahead.

After several days of filming in Samburu villages, where family life follows age-old patterns and savage thorn-hedges still protect the livestock from prowling night-time predators, we finally return to the capital city of Nairobi to sort ourselves out for the flight home. There is time for a little shopping and I manage to acquire a delightful oddity in the shape of a tiny tribal loincloth complete with a zip-fastener. For our final evening we unwind by seeking out Nairobi's most notorious nightclub. One of the great advantages of travelling with a film crew is that you can take risks you would never contemplate on a family holiday. Nairobi night-life is well known for its dangerously shady characters, but by arriving at this club in a group we have safety in numbers.

This is the kind of joint where you expect to see Humphrey Bogart and Peter Lorre playing poker at a round table in the corner. It attempts to be chic and classy in a wonderfully seedy way and I love it. I feel as though I am entering a scene in one of those classic films I watched so avidly in my childhood. Where movies are concerned I have always been a hopeless escapist. As soon as the cinema lights go down I am away, carried off into whatever make-believe world there is on offer. My wife claims that I have watched more bad movies than anyone she has ever known. But they are not bad to me: they are my way of unwinding. As a writer, the last thing I want to do after hours of typing, surrounded by piles of reference books, is to sit down and read a novel. If I am to relax, I need to get away from the written word, and a movie is the perfect answer. For a few hours, fantasy can be allowed free rein.

So here I sit, late at night in a smoke-filled room in an African city, sipping my drink, listening to the music, watching the lazily dancing couples, and absorbing the richly fictional atmosphere. After days in the bush, this is perfect. And to top it all I get to play a bit part in my imagined movie. At the bar, straight from central casting, there is a ginger-haired, bull-necked brute of a man with a guttural European accent. Slouched on a tall stool, fumbling for cigarettes in the pockets of his khaki bush shirt, he has obviously been drinking heavily.

He beckons to someone with a fleshy paw and a slender young Kenyan girl in a skimpy dress, with big eyes and an appealing vulnerability, emerges from the shadows. There is a brief, angry discussion between the two and she looks distressed. She moves away from him and hesitates. Then she sits at a table near to me and smiles the sad smile of someone with a duty to perform. It is clear that I am supposed to ask her to dance, so I do. She has a lovely, lithe body and at close quarters her skin has an intensely erotic aroma. With a soft, almost whispering voice she asks me where I am staying. I mention the name of the hotel and, after a short pause, she says: 'I have nowhere to stay tonight. May I sleep with you in your hotel room?' It is said with a soft sadness. There is none of the usual professional banter. I have been chosen as the central player in one of the oldest scams in town – the dear old Badger Game. I have seen it in so many movies and now here it is for real. (She would come to my room, get into my bed, Bullneck would break in and threaten me, and I would pay them off. Or one of many variations on this theme.) My fantasy evening is complete.

I decline her request as gently as I can and as the music stops we separate. From my table I watch as she returns to the bar where, after a few brief words of explanation to the bull-necked thug, there is an explosion of angry cursing and shouting. She has failed and is now looking even more vulnerable and sad. Bullneck is still fuming when we decide it is time to leave and I make sure that we do so in a group. Outside in the street there are lurking figures watching our departure into the dark night and once again I am glad to be part of a team.

Waiting for our transport at the hotel the following morning, I pass my time in one of my favourite Kenyan pursuits – reading the local English-language newspapers. They can always be relied upon to contain a few gems. In this edition of the *Nairobi Standard*, for instance, I see that the ousted Ugandan dictator, Idi Amin, famous for keeping body parts of his enemies in his refrigerator, is describing himself as a 'devoted homemaker who is appealing to the US to educate his twenty-two children'. There is also a report about the way that human urine collected from public toilets in the Philippines is helping to treat cancer sufferers in New Zealand. It gives 'taking the piss' a whole new meaning. But my favourite items are the *Nairobi Standard* obituary notices. There was one I saw, on another visit to Kenya, that I tore out and kept. It went as follows:

IN LOVING MEMORY

Since you have gone, we feel
The pinch a great deal

As if the rose is gone
And the thorns are on

Despite the fact that there is
A rose-bud – a bliss

Which you couldn't see and adore
And that pinches us all the more.

British newspapers are going to seem rather dull after this.

## NOTE

AFTER OUR TRIP TO AFRICA, A CRISIS HIT *THE HUMAN RACE* PROJECT. THERE WAS A MASSIVE BUDGET-CUT IN THE PRODUCTION WHICH PUT SEVERE LIMITS ON THE AMOUNT OF TRAVELLING THAT WAS POSSIBLE. AS ONE OF THE ECONOMIES, IT WAS DECIDED THAT, INSTEAD OF CHASING AROUND THE WORLD, I WOULD DO ALL MY TALKING, WHEN SEEN ON CAMERA, FROM MY OXFORD LIBRARY. AS FAR AS I WAS CONCERNED, THIS WAS A MAJOR BLOW, BUT THE SERIES WAS WELL UNDER WAY BY NOW AND IT WAS TOO LATE TO CANCEL IT. IT DID MEAN THAT THE FINAL PRODUCT WOULD FALL WELL BELOW THE STANDARD TERRY DIXON AND I HAD HOPED FOR WHEN WE STARTED OUT. IN THE END, IT WAS AN INTERESTING ENOUGH SERIES, BUT NOT THE GROUND-BREAKING PRESENTATION WE HAD DREAMED OF. AND SADLY, ALL THE WORK I HAD DONE IN FRONT OF THE CAMERA IN AFRICA HAD TO BE SCRAPPED. I COULD HARDLY APPEAR IN JUST ONE FOREIGN LOCATION AND NOWHERE ELSE. SO I NEED NOT HAVE MADE THAT EXTRAORDINARY JOURNEY. MARTIN COULD EASILY HAVE FILMED THE TRIBAL ACTIVITIES WITHOUT ME. BUT ALL WAS NOT LOST, BECAUSE THE FIRSTHAND EXPERIENCE I HAD GAINED DID AT LEAST GIVE ME A SPECIAL INSIGHT INTO THE TRIBAL PEOPLE I WOULD BE TALKING ABOUT, WHEN SITTING COMFORTABLY IN MY LIBRARY CHAIR.

THE THAMES TV SERIES, *THE HUMAN RACE*, WAS FIRST SHOWN ON ITV IN BRITAIN IN APRIL 1982. ONE CRITIC DESCRIBED ITS APPROACH TO THE HUMAN CONDITION AS 'DETERMINEDLY OPTIMISTIC', WHICH PLEASED ME, AND TO SOME EXTENT MADE UP FOR THE FACT THAT MY OPTIMISM ABOUT THE BUDGET HAD BEEN SO MISPLACED.

# MANWATCHING IN JAPAN

## (1982)

———◦◦◦———

IN 1982, I WAS INVITED TO FLY TO THE FAR EAST TO EXAMINE THE CUSTOMS AND BODY LANGUAGE OF THE JAPANESE PEOPLE. IT WAS PROPOSED THAT I WOULD BE FOLLOWED EVERYWHERE BY A JAPANESE FILM CREW AND MY COMMENTS WOULD BE SHOWN ON TELEVISION THERE. THE IDEA FASCINATED ME BECAUSE THERE ARE SO MANY CULTURAL DIFFERENCES BETWEEN EAST AND WEST. AND OF ALL THE EASTERN CULTURES, IT IS JAPAN, ISOLATED FROM THE WEST UNTIL THE SIXTEENTH CENTURY, THAT HAS DEVELOPED THE MOST DISTINCTIVE REPERTOIRE OF BODY SIGNALS, ACTIONS AND RITUALS. MANY OF THE EARLY BEHAVIOUR PATTERNS HAVE SURVIVED UNTIL THE PRESENT DAY, BUT THESE ARE NOW COMING INTO CONFLICT WITH RECENT IMPORTS FROM NORTH AMERICA AND ELSEWHERE, CREATING AN EXTRAORDINARY MIXTURE OF ANCIENT AND MODERN.

## THE SECRET LANGUAGE OF THE GEISHA

———◦◦◦———

FOR THE FIRST TIME in my life I am sleeping in a bed at 30,000 feet. In the past I have often tried to snooze in an upright seat, a semi-reclining seat, or a nearly fully reclining seat, but never flat out in a proper bed. This is the height of luxury and, as I stretch my long legs out to their full extent and sink back onto the flat mattress, I swear I will never travel on long-haul flights any other way again. This magical service, called the 'Sky Sleeper', should be compulsory on all transcontinental flights but sadly it is only available at the present time on Japan Airlines. What the cunning Japanese designers have done is to restyle the upper level of the Boeing 747, converting it into a small dormitory. After dinner and a movie, honorable passenger goes upstairs to bed and then, after a good night's sleep, descends for breakfast and, hey presto, here is Tokyo airport.

It may appear that I am being spoiled by Japanese TV but they have asked me to do something that I do not relish, and I need to be fully awake to accomplish it. The script demands that, as I push my trolley through customs at the airport, I should already be talking to the camera to announce that I have just arrived in Japan to take a close look at the behaviour of the people there. As the flight from England to Japan is one of the longest it is possible to fly without actually going to the moon, I knew that I would be too woozy to speak coherently, and so I asked them to delay my introduction to the programme. They did not wish to do this, but they overcame my worries by ensuring that I arrive rested after the most expensive night's sleep I have ever taken. Fresh from my long slumber I manage to speak my piece without any errors and then guide my trolley through the crowded airport lounge to the waiting car.

Almost before taking breath I am off again to study the local train system. At the station I am lucky to arrive at the same moment as a farewell party seeing off a junior colleague who is being transferred to a new branch of his firm. All the company men are there to witness his departure. There are thirteen dark-suited figures arranged in a semicircle and they are clearly itching to get back to their offices and their computer screens. But they must wait politely for the social rituals to be performed.

The ceremony begins with a young woman presenting the departing employee with a large bunch of flowers. In response, he bows four times. Then a friend of his leads the whole group in a rousing 'three bonzais', which I assume is the same as our own 'three cheers'. After that, the departee walks over to the semicircle, bows and shakes hands with the young man on the extreme left. It is possible to detect the precise relationship of every man present, simply by the way he bows. This first man is even more junior than the departee and bows even lower. So does the next man. The third one bows to precisely the same angle and must therefore be of identical professional rank. The fourth, and all the others, right around to the thirteenth, give only short bows, indicating that they are his superiors. Every one of the departee's own bows to his superiors is as deep as possible. Any deeper and his head would disappear into his navel.

Now he steps back into the train and, with the doors still open, bows some more. The train should leave but is held up for some reason. Everyone waits patiently. Finally the doors shut and our man performs four more bows through the glass, as the crowd of colleagues on the platform wave and clap. Finally, at last, the train pulls out, and the ritual is over.

I can't recall ever seeing a farewell of this type in any Western context. How many young businessmen in the West would expect to see their colleagues and bosses form up in a large semicircle on, say, a platform at Paddington Station, to bid farewell to someone who has been transferred to another branch? These elaborate courtesies are typical of the Japanese culture, as is the repeated bowing. I take the trouble to count the number of bows the departing figure performed, and find that it is no fewer than thirty-three. Each bow is angled to a precise degree. The subordinate bow comes from the waist, the dominant bow from the neck only. And, to make social life more complicated, there is a special three-gear bow in which the head jerks down, then lower again, then even lower, to end in a deep bow that is achieved not by a long, smooth dipping action, but by a segmented, three-stage descent.

For those who like statistics, it has been calculated that the typical Japanese salesman bows on average 123 times a day. The Japanese escalator-girl working in a department store easily beats this – her daily average is 2,560 bows.

Anyone from the West coming to Japan for the first time and imagining that they can bow with the best of them is sadly mistaken. It is a refined art form that is only learned through long exposure to the culture. Western visitors here often make mistakes and this can cause their polite hosts intense embarrassment. It is far better not to bow at all than to bow badly. The worst crime is for a dominant figure to bow deeply to a lowly subordinate. This often happens when a rich Westerner arrives in Japan and is shown to his hotel room. As the hotel porter puts down the bags, hands over the keys and makes ready to depart, the generous visitor hands him a tip and, at the same time – to show how well he understands the local protocol – executes a deep, deep bow. This causes the porter extreme discomfort. It is roughly the equivalent of a Japanese visitor to the West going down on one knee to give his hotel porter a tip. One must never, ever bow deeper than one's subordinate. A slight forward dip of the head from the neck is all that is needed – and all that is appropriate.

The status relationships between individuals here in Japan are a minefield for the unwary, and I soon commit a cardinal error. As none of the film crew speaks English and I have flown here on my own, I am somewhat isolated and unable to join in the usual crew small talk. But they have provided me with a lifeline, a gentle, modest interpreter called Masako. She stays close to me throughout the shooting, always ready to explain what is happening and what is required of me. I am puzzled by the colour of her skin which is unusually pale and white. Somehow it doesn't look natural, but I say nothing. After days of working together I become very fond of her and grateful for all her hours of translating. We are about to enter a building where our next sequence will be shot and, as a simple Western courtesy, I reach forward and open the door for her. She stops dead in her tracks and looks embarrassed. I indicate with a sweep of my arm that she should go though the open door. She shakes her head and hangs back. 'After you, Masako,' I say, smiling. Still she will not move, and is looking increasingly uncomfortable. To put her out of her misery I walk through the door and she follows me immediately. Before I can quiz her about this little incident, we are being introduced to people inside the building and the moment passes.

Next day, the same little drama occurs. I open a door for her and she refuses to go through. This time I have it out with her and she explains that it is impossible for her to pass through before me because I am senior to her. In fact, my opening of the door for her is already a social gaffe on my part. I promise not to offend her by doing it again.

Now Masako and I are walking down the street talking to one another and her boss, Yutaka, the television director, catches up to talk to me. Masako quickly drops back three paces, which is crazy because she cannot act as my interpreter from there. I try to persuade her to join us but she smiles and shakes her head. My director does his best, in his very broken English, to describe to me what he wants. Later, I ask her about this and she explains that we are both senior to her and that while we are talking together she cannot walk with us, but must walk a little way behind us. Part of me wants to confront her and tell her not to be so hopelessly traditional, but another part of me knows that any attempt on my part to interfere with her status-customs will only cause further offence. That is the last thing I want to do with such a charming young woman, so

I give up the struggle and do my best to adapt to the Japanese system of etiquette, even though it rankles.

On another day, when Masako and I are sitting together waiting for better light for a particular shot, I try a little small talk. 'Where are you from, Masako?' My God, even this embarrasses her. What have I said now? After a pause, she answers me in a softer than usual voice, her single-word reply accompanied by an apologetic smile. 'Hiroshima,' she says. There is no answer to that. She is staring sadly out into space, and I cannot conjure up the right phrase to reply. Anything I say will sound trite, so we sit in silence. I have no idea what she is thinking, but inside my head a voice is saying: '*She* is apologizing to *me* for *that?*' But no, that's not it. She is apologizing for embarrassing me by having to mention the name of that devastated city.

I have come to Japan in late March, which means that I will be able to witness the curious Tokyo festival of *Hanami*, or Blossom Viewing. Each year, when the cherry trees in the capital's Ueno Park come into full bloom, huge numbers of urban Japanese abandon their offices and homes and spend a day contemplating the beauty of nature. It starts early in the day, with people claiming small territories on the ground along the avenues of trees. Each territory is marked out with a groundsheet, some boxes, or other markers, and once this has been done, others will respect it and go elsewhere. The big bosses, who feel they should participate, but cannot be bothered to squat, shoeless, on their company groundsheets all day, send junior employees to stake their claims for them. As the day wears on, people gather in clusters on their little rectangles of personal space and enjoy themselves. They drink large quantities of the strong rice wine called saki, they dance and they sing, or they simply enjoy looking up at the dense, endless white clouds of exquisite cherry blossom.

There is only one patch of ground here that has been left

bare and this, I notice, is surrounded by a group of young men, squatting in a circle, wearing black tunics. I am told that this is a martial arts group and that their lack of a territorial marker is a status display, the idea being that nobody would dare to intrude on their space and that their own bodies are the only markers they need.

We film the activities in the park and I describe my impressions for the camera. Then we take a break and wander across to the nearby Ueno Zoo. The animals are sitting in rather bare cages looking bored. I spot a beautiful tiger lying listlessly on a concrete platform and wander over to exchange a few words with it. (I am fluent in Tiger, but I only have restaurant Lion.) I greet the great animal in its own tongue and it nearly dies of shock. It jumps up and stares at me as though it has seen a ghost. The poor creature is housed alone and has probably not heard the 'phfff-phfff-phfff-phfff' tigerine greeting for years. It responds with a similar utterance itself and then starts rubbing its flank up and down the bars of its cage like a pussy-cat excitedly greeting its owner. My Japanese colleagues are astonished at this interaction and I have a hard time explaining to them that it is easy to learn the language of any species if you just stop talking in your own tongue and listen to theirs. It is something that never seems to have occurred to them. Perhaps I will have started a trend.

Back at the cherry blossom, many people are getting seriously drunk and the usual Japanese reserve is collapsing under the special licence of the festive occasion. One group of four young men, however, remain seriously sober. They are the office juniors who are still awaiting the arrival of their must-be-obeyed-at-all-costs bosses. Visibly and painfully unhappy, they exhibit the tightly contorted misery-faces unique to the Japanese. Then the wind starts to blow and they sit in what looks like a snowstorm of white petals. The carefully laid-out groundsheets of other revellers begin to fly up into the air, but not the immaculate covering laid out by our diligent office juniors – for they have come armed with rolls of sticky tape and their sheet holds firm. Their bosses will be impressed. But then, disaster, the rains come and people begin to run for cover.

The whole park is rapidly becoming a ghost town of little territorial markers. Among the few people left now are these wretched young men who dare not leave their post. Somehow they must protect their smart office suits from the downpour, so one of them starts ripping up their taped ground sheet and hiding beneath it. The others join him and carry their provisions and crates of drinks beneath their impromptu 'tent'. Invisible to the outside world, they crouch there wretchedly, waiting for the storm to pass. The skies grow darker and we continue to film their brave stand. Surely their bosses will not come now? At last, sodden and downcast, they emerge and abandon their post, ripping up their sheeting and dumping it in a nearby rubbish bin. Then, eyes downcast, they drift away, carrying the heavy crates of drinks back to their offices. The cherry blossom festival is over for another year.

Spring is a busy time for Japanese festivals. I was too late to experience the Doll Festival on March 3rd, or the Knickers Giving Day on March 14th (don't ask, I have no idea) and I will be gone before the Golden Week at the end of April. But I have at least been able to view the cherry blossom and I shall cherish the sight of a middle-aged Japanese gentlemen who, having emptied an unusually large bottle of saki, was using the empty bottle as a microphone, into which he was crooning, with great concentration, a romantic Japanese melody. He was oblivious of our camera, oblivious of the wind and the rain, and was floating off in a personal bubble of joyously unrestrained excess that will probably have to last him a full twelve months. Tomorrow, duty, conformity, regimentation, company loyalty, and all the other restrictions of modern Japanese business life will come crashing down around his shoulders once more, like an invisible suit of cultural armour that allows for little freedom of movement. But on this one spring day, at least, when the cherry trees bloomed in Ueno Park, he was able to unwind and fleetingly expose his secret dreams.

Tokyo is famous for its incredibly efficient 'bullet trains'. These are popular with commuters because they are so fast, but their popularity has been their own undoing. They have become so overcrowded that students are now employed during the rush-hour periods to push, squeeze and shove people through the doors before they slide shut. I have heard of this drama but I have never witnessed it. Now I am to endure it. Masako has taken me to the station *before* the one where the film crew is waiting. As soon as the train arrives, I have to ram my body into the very centre of the compartment so that, when the train stops at the next station, they can film my desperate struggle to get off again.

Before the train departs, more and more commuters arrive and literally fling themselves at the solid knot of humanity that is already crushed into the available space. By the time the doors have shut I realize that my feet are no longer touching the floor. And this is happening in a culture where non-contact bowing is the preferred greeting and where it is quite improper to embrace an old friend in the street. But, of course, the bodies flattened against me are total strangers and I will never meet them again, so they are more like furniture than individual beings.

At last the train stops at the next station and I can just make out the film crew on the platform. People start to cascade through the open doors, but I am unable to move. I am still completely hemmed in and the seconds are ticking by. Soon the doors will slide shut again and I realize that, if I don't make it to the outside, I will be carried off on a Japanese train to an unknown destination, speaking no Japanese and without the faintest idea how to get back. This thought spurs me on and I try to revive in myself the brutal mood of the rugger scrum that I have happily been able to avoid since my schooldays. I writhe and twist, lean and elbow, hunch and thrust until eventually I can feel the crush easing and then, with a final cork-popping explosion, I am out onto the platform, staggering towards the camera. The director is delighted. I have demonstrated a very Japanese moment perfectly and I have done it without having to resort to non-existent acting skills.

The next day brings the most amazing contrast. From the chaos of urban Tokyo, we have travelled to the peace and serenity of the Ryoan-ji Temple near Kyoto – with its world-famous gravel-raked garden of the fifteen rocks. This uniquely minimalist, Zen rock garden, completely free of any botanical intrusions, has been lying here like this in its long, rectangular space for over five hundred years. It is said that, wherever you sit, you can only see fourteen of the fifteen rocks. But it is promised that when you have attained spiritual enlightenment by prolonged meditation, you will also be able to see the fifteenth, invisible rock, in your mind's eye.

Of course, even this sacred place will be teeming with swarms of excited tourists later in the day, but we have been allowed to come here at dawn, before the public is admitted, so that I can be filmed, squatting in solitary splendour, cross-legged and barefoot, in front of the fifteen rocks. The director asks me to sit motionless like this and meditate until the shadows cast on the rocks by the rising sun have moved significantly.

The air is sharply cold at this hour and as the minutes pass I can feel myself losing body heat at a steady rate. This is a magical place and I will never forget its haunting atmosphere, but my personal serenity is slowly giving way to acute discomfort. If I attain anything here, it will be physical cramp rather than spiritual enlightenment. Quite apart from the fact that I prefer heat to cold, I have never been very good at prolonged squatting. It is a game for the emaciated and I am too heavily built to excel at it. I concentrate as hard as I can on the immaculate ocean of white gravel, the meticulous waves of rake-lines, and the jagged islands of black, protruding rocks, but in the end I am as eager to leave this temple as I was to see it.

I am not at all sure why the immensely sensible custom of using tables and chairs has somehow managed to elude the Japanese culture. Today they have imported the idea from the West on a large scale, but given half the chance they are back on the floor again, where they obviously feel wonderfully at ease. This has been happening at many of our meals together, and I have still not worked out a pain-free way of positioning my clumsy Western body. I look around me at their elegant cross-legged postures, effortlessly maintained with the grace of ballet dancers, as they consume another colourful spread of unidentifiable food objects and the inevitable raw fish. I start out by imitating their leg-crossing, but my back soon rebels against this tyranny. Then I try a one-leg squat, then a sideways squat, then a half-squat, then a bent-leg sit, then a bent-kneel and so on. I am inventing new low body postures unknown to the human species. Each one lasts for a few minutes before muscular agony sets in. I am trying to do this without anyone noticing, so my body shifts have to be cunningly disguised as food-reaching actions. Finally I decide there is only one solution. I must sit on the floor with my aching legs stretched straight out in front of me, under the low table. The relief is enormous but I'd give anything for a backrest.

After two weeks of floor-level raw fish and mysterious vegetable packets, I plead exhaustion one evening and excuse myself from yet another beautifully presented dinner. They are concerned that I am not well, but I assure them that all I need is a little extra rest before the next shoot. Then I sneak off for an evil, greasy Western hamburger, greedily devoured in a standing position. On the way I bump into one of the Rolling Stones, who is probably making a similar escape.

My hosts are keen for me to experience every major Japanese obsession – sumo, kabuki, geisha houses, baseball … baseball? Yes, they are passionate about this American sport. In fact, there are those who claim that, head for head of the population, it is more popular here than in America. Many people in the West believe that Japanese baseball is a recent import, brought here by GIs after World War II. In fact, baseball began here well over a century ago. The first games were played on Japanese soil as long ago as 1873, and the professional game started here in 1934.

The sense of ritual at Japanese baseball is overwhelming. The followers are equipped with elaborate costumes and symbols, and many of them hold drums or other musical instruments. They spend hours during games beating time to synchronized chants and cries, with a colourful pageantry to match anything that international soccer can offer. I am allowed to study this at close quarters and manage to analyse the timing of their chanting. Using a stopwatch I find that, when their team is doing moderately well, the fans (unknowingly) beat and call out their rhythms precisely at heartbeat speed – seventy-two strikes per minute. When fortunes improve and their team is doing extremely well, they increase their speed to eighty strikes per minute. Then, when a home run or some other moment of triumph occurs, they lose their synchrony and the noise disintegrates into a cacophony of irregular sound, as each individual leaps about screaming, going independently wild with joy.

The baseball match we have come to film is the college baseball final and emotions are running high. When it is over we are allowed to film the two teams in their dressing rooms. The members of the winning team are behaving like winners the world over, laughing and shouting, but the losing team is

ABOVE AND BELOW: *Baseball has been popular in Japan for many years and has developed its own special rituals and displays. Each game is accompanied by music, chanting, drumming, and the waving of colours and emblems.*

ABOVE: *Each year in Japan there is a special celebration of the blooming of the local cherry-blossom trees. In Tokyo this takes place in Ueno Park, where huge crowds gather to drink and dance.*

ABOVE: *The author in a traditional geisha house in Kyoto, where ritual, elegance and decorum take precedence over the activities more usually associated with such establishments in the Western mind.*

OPPOSITE PAGE, BELOW: *The preliminary rituals that must take place before a sumo contest can begin. This particular contest, or* basho, *was staged in Osaka.*

RIGHT: *Interpreter Masako at the famous Japanese garden-of-the-rocks, in the Ryoan-ji Temple near Kyoto.*

ABOVE: *Gangland in Los Angeles, where every square inch of wall-space is densely covered in graffiti.* [PHOTO: JOHN MACNISH]

BELOW: *Filming a Drive-in Wedding in Las Vegas.* [PHOTO: CLIVE BROMHALL]

ABOVE: *The million-dollar winner of the World Poker Contest held at Binion's Horseshoe Casino in Las Vegas.*
[PHOTO: CLIVE BROMHALL]

RIGHT: *One of the uninhibited dancers at the 'Dream Girls' nightclub in Las Vegas.*
[PHOTO: CLIVE BROMHALL]

ABOVE: *The amazing, bus-riding crows of Bombay, travelling around the city on the lookout for food. When they see some, they hop off, feed, and then catch the next bus.*
[PHOTO: CLIVE BROMHALL]

LEFT: *To show the effects of living in a high-density human population we filmed in the streets of Bombay.*
[PHOTO: CLIVE BROMHALL]

OPPOSITE PAGE: *The impressively decorated official birthplace of Jesus Christ in an underground cavern in the holy city of Bethlehem.*

LEFT: *Ancient olive trees in the Garden of Gethsemane. Carbon dating is said to have proved that these same trees were witnesses to Christ lingering here after the Last Supper.*

BELOW: *Long-suffering Bedouin camels in the Sinai Desert, on the route to the spot where Moses had his little chat with God.*

OPPOSITE PAGE, ABOVE LEFT: *The sanitized island of Singapore, where cleanliness is almost a religion.*

OPPOSITE PAGE, ABOVE RIGHT: *In Singapore today the statue of the colony's founder, Sir Stamford Raffles, is dwarfed by modern skyscrapers.*

BELOW: *In the heart of Singapore, bronze figures of a Singapura Cat and her kittens commemorate this unique local breed.*

BELOW: *Despite its recent use, by China and America, as a super-powers' battlefield, Vietnam remains one of the most beautiful countries in the world, as this Water Pavilion near Hue illustrates.*

ABOVE: *The new mosque in Brunei, which was built by the second-richest man in the world, and houses the world's largest chandelier.*

RIGHT: *Nothing is left to chance in Brunei's super-efficient new mosque.*

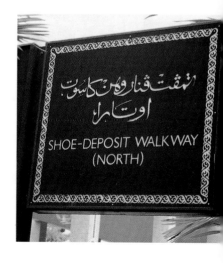

اتمقت قنار وهن كاسوت
اوت ارا
SHOE-DEPOSIT WALKWAY
(NORTH)

OPPOSITE PAGE, ABOVE: *The ornate gaudiness of this Vietnamese restaurant in the old capital of Hue is strangely at odds with the image one has of this Communist state.*

ABOVE AND BELOW: *In Bali the famous Kejak dance is now performed as a spectacular theatrical production for tourists.*

ABOVE: *The interior of a sacred monkey temple in Bali, where female monkeys may menstruate, but female humans may not.*

RIGHT: *A startling sign-board outside the monkey temple, showing that primitive superstitions towards women still survive here, despite the recent advances of the feminist movement in many other parts of the world.*

## ATTENTION

To maintain the religious puri
and cleanliness of this temple
 Women during menstruation
 should not enter the temple
Do not climb on or deface -
temple structures .
Wear suitable clothes and
observe polite manners .

OPPOSITE PAGE: *For the European visitor to Australia almost every plant and animal is novel and exciting. Where else would one encounter a treeful of white cockatoos?*
ABOVE: *The banded sea snake, on a rocky beach in Fiji, that nearly cost me my life.*
BELOW: *A delightfully bold* mola, *a fabric panel depicting a dog biting the moon. Made by the Cuna Indians from the San Blas archipelago in Central America.*

ABOVE: *A cultural contradiction – Dutch architecture in the Caribbean – on the island of Curaçao.*

BELOW: *Striking graffiti at a crossroads on the relaxed Caribbean island of Barbados.*

reacting in a way I have never observed before. They are silent, they are not moving and their heads are down. As they sit on their benches, slumped forward, long glistening threads of liquid stretch from their faces to the floor. They are weeping in an eerily motionless tableau. It is painful to watch and we find ourselves eager to cut short our visit and leave them to their mute despair.

Baseball is the second most popular sport in Japan. The top sport of all is sumo, and I am lucky because we have arrived in Osaka in time to see the final day of the Grand Tournament that is staged here each spring. Sumo wrestling has been a noble spectacle in Japan for over two thousand years and has managed to retain many of its ancient ceremonial qualities.

The massive, rectangular arena is already packed by the time we arrive, and the atmosphere is crackling with intense anticipation. It reminds me of something I have witnessed before and I am trying hard to place it. Then it comes to me – the last time I experienced this sort of audience tension was when I was unfortunate enough to be shown a cock-fight in a Balinese temple. The arena is the same shape, the ritual combat involved in both cases is endowed with religious significance, and the focus of attention is a brutal, one-on-one, face-to-face encounter, starting from a crouched position, in a tiny, central ring.

Our small group is shown to our seats and I realize, as I look about me, that for a non-Japanese to be allowed in here is something of an honour. It is clear that everybody in this great arena – everybody except me, that is – is a fanatical expert and has been following the sport since birth. Did I say 'seats'? Correction: there are no seats. It is squatting time again. Our little group must share what looks to me like an oversized cat's litter-tray. We squeeze in and settle down as best we can. The middle-aged man in the tray next to ours, whose face is about an inch away from mine, is delighted to discover that I am from England because he prides himself on his English. As the opening ceremonials draw to a close and the first pair of gigantic wrestlers clamber into the ring, he asks me which one will win. As I have a fifty-fifty chance of getting it right, I study their warm-up body language, as though I know what I am doing, and give him my answer. He gives a noisy intake of breath which suggests that I am either a genius or an idiot. I am not sure which.

The bout begins with the three key ritual gestures: the downward stamp of the foot, to crush the devil; the spreading of the arms, palms-up, to ask for help from the gods; and the throwing up of a handful of salt, to honour the ancestors who came over the (salty) sea. This done, the two giants crouch in front of one another and then, on a signal, launch themselves at each other's chests, both of which are sporting breasts any Western showgirl would kill for. Their bodies bounce off one another with what can only be described as blubber-judder. Then they grab at one another's modesty-belts, and set about a mutual toppling struggle until one of them crashes to the ground.

To my surprise, the winner is the one I predicted. My neighbour is impressed. He asks me to guess the outcome of the next bout. I watch the warm-up actions and name my winner. I am right again and now my neighbour is looking puzzled. So am I. I keep going with my predictions and my overall score is about eighty per cent correct – significantly higher than chance. All I am doing is checking the levels of anxiety and confidence in the body language of the two fighters as they measure up to one another. I am feeling cocky but I am about to come unstuck. The wrestlers we have been watching so far are the minor ones, the supporting cast. The champions are yet to come. When their bouts start, my predictions sink to the random, fifty per cent level. As with great poker players, the success of these champions involves an ability to conceal their true feelings. During their warm-up they give nothing away. With great skill, both contestants manage to send out signals insisting that they will win. All bets are off.

Finally the great moment arrives. The two top champions are pitted against one another. The older one is a Mr Obata, who fights under the name of Kitanoumi. The younger man is a Mr Akimoto, who is known professionally as Chiyonofuji. It is the old lion against the new pretender. Chiyonofuji is exciting everyone because he is so handsome and so quick. He lacks the huge belly of the others but makes up for his lighter weight by his agility. When he fights someone like the Hawaiian giant Takamiyama, the contrast is extraordinary. Chiyo weighs only 260 pounds, while Taka clocks in at a staggering 432 pounds. It is wolflike cunning against whalelike bulk. And the wolf is winning, time and again, making him the most feared of the new stars. He wins again today and I find myself getting swept up in Chiyo-mania. If I lived in Japan I know I would become an addict, like most of the rest of the population.

Outside the stadium, huge, black, stretched limousines are waiting. Their interiors are screened by ornamental, tasselled curtains that hang regally inside the windows. These are the carriages of the gods – the grand champions (the *yokozuna*) of the sumo world. At the end of the tournament (the *basho*) they will whisk these deities away to their special quarters, where they will once again start their intensive rounds of competitive eating and physical preparation for the next big event. (There are six fifteen-day bashos each year.)

These amazing figures should not be begrudged their deification or their pampered existence, because they literally give their lives to their sport. Most sumo wrestlers die young, victims of the physical excesses to which they must subject their huge bodies. But theirs is a proud existence, controlled

and disciplined for most of the time, then explosively
unleashed for a few brief moments, when the occasion
demands. They are anatomically so distinctive and so different
from the rest of the Japanese population that it is almost as
though they belonged to another, grander species. And for me
personally, watching them bouncing about in their giant
nappies, they have a special appeal – for the first time since I
was a teenager, I feel skinny.

Now we are in Kyoto, where the best geisha traditions are
upheld and the old-style geisha houses still exist. Many in the
West still imagine that geishas are little more than classy
prostitutes in fancy costumes, but the truth is very different, as
I am about to find out. We climb the stairs of an antique wooden
building and settle ourselves on the floor-mats of a rectangular
room. A Geiko and a Maiko enter and begin to tend to my
needs. A Geiko is a senior geisha and a Maiko is a young
trainee. You can tell which one is still an apprentice because she
is not allowed to have lipstick on both her lips, only on the upper
one, which gives her a strangely appealing face.

The Maiko is beautifully dressed in her traditional Japanese
costume and so delicately graceful that she would make an
antelope look clumsy. She does a great deal of smiling and
deep bowing and creates the impression that she is there to
satisfy my slightest whim. She serves me with drinks and food
and lights my cigarette so lovingly that it feels like a sexual
act. And yet the whole atmosphere is curiously chaste. I feel
as though I am in a religion-free nunnery where the inmates
have only one goal in life, which is to please me. (One
disappointed American visitor once described a geisha party
he attended as 'something like a church supper – with sexy
overtones'.)

This, in a nutshell, is the essence of the geisha. They are
ladies of pleasure in the strict sense. Rich Japanese businessmen
come here for an afternoon or an evening to forget their worries

and to sit quietly with these elegant, subservient women, who soothe them, serve them, dance for them, play musical instruments, sing to them and listen to them. Their skills are refined to the point where, by the time their male guests leave and plunge back into the harsh reality of the twentieth century, they are feeling like pampered princes.

Unfortunately, many customers today arrive at traditional geisha houses with little idea of what to expect, other than something vaguely erotic. They are puzzled by the stilted performances and find it difficult to tune in to the archaic atmosphere. One observer has described this culture clash as 'like an Elizabethan costume play performed for uncomprehending football supporters'.

But what about the geisha's worldwide reputation for providing exquisite sexual pleasure? Yes, I am told, this may happen, but it is not common in the best geisha houses. If a rich guest becomes enamoured of a particular geisha, she may agree to provide him with the ultimate in intimacies, and he may then go to the lengths of setting her up in her own apartment. She will be available exclusively to him and will wait patiently for his occasional visits. But to afford this extravagance today, one must be at least the head of a major company, a captain of industry or a top politician.

I try to find out more about the private life of the geishas, but I am met with polite giggling and shy glances. What do they think of their guests? More giggling. Then, one of the senior geishas admits that they have a secret gesture which is used to indicate that a particular guest is not very pleasant. After much probing I get them to demonstrate it to me and I am duly astonished. It is an ancient European gesture that I know well, and I am amazed that it has travelled this far. It is the *fico* – the fig-sign ... a sexual gesture known from ancient Greece. The hand is closed, with the thumb thrust between the first and second finger. The tip of the inserted thumb peeps out through the knuckles and symbolizes sexual penetration. The ancient Greeks considered this gesture to be a powerful defence against the Evil Eye and many wore a small carved hand, displaying this sign, as a protective amulet.

It has survived the passing of the centuries and still occurs, both as a gesture and as an amulet, in many Western countries today. But a change has taken place. In most places it has taken on the role of an obscene insult and has lost its protective significance. There is only one European country where it is still widely used as a 'good luck' charm, and that is Portugal. And it was the Portuguese, of course, who were the first Europeans to visit Japan, back in the sixteenth century. Could it be that this modern geisha gesture, used secretly to share a dislike of a particular visitor, has roots going back to the first Portuguese contact with early Japan? Or is it merely a coincidence, with the same gesture being invented separately in the two places? I favour the Portuguese origin and I am intrigued by the fact that the modern words for 'thank you' in Japanese and in Portuguese are the remarkably similar *arigato* and *obrigado*. Perhaps the Portuguese explorers left more behind here than most people imagine.

The geishas also have their own specially invented mime language with which they can silently indicate the names of their guests. I ask them to give me a mime for Morris and they make a horn-sign, followed by the ringing of an invisible hand-bell, followed by the circular action of grinding corn. They explain that the horn-sign indicates a cow, which makes a 'mooo' sound; the bell makes a 'rrrring' noise; and the grinding of corn makes a 'ssssssh' noise. Put these together and you have 'Mooo – rrrrri – ssssh'. Morris. Simple. I feel proud to have learned my code name in geisha language, but what possible use this will ever be eludes me. Not being a senior official of Sony, Nikon or Toyota, I decide against the idea of setting up one of these delightful beings in a private apartment, to relieve my tensions on future trips to Japan, and reluctantly step back into the crude, hard, harsh outside world.

My journey around Japan is coming to a close. Yutaka, my Japanese director, is happy because he has a total of thirty-three hours of videotaping from which to edit his programme. I have been here only three weeks, but it feels like three years. I don't mean that time has dragged, but rather that, travelling with a film crew, I have been able to absorb so much more of the culture than would have been possible as a tourist or a private traveller. Film crews can get you to places in favoured circumstances in a way that cannot be matched even by the best tour-guides. In this television age people automatically recognize what is going on and wonder whether perhaps one day they will see the scenes being shot, on their own screens back home. They rarely object when asked to give way to the camera.

I have often thought that, if one wanted to be a successful bank robber, all you would have to do is to take a film crew with you and everyone would think it was being done for a movie. By the time the truth came out it would be too late. Certainly this Japanese crew has been brilliant at injecting me into dozens of exclusive situations. I have come away with a very clear picture of the contradictory state of modern Japanese culture, with its ancient and modern elements standing side by side, staring at one another across the divide of centuries. It has been said that all new technology has been invented in the West and then developed by the Japanese. They are brilliant at improvements and refinements, but weak on innovations. There is an element of truth in this, but I have been keeping my eye open for signs of innovations and have spotted a few small ones that amuse me.

The first concerns the front walls of houses. Some of them, I notice, have rows of symbols painted on them, low down at ground level. 'What are they for?' 'Ah, yes, sacred symbols, like your Christian cross.' 'But why paint a row of them along your front wall?' 'Because dog-owners will never allow animals to cock legs on holy signs.' Ingenious.

The second concerns taxi doors. When your Tokyo taxi stops to let you out, the driver pulls a lever in the front of the car and it opens your back door, for you to alight with ease.

And the third concerns my own Japanese cameraman. He has been taking candid camera shots as we have been touring the country, and knows that everybody here is sophisticated enough to be aware that, when a television camera is switched on, a little red light shows that it is active. When the camera is switched off, the light goes out. So he has reversed this switch and, when his light goes out, his victims relax, not knowing that this means that his camera has only now become active.

OK, so these are three trivial innovations, but it is a start. And there is a feeling of creative rebellion among many of the young Japanese that bodes well for the future. The slavish following of authority and the unquestioning respect for old age that inevitably favour rigid thinking are beginning to waver. If the Japanese can keep their graceful, ancient ways and somehow marry them to modern freedoms, they will remain a major culture on the world stage in the third millennium. It remains to be seen whether they manage to achieve this, or whether their deep bows to seniority will keep their gaze diverted from tomorrow's cultural horizon.

### NOTE

ON MY RETURN TRIP TO ENGLAND FROM JAPAN, I STOPPED OFF BRIEFLY IN NEW YORK. ON A SHOPPING TRIP THERE I WAS LEAVING A BIG DEPARTMENT STORE WHEN I SAW A SMART FEMALE NEW YORKER APPROACHING. I STOOD BACK AND HELD THE DOOR OPEN FOR HER TO ENTER. THIS TIME, I THOUGHT, I WILL HAVE NO TROUBLE. THERE ARE NO SHY MASAKOS HERE. THIS BRISK YOUNG WOMAN IS HARDLY GOING TO REFUSE TO PASS

THROUGH BEFORE ME. INDEED, I WAS RIGHT. SHE SWEPT PASSED BUT, AS SHE DREW LEVEL, SHE STARTLED ME BY HISSING IN MY EAR: 'PIG!' THE POLITE EUROPEAN MALE HAD GOT IT WRONG AGAIN. HERE, AT THE VERY CORE OF FEMINIST REVOLT, I WAS GUILTY — BY HELPING HER WITH THE DOOR — OF IMPLYING THAT SHE WAS TOO WEAK TO DEAL WITH IT HERSELF. SO ONCE AGAIN I HAD UNWITTINGLY CAUSED OFFENCE. AFTER THAT, IT WAS A RELIEF TO GET HOME TO ENGLAND AND THE STATUS RELATIONSHIPS I UNDERSTOOD.

ON A SAD NOTE: THE DELICATE, SENSITIVE, WHITE-SKINNED MASAKO, ALTHOUGH STILL YOUNG, DIED ONLY A FEW YEARS AFTER MY VISIT TO JAPAN.

# TRAVELS FOR *THE HUMAN ANIMAL*

## (1993–1994)

—◦◦◦◦—

IN THE EIGHTIES, I WAS BUSY WRITING AND PAINTING. THEN, IN 1990, MIKE BEYNON, A SENIOR PRODUCER WITH THE BBC'S NATURAL HISTORY UNIT, ASKED IF I WOULD MAKE A TELEVISION SERIES ABOUT MY VARIOUS STUDIES OF HUMAN BEHAVIOUR. EACH PROGRAMME IN THE SERIES WOULD BE LOOSELY BASED ON ONE OF MY BOOKS, BUT WOULD INCLUDE A GREAT DEAL OF NEW MATERIAL AND BE FILMED ALL OVER THE WORLD. AT FIRST I WAS RELUCTANT TO AGREE BECAUSE I KNEW FROM PAST EXPERIENCE THAT TREATING HUMAN BEINGS AS NATURAL-HISTORY SUBJECTS CAN CREATE ALL KINDS OF PROBLEMS. THERE ARE ETHICAL ISSUES CONCERNING INTRUSIONS INTO PEOPLE'S PRIVATE LIVES AND LEGAL HAZARDS REGARDING PER-MISSIONS TO SHOW CERTAIN MATERIAL. ABOVE ALL, THERE ARE CEN-SORSHIP RESTRICTIONS. IT IS POSSIBLE TO WRITE ABOUT SEXUAL BEHAVIOUR IN GREAT DETAIL, FOR EXAMPLE, BUT TO SHOW IT ON A TELEVISION SCREEN IS ANOTHER MATTER, ESPECIALLY AS I DID NOT WANT ANY SEQUENCES IN THE SERIES TO BE FAKED BY ACTORS. BUT MIKE WAS PERSUASIVE AND I EVENTUALLY AGREED. THE PRODUCTION TEAM WAS ASSEMBLED IN 1992 AND MY FIRST LOCATION FILMING FOR *THE HUMAN ANIMAL* STARTED IN THE SPRING OF 1993.

THE GREAT REWARD FOR ME WAS THE WORLDWIDE TRAVELLING THAT THE PROJECT ENTAILED. ONCE AGAIN, I WAS OFF TO FARAWAY PLACES WITH ALL THE ADVANTAGES THAT AN ACCOMPANYING FILM

CREW CAN BRING, EXPERIENCING EVENTS AND ENCOUNTERS THAT WOULD OTHERWISE HAVE BEEN BEYOND MY REACH. TO RECOUNT THEM ALL WOULD REQUIRE A BOOK TO ITSELF, BUT I HAVE SELECTED FOUR — TWO FROM THE UNITED STATES, ONE FROM INDIA AND ONE FROM AFRICA — TO GIVE THE FLAVOUR OF THE UNDERTAKING.

## A HASTY RETREAT FROM GANGLAND

GAZING DOWN AT the interminable spread of Los Angeles as you come in to land at the airport, you get the sensation that, in this disposable age, this is a disposable city. Watching intersection after intersection slip past the window, it looks as though someone has thrown a rug of suburbia over some rather nasty cracks in the floor. And cracks there are. In this city it remains unspoken, but deep down, nobody ever forgets that they are at the leading edge of a gigantic continental plate which is grinding its rim on the Pacific coastline. One day soon, LA will be either beneath the waves or high on the slopes of some new Rockies.

Here, more than anywhere, it is clear that nothing is for ever. In fact, LA will be lucky to find itself still standing when it wakes up in the morning, so why bother with serious architecture? Why not construct a vast 'back lot' and watch it collapse when the 'Big One' strikes? It used to be said that John Paul Getty had a lot of money but no sense of humour. That is rubbish. It takes a very special sense of humour to gather together many of the world's greatest masterpieces and place them in museums that are perched on the San Andreas Fault – the most livid scar on the face of the earth.

I am here to film in gangland. I have been warned against it, but the idea fascinates me. I want to show on television the

way in which a parallel culture has sprung up right in the heart
of one of the richest societies in the world. This subculture
has not been fostered by outside forces, nor encouraged by
the state. Indeed, the authorities have been doing their best to
stamp it out. But it has refused to die away and instead has
gone from strength to strength, creating its own remarkable
social structure as it grows. I have a feeling it will teach me
something about the tribal nature of the human species, and I
want to catch this if I can, on film, for *The Human Animal.*

But first I must settle in to my hotel. I love the hotels in this
city and it is hard to choose. My long-time favourite is the
Beverly Hills Hotel, with its Polo Lounge full of anxious movie
stars and their agents. For every star who is overworked there
are a hundred who are underemployed and, for them, the
business of being seen and making contacts is ever on their
minds. So every table has a telephone socket, ready and
waiting for that important call. For the lucky ones, the
superstars, there are discreet bungalows in the grounds of the
hotel. Each bungalow is reached by a path that winds its way
from the hotel foyer through tropical vegetation into an area
of total privacy. A small side-road runs along the back of the
bungalows, enabling the megastars' lovers to visit them
without the indignity of having to pass through the main
reception area.

Sadly, the Beverly Hills Hotel is closed for the time being,
having been bought by the Sultan of Brunei in case he ever
needs to spend a weekend in LA. He buys hotels all over the
world, as if someone forgot to tell him that Monopoly is only a
board game, and this is his latest bauble.

There are several other special ones to choose from. There
is the architecturally amazing Bonaventure in downtown LA,
with a mall-sized lobby and little indication of where one
should go after obtaining a room-key. When I paid the hotel a
visit on my last trip to LA, nobody was available to take my

luggage but, after a long trek, I did manage to find the correct elevator and climbed in gratefully, only to suffer the shock of being stranded aloft in a glass bubble. This little bubble, skimming up the outside of the building, started to slow down about twenty-five storeys up and then stopped between floors. It was at this point that I remembered that the Bonaventure had been the basis for the disaster epic *The Towering Inferno*. Not a comforting thought.

Nothing I could do would force my little glass bubble to rise further, to the twenty-seventh, where my room was located. The only button that would respond was 'down', so down I went, back to the vastness of the lobby. Feeling foolish I tried again and shot skywards, only to slow down once more, just before reaching my floor. This time, when I descended, I wheeled my suitcase back around the expanse of the lobby and enquired whether there was some way I could be propelled up into my room before I fell asleep. The matter-of-fact explanation was that there must have been a 'tremor'. The elevators were programmed to cut out if there was an earthquake, to stop people from being stranded at high levels when the whole edifice came tumbling down. A full analysis of the logic of this statement was more than I could face, and luckily I was tired enough, when I finally reached my room, to fall asleep despite the lurking feeling that the entire building was about to restyle itself as a flat-pack for easy removal.

Then there is the bizarre Chateau Marmont on Sunset Boulevard. The film crew have decided to take a suite there to accommodate all their technical gear. A dark and sinister hotel that makes no concessions to modernism, the fascinating Chateau Marmont is one of the few hotels in America that is said to be haunted. (The ghost is a man who climbs into bed with female guests, if you can believe that.) It opened in 1929 and has a longer and more colourful history than any other hotel in Los Angeles. This is the place where

Garbo had a permanent room, swam in the small pool and smoked a cigarillo; the place where Howard Hughes used binoculars to watch from his window as girls in swimsuits lay sunbathing; the place where rock star Jim Morrison, one drunken night, fell out of a window and damaged one of his lungs, leading to his death in a Paris bathtub a month later; the place where John Belushi killed himself with a mixture of heroin and cocaine.

Walking down one of the dark corridors at the Marmont, one of our young researchers, who has just been to see an unusually grisly horror film starring Christopher Walken at his most terrifying, turns a corner and there Walken is in the flesh, emerging from the gloom and padding straight towards her. Her mind is on other things and she only recognizes him when he is a few feet away. She lets out a piercing scream and then, as her brain snaps into focus, starts apologizing profusely to his retreating back. She is still suffering from acute embarrassment at her reaction the following day, but I point out to her that, in a strange way, she has paid the actor a huge compliment.

Having recently seen the movie *Pretty Woman,* I decide this time to stay at the Beverly Wilshire, the hotel featured in that engaging film. Some of my friends have been very sniffy about the plot of the film, but it is simply dear old Cinderella, with condoms added – nothing but a light-hearted fairy tale. Anybody who takes it seriously enough to debate its ethical message or its moral posture either is in need of a therapist, or is one.

Arriving at the hotel, I am amused to discover that the assistant manager who shows me to my room has groomed himself to look exactly like Hector Elizondo, the actor who plays the hotel manager in the movie, complete with trimmed moustache, elegantly groomed hair and precisely restrained mannerisms. It is a nice touch and I am dying to ask whether it is hotel policy, or private enterprise. I suspect the latter but am too polite to ask. Unfortunately, this is as far as the charade goes. There is no sign of Julia Roberts.

The next morning, with jet lag receding, we set off for gangland in south-central LA. John Macnish, our producer, has only been able to obtain permission for us to film there if we are accompanied by Trevor, a gang liaison officer, whatever that is. It seems that, if we had a police escort (of the kind we will later use in Las Vegas), we would be killed. But Trevor is OK – he is a recognized go-between and is accepted by the gangs.

From the multimillion-dollar villas and mansions of Beverly Hills and the swank shops of Rodeo Drive, it takes no more than twenty minutes to reach the heart of gangland. I am foolishly childlike in my enthusiasm, as though I were viewing the whole scene from the safety of a cinema seat. Trevor is not so relaxed and insists that, at the slightest sign of any trouble, we must all immediately pack away our gear and depart as swiftly and silently as possible.

We are to film on the fringe of the territory of the most feared of all the gangs – the 18th Street Gang. But this is not the sort of gang familiar to us all from the gangster movies. Organized crime has grown old and respectable. It owns corporations, runs casinos and influences politics, but keeps a very low profile. The new gangs are defiantly high profile and in-your-face. They are outside society, in their own world, with their own rules. It is these rules that intrigue me, because they reveal the way in which, no matter how a social structure develops, it quickly settles into an accepted pattern of behaviour. The gangland we are entering is a complete community, with all the social trimmings.

These are essentially youth gangs, if only because no males live long enough to become elder statesmen. It all began back in 1968 when teenagers who were too juvenile to belong to the earlier, serious rebel groups, such as the Black Panthers or Hell's Angels, formed their own precocious organization called the Baby Avenues. Because babies live in cribs, they soon became known as the Avenue Cribs. Then, for some unknown reason, the word Crib was modified to Crip, and new Crip gangs started to spring up everywhere, always consisting exclusively of very young males, nearly always teenagers. There were the Avalon Garden Crips and the Inglewood Crips, each defined by its home territory, and many more, all loosely affiliated to the larger Crip brotherhood.

Then in 1972 there was a major rumble between two of the Crip gangs, when the Piru Street Crips were outnumbered and defeated by the Compton Crips. The Pirus split away and formed a new alliance with some other gangs. They set themselves up as a major rival force. The Crips wore blue bandannas, so their new rivals chose the opposing colour, red, and named themselves the Bloods. When writing, the Bloods crossed out the letter 'C' wherever it appeared, as an insult to the Crips. The Crips, for their part, always wrote the letter 'C' wherever the letter 'B' was required in their writing. The Crips did, however, make an exception when writing the initials 'B K', because these stood for another name they gave themselves, namely 'Blood Killas'.

One gang after another joined either the Crips or the Bloods, as a way of gaining protection and power for times when they might come under threat. Just as with the bi-partisan politics of orthodox society, a two-party system was growing naturally out of the chaos of small, independent war-parties. Gangland was unconsciously echoing the greater world outside.

Today there are over 300 Crip and Blood gangs in Los Angeles County, with a total of more than 150,000 members. Each gang has its own well-defined territory, its special symbols, graffiti and tattoos, its hand-signs and gestures, its style of clothing and tribal colours, and its gang affiliations. Some groups are racially aligned, but others are multiracial. Most have brutal initiation ceremonies in which the new recruit has to submit himself to an eighteen-second beating by a group of established gang members. It is a curious ritual, involving heavy punches to the head, shoulders and chest, but is then followed immediately by hugs and embraces from the attackers, and a celebratory toast to the new member. The next day he proudly shows off his bruised and swollen face. What he has gained is a sense of belonging, shared honour, and strength through membership. What he has lost is individuality and independence of action.

There was a major change in gang society in the early eighties, when they began to deal in narcotics. With the introduction of crack cocaine, they became rich almost overnight. The gang members became landlords, in the true meaning of that word. They discovered that they themselves did not have to deal in drugs. All they had to do was to rent their individual territories to the drug suppliers. If these drug dealers paid a particular gang a substantial rent, they were allowed to sell their wares in the territory of that gang. If they failed to pay, they were killed. This led to increased competition between neighbouring gangs, and the number of homicides rose higher and higher throughout the eighties. Now, in 1993, it has reached a level that makes other trouble spots, such as Northern Ireland, seem like oases of peace and calm. The astonishing total of 'gang-related homicides' in Los Angeles for the last twelve months is 861.

However, the 18th Street Gang, whose territory we are entering, is a special group. According to the *Los Angeles Times*, this is 'the biggest and deadliest street gang to rise from the nation's gang capital, reshaping Los Angeles' criminal underworld.' Sounds impressive. With no fewer than 20,000 members (sixty per cent of which are thought to be illegal immigrants), this gang has become a law unto itself, 'dwarfing even the notorious Bloods and Crips'.

So, the old bipartisan system is already changing. The 18th Street Gang has grown and grown and driven a wedge for itself into territory previously owned by the earlier gangs. Doubtless this will lead to even more bloodshed. The 18th Street males have already executed large numbers of rival gang members in the last few years – three times the killing rate of even the worst of the other gangs.

It is little wonder that there are no elderly gang members. As one reporter said, there is no 18th Street Godfather. Even the more senior members, the 'veteranos', are still short of middle age. A twenty-year-old may be called a veteran. They recruit new members from the local schools, targeting children as young as thirteen, offering them the promise of guns, drugs, women and, above all, backup. Many are excited by the idea and others are too scared to refuse. Where there is poverty, recruiting is easy, and what has been described as a 'children's army' is the result.

The gang is made up of a network of small cliques and is so loosely run that it has shown no indication of becoming the new face of organized crime. But despite this it has developed its own form of society. The boys hang out together, in a manner reminiscent of the hunting parties of the primeval hunter-gatherer societies. The girls live in 'female houses', where they rear the children resulting from their brief sexual attachments to the various male gang members. The males, now drug-rich, support their females financially and defend them against any interference from rival males. Identity can always be established by displaying the gang-symbol tattoos, which act like unforgeable passports. Status is displayed by parading the scars of numerous bullet wounds.

The 18th Street Gang, largely but not exclusively Latino, has formed strong links with the Mexican and Colombian drug cartels and deals directly with them. The gang has refined the landlord system to a point where specific street corners are now rented to non-gang drug dealers on an hourly basis. These short-term rents are referred to as gang 'taxes'. And as tax collectors, these young men employ methods that governmental taxation authorities can only dream about.

These, then, are the people we are coming to film. Thank goodness it is broad daylight. As we approach the heartland of gang territory, the landscape changes dramatically. Gone are the neat façades of Beverly Hills, gone are the bleak frontages of the poorer districts. Now what we observe is a seething landscape of endless, densely packed graffiti. They stretch as far as the eye can see, covering every inch of every vertical surface. Some are so high up that it is hard to work out how the graffiti artists managed to place them there.

We park our vehicle near an empty triangle of rough land and proceed on foot, led by the trepid Trevor. On a raised platform, in front of a gutted, deserted building, there are several derelict chairs, placed as if on the terrace of an elegant hotel. We set up our cameras and start filming the graffiti. We are blissfully unaware of the fact that this was recently the site of an unusually violent gangland assassination, when two 18th Streeters opened fire with AK-47 assault rifles on a Mexican Mafia bagman and his girlfriend. The execution was carried out with a firepower of such ferocity that the victims' skull fragments were scattered over half a block.

I am engrossed in the aesthetic qualities of the graffiti jungle, comparing it in my mind to the work of the greatly overrated Jackson Pollock, when two young men approach. It would be wrong to describe them as walking towards us. They are not walking, they are padding, the way lions pad on the African savannah. Their limbs move loosely, almost gently, but with a predator's confidence. Their progress is as silent as the flight of an owl. They mount the terrace in front of the paint-splattered building and, without hesitation or introduction, sit down on two of the chairs. I notice that, incongruously, the table next to them is covered with a tablecloth. One of them keeps his face averted, but the other doesn't seem to care. Trevor explains that they are two of the most cooperative of the gang members and that they do not mind being filmed by us. So we set up the camera with them in the background and I say my piece, explaining the significance of the graffiti.

To most people these paint-sprayed markings are nothing more than vandalism, but to anyone who takes the trouble to analyse them in detail they are much more. The graffiti are of several types. There are the large, decorative designs carrying no specific gang messages. There are also the individual signatures, placed by well-known 'taggers', who roam around many territories and who seem to be generally accepted by the gangs. Forming a third category are the gang-symbols sprayed by gang-taggers associated with particular groups. Finally – and this is the dangerous type – there are the obliterations of gang-symbols, added by 'tag-bangers'. These tag-bangers deliberately set out to over-paint rival signs and, if possible, to kill rival taggers. Their actions are symbolic insults of such gravity that they usually provide the excuse for an outbreak of extreme violence.

Contemplating all this paint-spraying activity, the metaphor of the padding lion comes back to me. These young men not only pad along like lions, they also spray like them – for it is urine-spraying that male lions employ to mark their territories in the wild. The only difference is that the lions' territorial markers are olfactory, while the gang members use a visual display.

After a while, our cooperative gang members decide they have had enough and lope off into the distance, their elongated baggy shorts flapping around their knees as they go. Not long after their departure, we complete our filming of the details of their graffiti and are in the process of packing up our gear when a group of young men appear and walk (rather briskly this time) down the long slope of the rough land towards us. They exchange words with Trevor and he becomes agitated. We must leave immediately. This is most unfortunate. These are tag-bangers and they have come to obliterate the local gang-signs. Gunfire is expected at any moment.

I am sure he is exaggerating. It is still broad daylight, and I know that most of the gang shootings occur late at night, when the gunmen are high on drugs, drink and nocturnal bravado. I insist that we wait a few moments longer, to give me a chance to describe to the camera what is going on. This is counter-territorial behaviour of a kind that underlines the deeply ingrained, tribal nature of the human species, and I don't want to miss it. We reach a compromise. He agrees that, with our vehicle standing by and shooting on a long lens, I can say my piece. In the distance we can hear the characteristic rattling sound as the spray bottles are shaken in preparation for the first squirt. The tag-bangers are poised for action. Then off they go, covering whole areas of already decorated wall. At first they only obliterate the decorative elements, but then one of them sprays over a sacred gang-sign and that is enough for Trevor. Now we *must* leave, now, now, now. Reluctantly we pile into the van and speed away.

As we are bowling along, returning to that other, more familiar Los Angeles, the LA of Versace and Dior, of Cartier and Louis Vuitton, our producer, John Macnish, suggests to our greatly relieved gang liaison officer, Trevor, that we might have been left in peace in gangland if we had explained that we are members of the BBC. Trevor shakes his head faster than usual and stutters: 'No, no, no, no! Never say that. There is another gang that goes by that name. The Bonnie Brae Crew are known here as the BBC. If you'd said that in this territory we would all be dead.' Privately, we think he is exaggerating again, but you never know ...

———◦◦◦◦———

Before leaving California, we have a date at a cryonics centre, where I am going to investigate the latest bid for human immortality – the preservation of human bodies by deep freezing. To give it its proper name, it is the Alcor Life Extension Foundation, and it already has quite a bevy of frozen bodies in its huge, silvery containers.

The basic idea is simple enough. When you die, technicians from Alcor hasten to your deathbed, where they quickly replace your blood with a cryoprotectant liquid affectionately referred to as 'biological antifreeze'. This reduces the damage done to the body cells when they are deep frozen. Your body is then rushed to the Alcor centre where it is submerged, head-down, in liquid nitrogen.

The reason you find yourself in this rather undignified, inverted position for the rest of eternity is that your head is considered to be the most valuable part of your body. Some of the liquid nitrogen turns to vapour as the days pass and each of the giant vacuum flasks in which the bodies are stored has to be topped up from time to time. If a local disturbance – earthquake, riot, flood or some such catastrophe – were to prevent the Alcor staff from attending to their regular topping-up duties, the inverted position would mean that the heads would be the last part of the bodies to suffer from a lowering of the level of the liquid nitrogen. Since you may be kept hanging around at Alcor for a very long time, they have to allow for every eventuality.

The long-term object of this bizarre exercise in cheating death is, of course, to revive the suspended bodies at some point in the distant future. This will be attempted when medical science has advanced to a point where it can offer a certain cure for whatever caused the death.

As we approach the centre I am slightly apprehensive. There is something vaguely unpleasant about the idea of being in a room full of inverted, deep-frozen hopefuls. We expect the centre to look like an elegant funeral parlour or a memorial hall of some kind, but what we see as we clamber out of our American hire-car looks more like a garage on an industrial estate. At least they don't waste money on pretentious displays of a kind that their suspended customers are not in a position to appreciate.

In the entrance passage there is a collection of framed photographs of some of the hopefuls. Further inside the building, the main room is bristling with highly technical equipment and has the air of an efficient medical laboratory. The only oddity is the presence of a copy of an ancient Egyptian wall-painting, hanging on one side of the room. I ask one of the officials why it is there and he explains that Alcor sees itself as the modern, scientific equivalent of the ancient Egyptian embalmers. The techniques may be different, but the goals are the same. I enquire whether the hieroglyphs in the painting have any special significance, but the official is not sure. I take a photograph of it so that I can show it to my son, Jason, when I get home. He is reading Egyptology at Oxford and will be able to decipher it for me. (He did so, and pronounced it gobbledegook.)

I am taken into a smaller room and this is where the mood changes. It is full of tall, shiny containers standing silently side by side. We all know what is inside, but it is hard to visualize the details. In one corner there is a rectangular tank that is not tall enough to contain suspended human bodies and I enquire about its contents. The Alcor official explains to me, in a matter-of-fact way, as though we were discussing frozen vegetables, that this tank is full of human heads. They call it 'neurosuspension' and the idea is that, when reviving the brains inside this tank, they would be given new, artificial bodies of some kind. It is the contents of our brain that makes us who we are and if that essence can be revived, then we stand a chance of regaining some kind of future existence. This brings up the intriguing question of whether, when you freeze brain cells, you also manage to preserve the knowledge inside them. Or would dying, and then being frozen, wipe the 'hard disk' of the brain clean? I can switch off my computer without losing its contents, but could I switch off my brain in the same way?

When I voice my doubts about the cryonics process, the Alcor staff make no attempt to sell it to me. Indeed, they are keen to explain the shortcomings. Not only do we not know how easy it will be to revive the dead or cure them of their cause of death, but in addition, we do not yet know how to prevent the damage done to body cells by the deep freezing. Even with the replacement of blood by the special preservative, some water will still seep from the frozen cells; this water will form tiny crystals, and these crystals will then puncture the cell membranes. So there are major hazards involved and the Alcor staff freely admit that the entire enterprise may turn out to be an expensive failure. But, they hasten to add, as long as there is even the slenderest of chances, it is better than no hope at all, and no hope is what you get with cremation and burial. So, if you can afford it, why not take the slender chance?

This introduces the question of cost and I am told that, if I want my whole body preserved it will cost me $120,000. If I want only my head done, that will be less, a mere $50,000. For an eternity, this seems reasonable enough. And with the advances we are seeing in genetics these days, perhaps all they will need in the future is a tiny bit of tissue to regrow the complete person. By the year 3000, who knows what may be possible?

As I am leaving, the staff ask me to remember that they are not concerned with death, but with 'life extension'; that there are no corpses at Alcor, only 'patients'; and that there is no mortuary, only a 'patient care bay'. Listening to this jargon, one has a strong inclination to treat their whole enterprise as a Californian weirdo-craze, but I have been impressed by their honesty and I promise to report objectively and leave it to others to draw their own conclusions.

When I return home to Oxford and explain to Ramona about the high cost of having me deep-frozen after I die, she ponders the problem for a while and then announces that she might consider running to a head-freeze, but not a whole body. She explains that her decision is based upon the fact that my head is the most interesting part of me. I am still trying to decide whether to take this as a wifely compliment or a wifely insult.

**NOTE**

THE LA GANGS HAVE SINCE SPREAD TO AT LEAST A HUNDRED OTHER CITIES IN THE UNITED STATES, AND THEIR NUMBERS ARE GROWING MONTH BY MONTH. IT IS NOT EXAGGERATING TO SAY THAT THERE ARE NOW TWO DISTINCT SOCIETIES EXISTING SIDE BY SIDE IN THE HUMAN POPULATION OF NORTH AMERICA — AN UNDERWORLD AND AN OVERWORLD.

WHEN ONE OF OUR FILM CREWS WAS ON LOCATION IN NEW ORLEANS FOR A SEQUEL TO *THE HUMAN ANIMAL*, WE NEARLY RAN FOUL OF THE GANGS THAT ARE OPERATING THERE. THE DIRECTOR, CLIVE BROMHALL, AND HIS CREW WERE IN A COVERED VAN WITH THE CAMERA POINTED AT A SMALL GROUP OF MEN AND PROSTITUTES TALKING TO ONE ANOTHER ON THE OTHER SIDE OF THE STREET. OUR LOCAL 'FIXER', WHO WAS IN A SEPARATE CAR, WAS EAVESDROPPING TO LEARN WHAT WAS GOING ON. SUDDENLY TWO MEN SPOTTED THE CAMERA AND BROKE AWAY FROM THE GROUP. AS THEY PASSED OUR FIXER SHE OVERHEARD THEM DISCUSSING THE KIND OF

HIGH-POWERED GUNS THEY WERE GOING TO COLLECT, TO EXECUTE OUR
ENTIRE CREW. SHE LEAPT INTO HER CAR AND DROVE OFF AT SPEED,
SIGNALLING THE CREW TO FOLLOW HER. LATER, AFTER THEY WERE WELL
CLEAR, SHE EXPLAINED TO THEM THAT THEY HAD INADVERTENTLY BEEN
FILMING A MAJOR DRUG DEAL BETWEEN ONE OF THE LOCAL GANGS AND
DRUG PEDDLERS. ALL WE HAD WANTED TO DO WAS TO RECORD THE
BEHAVIOUR OF STREET-WALKERS, BUT WE HAD ACCIDENTALLY STEPPED
OVER THE INVISIBLE BARRIER BETWEEN ORTHODOX AMERICA AND
GANGLAND AMERICA, AND IT NEARLY COST US DEAR.

## WHAT 'WORKING' MEANS ON THE STREETS OF LAS VEGAS

I AM WALKING DOWN a busy street, talking to myself. Nobody
seems to mind, but then, it is that kind of street. There are
plenty of crazies here who converse with invisible spirits every
day. One very thin, almost emaciated crazy is gently bowing to
a newspaper stand on the corner. So my odd behaviour goes
unnoticed for quite a while. But after I have strolled down the
street, talking animatedly, for the twenty-second time,
someone does approach me with a question.

The question has a certain appeal: Why don't I come inside
and meet the gorgeous girls of Glitter Gulch? But I must
resist, because I have travelled six thousand miles to speak
my few key sentences, and nothing must distract me now.
With a weak smile, I refuse the invitation.

I am in downtown Las Vegas filming for *The Human
Animal*. Far away on the opposite side of the street, half
hidden in a side door of the Golden Nugget casino, are my
camera crew and my producer. They are so distant that I
appear to be completely on my own. I am talking to the camera

but no one near to me can see it. My tiny radio microphone is hidden under my shirt. As people brush past me on the sidewalk, they whisper to each other about what drugs I might be high on. But they are not embarrassed. They have seen it all before, in this city consecrated to pleasure and risk.

Each time I speak my piece some kind of problem arises. A bus obscures the view or a group of tourists stops dead in front of me. It requires thirty-two takes to get the shot and eventually we succeed, but not before I have been made this attractive offer to leave my patch of sidewalk and step inside the topless, everythingless fun house. The girl who approaches me is unaware that she has just ruined yet another take. She has no idea that I am making a film. She is a sturdy blonde who clearly expects compliance from the apparently solitary male loitering before her. It is obvious that a simple refusal will not deter her and then there will be more delays. So I must explain. But not with too much detail or I will become embroiled in a long explanation about the kind of TV series I am making. I must be succinct.

'No, I am sorry. I am working ...' is what I blurt out. She stops in her tracks, looks me up and down, leers knowingly and, as she strolls away, shoots back over one unclad shoulder: 'Well, you are not having much luck tonight, are you, honey?'

'No, no,' I call out. 'Not that sort of work,' but it is too late. She grins and shouts: 'That's OK, honey, it's a free world. You do your thing.'

At this point my producer, Clive Bromhall, an elegant young Englishman dressed in white shorts, senses some kind of difficulty and comes trotting across the street. He joins me on the sidewalk and gives me a few words of encouragement. I glance across at the girl. She gives me a wink and a thumbs-up sign. Bless her heart, she is pleased for me that business is looking up and that I have struck lucky at last.

In show business they say one should never work with children or animals. I have worked painlessly with animals many times for several decades, but now my subject is the human species and I have never found the going so hard. I suppose it is because I am by nature a quiet observer. When you sit and watch an ape or an antelope, they don't walk over to you and ask questions. They get on with their feeding, fighting or mating and ignore you. But people ...

We have made the long trek to Las Vegas because there are so many strange happenings here. The whole city is an exercise in commercial surrealism. We are trying to find out what happens when people build a huge urban centre in the middle of a desert purely for play – adult play. How does their imagination react to this freedom?

To start with, there are no clocks in this city. Search as long as you like and you will not find a single one in any public place. Time-slavery is banished here, as it is in childhood. So is night. As soon as the sun sets behind the dark hills that ring the city, the sea of neons blink into action. Downtown it is as light as day: there are no hours, no minutes, no noon, no midnight.

In this timeless place odd things happen. Every hotel has a casino and every casino has something bizarre to offer. At one they proudly display the largest gold nugget in the world. At another there is a museum of lucky charms. At another there is a mountain of banknotes totalling one million dollars piled high on a poker table, to be won by the finalist of the World Poker Contest on a single draw of cards.

But even this huge win would not be enough to buy a small piece of paper displayed in one of the shopping-mall windows. On it are scribbled in spidery longhand some incomprehensible German sentences. This is the scrap of paper on which Einstein first wrote down his ideas about the theory of relativity, and it is being offered for sale for a cool one and a quarter million dollars.

At the Circus-Circus casino there are acrobats performing high above the acres of intensely preoccupied gamblers. High swingers above high rollers, with neither the slightest bit interested in the other.

At the Desert Inn a geriatric Frank Sinatra is still gamely doing it His Way. His voice may have lost some of its range and power, but his arrogantly bemused body language is as perfectly timed as ever. With his enormous wealth, it is surprising that he still wants to crank himself up to go out on stage each night, but the corner-of-the-mouth rumour around town is that when he is asked to perform here it is an offer he can't refuse.

At the Excalibur there are twice-nightly jousting contests in the basement, with men dressed in suits of armour complete with plumed helmets and lances, galloping back and forth at one another on huge, ornately bedecked horses. At the hotel's Camelot Level you can, if the mood takes you, get married by a Medieval Monk in the 'Canterbury', where each couple is dressed in elaborate cloaks and crowns as King Arthur and Guinevere. Afterwards you can dine on Sir Galahad's Prime Rib.

At Caesar's Palace the groups of Roman statues are electronically activated so that they can talk to one another. Purists are outraged at this, but I bet the Romans would have loved it.

At the Mirage there are live sharks swimming up and down behind the hotel check-in desks and just down the corridor there are equally live white tigers snoozing on plastic rocks, behind a vast sheet of glass. Outside the foyer there is a volcanic eruption at regular intervals. The enormous artificial volcano roars and rumbles, then sends jets of fire spurting high into the night sky. Simultaneously, flaming petrol is cascaded down the waterfalls around the volcano, setting them alight and eventually igniting the whole surface of the lake that surrounds the hotel entrance.

One night, when we are filming people's reactions to this volcanic extravaganza, a saloon car full of gangling teenagers pulls up and they rush towards us. No, not a mugging, but angry panic. A wandering weirdo has just punched his fist clean through their rear window. I inspect the damage. There is indeed a fist-sized hole right through the shattered glass. How anyone could have such strength is beyond me. The two motor-cycle policemen guarding our film crew move into action. Across the street the weirdo is spotted sauntering along. He is cornered and brought across to confront the scared teenagers.

He denies everything, but his right arm is covered in cuts and grazes. I watch with fascination his false denial gestures. His body is rigid. Like all acute liars he is trying to give nothing away. His hands are unnaturally inactive. He makes no gesticulations, no facial expressions. He is clearly guilty and eventually he confesses. But the police can do nothing because he is a vagrant. Although not badly dressed, he is homeless and penniless and there is no point in holding him. So he wanders off into the brightly lit night. Despondent, the teenagers depart to check their insurance for a weirdo clause. The volcano erupts again.

One of the motor-cycle policemen is being asked by a crew member what he thinks of President Clinton. He sticks out one hip, makes a limp-wrist gesture and winks. No words are necessary. But despite his intolerance he is a patient, kindly man. He allows tiny Japanese visitors to sit on his vast motor-cycle to be Nikonized by other members of their tourist party. Later, he hands out police badges to our film crew and finally powers off into the glare of the neon night.

A fax message has come through from our senior producer, back at base, asking for some sex scenes for one of the other programmes in the series. Strangely, sex is none too obvious in this city of fun. It is there, but it is discreet. There is a good reason for this. In Las Vegas, nothing must be done to divert the gamblers from handing over their money to the casinos. For this reason, all of Nevada's famous legal brothels are miles away, outside the city limits. It takes a determined lecher to reach them.

We have no idea how to go about this new assignment, but I spot a sex shop and suggest that they may be able to help us with our arduous task. Inside we find ourselves in a temple of phalluses. The endless display is overwhelming. How there can be so many varieties of technical paraphernalia for such a natural act as copulation is beyond me. Does anyone ever seriously consider buying such items as 'The Complete Bedside Orgy Kit'? A neat, bespectacled man beams at us and offers his assistance. When we explain our problem he is immediately understanding and, with the flourish of a professor putting his hand on a vital but obscure scientific treatise essential to his favourite pupil's research project, he brings forth an erudite volume entitled *The Best Cat Houses in Nevada*.

This is a remarkable book and, for those with a scholarly interest in such matters, its full title is 'The Official Guide to the Best Cat Houses in Nevada; Everything You Want to Know About Legal Prostitution in Nevada. Completely updated, with names, numbers and maps. By J R Schwartz.' It opens, astonishingly, with a quotation from a Neapolitan eunuch in Voltaire's *Candide*, who wails: 'O che sciagura d'essere senza coglioni.' The fact that Mr Schwartz has chosen an Italian quotation suggests that it is there to impress Mafia fixers despatched to find girls for their bosses.

The guide then proceeds to list the details of thirty-four houses, many with their own special features. The Mustang Ranch, for example, is praised for its work-rate – 200,000 'one-eyed monks' serviced each year. At the Calico Club the 'pleasure menu' includes a mystifying delight entitled 'binaca blast french'. At Penny's Cozy Corner (shades of Auden and

Isherwood, but without their orientation) there is a 54-inch-long walrus penis-bone on show in the downstairs bar. The Stardust Ranch has its 'own version of Elvis, a four-legged character that further enhances any visit to the Stardust Ranch'. The mind boggles. And Mabel's Whorehouse boasts 'Madame Butterfly's Love Tubs'. But all these perplexing oddities are put in the shade by the unique feature of Cherry Patch II where Agnes is a permanent exhibit. Who is Agnes? She is the oldest hooker in Nevada and her mummified body is displayed in an open casket. I can think of nothing more detumescing than an antique, taxidermized hooker. But this is Nevada, where the bizarre is commonplace.

Armed with this extraordinary literary document, our intrepid production assistant sets to work. Like all good PAs, she wields a telephone like a virtuoso violinist. But all is not well. She has tried cathouse after cathouse without success. None will throw open its doors to the BBC. Why? Because the girls do not want their grandparents to know what they are doing. Not their parents, please note, but their grandparents. An interesting comment on the changing attitudes of the generations. We give up. There will be no bawdy-house filming on this trip.

We must make do with covering the latest sex craze hereabouts, namely lap-dancing. There are several clubs in Las Vegas offering this new form of entertainment and we are told that there is one in particular that is well run. We make contact but encounter some resistance. Although the owners are keen to obtain free television exposure, they are deeply suspicious of the motives of documentary film-makers not known to them. Who are we? Are we covert puritans, out to attack them? Are we covert pornographers, out to exploit them? Are we phoneys, out for a cheap thrill without paying entrance money? Our application to film is subject to a preliminary meeting with the owners.

Clive Bromhall and I duly turn up at the club at the appointed time. As it is mid-morning, the place is closed and almost empty. We are ushered briskly through the main hall to a large back room where, seated formally around a huge circular table, are a dozen middle-aged men of Italian extraction and sombre expression. In the centre sits an older man, with silvery hair and a voice that sounds like a mastiff trying to clear its throat. We are in no doubt that he is to be taken seriously. 'OK,' he rasps, 'give us your schmeer.' Unfortunately I have no idea what a schmeer is. Is this man under the impression that we are here to audition and if so what on earth does he think we might perform for him? I look blankly at Clive, whose cheerful optimism has carried him through many a tricky situation in the past. 'Desmond Morris,' he announces, in his friendliest manner, 'is investigating human body language. He has some very interesting theories about female breasts. Desmond, would you like to elaborate?'

'Thank you, Clive.' Yes, thanks very much. Twelve pairs of unsmiling eyes are staring at me in disbelief and I have no choice but to give them a short lecture on human sexual evolution. I make it as academic as possible, explaining Wickler's theory of self-mimicry. Blank looks all around. I am sure we are going to be thrown out on our ear. But no, it seems we are so odd that we must be genuine. The Silverback male is rasping again: 'OK. OK, you are talking about human communication, right? That's what we're doing. We are in the business of communication. So, OK, you can film here tonight, but you must include shots of the rest rooms, OK?'

The rest rooms? What does he mean? Does something strangely kinky happen in there? But we readily agree to his condition and escape with great relief back into the sunny, fresh air outside. (It later turns out that they are very proud of their rest rooms and want the television audience to share their pleasure in the exceptional amenities of their establishment. This is not some cheap dump, this is a classy joint and it seems that a few shots of the well-appointed rest rooms will bring this home to the viewing millions.)

We return with the crew late at night and the mood has changed. Now that we have passed our audition, we are treated with great courtesy and offered every assistance. Surprisingly, the club really does have an elegant, exotic atmosphere. Although it is selling sex, it is not sleazy. The girls are stunningly beautiful, the décor and lighting are imaginative and the music is acoustically impressive. We settle into a corner and start quietly filming. Nobody seems to mind, neither the showgirls nor the male punters who are busy stuffing dollar bills into G-strings. Americans have become increasingly blasé about the presence of television cameras in their private lives – much more so than the British. This is confirmed by the fact that, when two young Englishmen arrive, later on, and discover that we are from the BBC, they hastily make for the exit.

There are two categories of girls, those that dance on the raised catwalk and those that perform the more intimate lap-dances. All are near-naked and it soon becomes clear that most of them have had their breasts surgically improved. This improvement consists of enlarging the breasts more and more until they become so firm that they are almost incapable of independent movement. Visually they may be perfect hemispheres, but in the process they have lost their feminine softness. We all agree that the few female performers who have not taken this step have much more sex appeal, but judging by the faces of the punters we are in a minority.

Away from the catwalks, the lap-dancers are busy. This form of dancing consists of a ravishingly attractive nude girl writhing about over a seated man's body, while the disco music struggles to burst his eardrums. She is not supposed to touch him at any point, although accidents do happen, and he is not allowed to reach out for her. Her breasts arc and sway, inches from his face, her long hair flicks rhythmically across his cheeks, her thighs graze his trousers.

This post-Aids, non-contact libido torment appears to be about as frustrating as any sexual activity can get. But the owner of the club reappears and assures us that there is a happy ending – that his girls send their clients home to their wives as better lovers. Wildly aroused they must surely be, but it is not hard to guess what images flash before the now closed eyes of these men as they position themselves over their spouses' bodies later in the evening.

The next day we are off to investigate marriage, Las Vegas style. Our target is the Little White Chapel where Joan Collins, Bruce Willis, Judy Garland, Frank Sinatra, Mickey Rooney (twice) and thousands of other lovesick rebels have come to tie a quick and easy knot (no blood test required), without having to face a ghastly gathering of their nearest and dearest. The ceremony, performed by Charlotte, the Wedding Queen of the West, is over in a flash and, for a small extra fee, can be climaxed with a serenade from a charming Elvis lookalike. The most expensive ceremony is the Joan Collins Special, which includes among other extras 'a Bride's Garter, a French Lace Handkerchief and a Free Love Recipe'.

For those in a tremendous hurry, there is a new facility, the Drive-in Wedding. In this, a white stretched-limo the length of a French lorry draws up to a little window-sill where the happy couple can say their vows without even alighting from their vce-hick-cull. Ever dynamic, the ingenious Las Vegans (not to be confused with vegetarians) are now working on a drive-in divorce.

We are told that it is a common practice for a religiously devout man to marry a good-time girl one day, spend the night with her and then divorce her the next morning. In this way he can have his fun without being disloyal to the strict marital requirements of his spiritual upbringing.

Before we leave we have one last assignment – to film the climax of the World Poker Contest at Binion's Horseshoe Casino. This is a curious annual ritual in which the 220 best poker-players in the world descend on this famous old casino in downtown Las Vegas. (Binion's has been there for over forty years, which, by local standards, makes it an ancient monument.) After four days of almost non-stop play, their number is whittled down to just two. At this point armed guards bring in a mountain of small-denomination bills, totalling one million dollars, and pile them up on the table. The atmosphere is tense, because this million dollars will be won or lost on the final game.

My interest in this event has nothing to do with gambling. My aim is to study the ways in which the various players manage to suppress their body language and prevent their rivals from knowing what is in their hands. Is there really a 'poker face'? After studying the earlier stages of the contest, it soon becomes clear that there are three poker strategies: what I call the Statue, the Clown and the Liar. The Statue suppresses all his body language, shows no expression and keeps completely still. The Clown tries to put the others off by joking and teasing his way through the contest. The Liar shows strong emotions, but tries to dissociate them from his true mood. All three strategies are difficult to handle well, but there is one player, a large, bespectacled man wearing a baseball cap, who is a supreme example of the Statue. Known to the onlookers as Arizona Jim, he is immobile to a superhuman degree. If he ever became famous enough to be exhibited at Madame Tussaud's waxworks, he could save them the trouble of fashioning an expensive model: they could put the real thing on show.

I fancy Jim for the championship and I only wish I were a gambling man, because, as it turns out, I am correct. He immobilizes himself right into a million dollars. But so powerful is his suppression of feeling that he shows no emotion whatever at his moment of triumph. He remains completely deadpan until he later greets his family.

Lesser players have fallen by the wayside for a variety of reasons. The most common mistake is to allow the eyes to be seen when looking at a new hand. If it is unusually good, the blink rate will automatically increase and the pupils will dilate. These tell-tale signals can be avoided easily enough by wearing eye-shades or dark glasses, but some players are too arrogant to bother with this kind of protection.

On seeing a good hand, a player is more likely to glance briefly at his pile of chips, quickly look away from his cards, avoid eye contact with other players and place his bet in a controlled way. On seeing a bad hand, a player stares longer at it, then stares assertively at his rivals and finally places his bet with an exaggerated flourish. Needless to say, Arizona Jim did none of these things.

Looking at the huge pile of money on the table after the game is over, I ask one of the guards why he is so relaxed, when there is an open door to the street only a short distance away. A hold-up gang could be out and away in a few seconds. He looks at me, smiles a disdainful smile and drawls: 'Not a chance. They all know who the connections are here.' Come to think of it, Las Vegas is probably one of the safest cities in North America. I have certainly never once felt threatened here, and the only guns I have seen are the endless rows of them in the pawn shops, where even Americans will give up the right to bear arms in order to buy chips.

At the airport we walk past the rows of gambling machines that line the departure lounge, carefully positioned to entice the last surviving dollars from the pockets of the addicts. As we fly out, back to normal cities where there are clocks and jobs and boringly serious human pursuits, we look down on the famous Strip below and marvel at its oddity.

There, near the Mirage casino, a new monster is being constructed. This one, soon to open, is called Treasure Island and will feature as its entrance a complete, full-scale pirate village with a full-size pirate ship at anchor in the artificial harbour. On the night it opens the megamillionaire who has built it will symbolically blow up the magnificent (but old) Dunes casino down the road. There is nothing wrong with the Dunes – it is world-famous and was operating successfully until only a few months ago. But its destruction will draw attention to the new attraction and that is all that matters. There are no 'listed buildings' here.

Farther down the strip, next to the Excalibur Hotel – with 4,032 bedrooms and 7,000 parking spaces, the largest in the world – they are building a full-scale Egyptian pyramid. It is covered in shiny black glass, giving it the smooth surface once displayed by the original pyramids before they were stripped of their fine marble finish. So although, once more, purists will grumble, I am sure that the ancient Egyptians would love it. It is fronted by a full-scale sphinx, between the giant paws of which the visitors will enter this latest, strangest hotel of all. Once inside, guests will ascend to their rooms, not in a boring old elevator but in a scary new 'inclinator'. Each inclinator rises from the bottom edge of the pyramid and climbs, at a steep angle, up towards its central peak. The thousands of hotel rooms are 'seemingly plastered on the sloping walls like honeycomb'. It is not for the vertiginously challenged. The fact that a pyramid is traditionally a tomb for the dead does not seem to deter them. Nor does the fact that there are no pyramids in Luxor deter them from naming it the Luxor Hotel. Luxor has a better ring to it than Giza or Saqqara, so who cares?

What will they build next? What further excesses can they imagine? Las Vegas is a play-town and just as children quickly tire of their playthings and crave novelty, so do adult play-people. Unless something goes terribly wrong, you can be certain that the Las Vegas of the year 2000 will look very different from the glittering gulch of today. Only one thing will remain constant, and that is that nobody entering the city will be allowed to contemplate anything profound for the duration of their stay – no politics, no religion, no smugly correct puritans, no pontificating pundits, no sanctimonious health-gurus. No wonder I enjoyed it so much.

### NOTE

NOT LONG AFTER OUR VISIT TO LAS VEGAS, THE EXCALIBUR HOTEL LOST ITS RECORD AS THE LARGEST IN THE WORLD. THE NEWLY COMPLETED MGM GRAND, ALSO ON THE STRIP, HAS NO FEWER THAN 5,005 ROOMS COMPARED WITH THE EXCALIBUR'S PUNY TOTAL OF 4,032. AND THE HUGE CONCRETE TRIPOD WE SAW UNDER CONSTRUCTION WHEN WE WERE THERE HAS ALSO BEEN TOPPED OFF TO CREATE AN OBSERVATION TOWER THAT IS (INEVITABLY) 28 FEET TALLER THAN THE EIFFEL TOWER, CAPPED BY A REVOLVING RESTAURANT, FOUR WEDDING CHAPELS AND A CARNIVAL RIDE.

## THE EUNUCHS ARE ANGRY

INDIA BREAKS YOUR HEART. What is worse, it then proceeds to harden it. The first pathetic beggar you see makes you want to cry and reach for your wallet. The second does the same, and the third. Then the floodgates open and there are thousands of them. You cannot cope. You cannot move. You are besieged. In no time at all you have become dismissive, then finally, hostile. And you end up hating them for making you so callous.

We are here in Bombay to film scenes for the episode of *The Human Animal* called *The Human Zoo*. We are not here, like the usual tourist visitors, for the exotic beauty of this fascinating and complex culture. We are here for the overcrowding, the slums and the chaos of urban survival. So we have only ourselves to blame. We knew it would be tough going, but some of the scenes that have met our eyes will stay in our minds for ever.

I am haunted by the split-second glimpse I have of a pretty, skinny, bedraggled little girl, as we are driving along a grubby dual carriageway in heavy traffic. She is crouching down on the exhaust-blackened central divide, with lorries and cars spewing hot fumes over her from both sides. She has one upturned palm outstretched towards the slowly moving traffic, hoping it will come to a complete halt and she will see a window turned down and a hand holding out a little money. It is a forlorn hope and you can see in her eyes that she knows it is hopeless, but she crouches there all the same, her lungs slowing filling with chemical treacle.

The traffic does not stop, and she vanishes from view. We are on our way to the slums near the airport. Bombay's slums have the dubious distinction of being the largest in the world. I am to be filmed walking through the warren of narrow lanes, while my commentary discusses the problems of overpopulation. I am already dreading it, but I am in for a surprise. Somehow, this huge community has managed to create a special world for itself. It may be ramshackle and crowded, but there is organization here and even, to my surprise, an atmosphere of defiant cheerfulness. It is a testimony to the resilience of the human personality, that people can still smile in such densely packed quarters, with so few of the luxuries of life to ease the passage of time. Significantly, there are no beggars here, because no one with any money to spare ever comes near this place.

Instead of being depressed by the vast shanty-town community, I am relieved. I am grateful that conditions there are not as bad as I had imagined, because the brutal fact is that slums like this will be around for many years to come. It will take a major shift in thinking for the Indian authorities to control the relentless growth of their nation and to bring an acceptable level of affluence to the whole community.

Back at the hotel, my discomfort quickly returns. Waiting outside the towering façade of the Taj Mahal Inter-Continental there are young women carrying babies. Each is desperate and each has trained her tiny infant to beg in a special way. The one who approaches me waits until she is very close, then hits her baby. Instead of crying like any normal infant when given a hard slap, this poor little mite instantly responds by whipping up its right arm in a brisk military salute. I am so angered at its exploitation that I refuse to give the mother anything and then walk away feeling disgusted with myself all over again.

The contrast inside the air-conditioned sanctuary of the hotel is shattering, for today happens to be the day of a Bollywood festival. The great stars of the Indian cinema are arriving in droves, wearing costumes that make the Oscar ceremonies in Los Angeles look positively dowdy. The outrageous flamboyance, the dazzling, richly coloured silks, the self-conscious, sauntering gait and the bright, birdlike chatter of the rich and famous of the Indian movie industry are all here. We are not sure precisely what the occasion is but we have to admit that when, later that evening, the winner of a national contest – the unbelievably, cartoonly beautiful Miss Condom – enters the bar where we are refreshing ourselves, we cannot take our eyes off her. This young woman, selected from the staggering total of 250 million Indian women to represent, well, sexuality, I suppose, is so sumptuously proportioned that her impact on every male within a hundred yards is seismic.

The next morning I wake up half-dead. Not, sadly, through a night of wild excess, but because it is Black Tuesday. We have been filming recently in countries where malaria is active, so I have been taking mefloquine, the powerful new anti-malarial drug. This is an extremely virulent substance and is causing one in ten people using it to suffer from serious side-effects. Some have hallucinations, while others become paranoid. Some even develop double vision. (Eventually air pilots will be forbidden to use it.) My own reaction is to become weak, unable to eat and quite unable to concentrate. I find that these reactions occur, like the disease itself, in a cyclical way, and this is the third time on location that, on a Tuesday, I have succumbed to a bad bout of mefloquine-itis. I have already learned from the previous experiences that it is hopeless to try to fight it, so I stay in a darkened hotel room while the crew sets off to film a sequence that conveniently does not involve me – namely eunuchs.

The next day, more or less recovered, I am told that I was lucky to have missed the eunuchs. Clive Bromhall, my producer, and his team were apparently forced to flee down a beach, with a gang of angry eunuchs in hot pursuit, threatening to lift up their clothing and reveal their hideous scars. I am still too groggy from my mefloquine to enquire precisely what triggered this curious revolt. Instead, I concentrate on learning my words for today's sequence. My task will be to talk about human family units and we are going to film this on Chourpatti Beach, where there should be plenty of large Indian families enjoying the seaside. I am slightly alarmed to discover that this is the same beach as the one that witnessed the attack of the massed eunuchs the day before, but Clive, who always suffers from chronic optimism, assures me that all will be well.

We arrive at the beach and there are indeed large Indian families sitting all over it, so we are in business. I am fitted with a radio microphone and despatched to stand in the middle of this carpet of humanity. Clive and the camera crew have found a high vantage point on a flat-topped sea-front building and have set up the tripod there. All is ready. A distant hand-signal indicates that I must now walk though the clusters of bodies, spouting words of wisdom. But, as I do so, a cry goes up. I have been spotted by the resident army of professional beggars. They cannot believe their luck. Here is the juicy prospect of what appears to be a lone tourist on a distinctly non-tourist beach. They converge on me, some scampering and weaving through the family clusters, others foot-dragging and limping. From all directions they come, closing in and in, until I am completely invisible to the camera team. I try breaking away and running to a new spot, but it is no use. No sooner have I started speaking towards the camera than they are on me again. A hundred palms are thrust out at me. The beggars closest to me are pulling my shirt, or jabbing me with their fingers. Those without any hands are prodding me with their stumps. And those without any stumps are chesting me, throwing their armless bodies at me, trying to get me to read the notices that are hung around their necks.

Again, I am horrified by the way they so quickly erode my sympathy for their plight. 'Later,' I keep saying, 'later, we will give you something, just let us film.' But of course they don't understand. The production assistant rushes down and attempts to distract them. She waves a few banknotes in the air and then runs off down the beach. They lurch after her and I quickly try to say my piece again. I manage something, but it is far from perfect. Then they are back, swarming over me again, having exhausted the few notes she was able to offer them. In the end, I admit defeat and we all make our way back to the van and glumly load away our equipment.

I am just remarking on how my admiration for Richard Attenborough has grown in the last hour or so and am questioning how he managed to deal with the thousands of extras when he was directing his epic film *Gandhi* here in India, when the swarm of beggars spots us in the car park. They quickly surround the vehicle and make it impossible for us to leave. In desperation, we shout out that if they line up in an orderly way we will give something to each one. This causes a massive status-battle within their ranks, but eventually, after much bickering and squabbling, some sort of line is established and we start doling out whatever small change we can muster. They are far from satisfied and keep up their harsh complaints until we finally get so fed up that we leap in and drive away. Not a good day's filming.

On the way back, Clive, relentlessly cheerful as ever, says: 'Well, at least it wasn't as bad as the eunuchs.' Not for him, perhaps, but then he was safely ensconced on top of a building for most of the time. For me, the memory of the sharp, jabbing fingernails and the soft, prodding stumps will linger for ever.

Our filming continues and the unforgettable images keep on coming: young mothers carrying heavy loads as part of a road-repairing team, breaking off every so often to squat by the roadside breast-feeding their babies; men high in the sky laboriously hand-painting the huge cinema posters that litter the city skyline; a taxi ride from hell in which the driver, lacking brakes, relies on hitting the cars in front to slow him down; large flocks of black crows riding along on the tops of double-decker buses and flying down to feed whenever they spot some promising refuse; poor people sleeping in the streets; posh people attending the resident hotel astrologer; people fighting to get into a cinema to see a popular film, leading to a street riot; a large fish, completely covered in a black-candy-floss of flies, for sale in a street market. And yet, despite all the agonies of Bombay that we encountered, this is a buzzing, throbbing, lively city, full of energy and ambition. The poverty may be appalling but this is not a depressed culture. If it can control its numbers and improve its politics, India has a good chance of becoming an affluent civilization once again. Especially if Miss Condom has her way ...

## THE OLDEST KNICK-KNACK IN THE WORLD

DURING THE MAKING of each TV series there is usually one event that stands out as the peak experience – a magic moment that could not be achieved in any other way. It is not always the most obvious one. During the making of *The Human Animal* series, for example, it consisted of nothing more than the simple act of holding a pebble in my hand. Let me explain.

Long ago, back in the early sixties, Kenneth Oakley, the anthropologist who uncovered the Piltdown forgery, asked me to carry out a small experiment for him. He had the cast of a pebble on which there was supposed to be a face. There was a pair of hollow eye-sockets and below them a half-open mouth. Above the eyes there was a distinct ridge suggesting hair. To any human observer this would clearly form a face, but Kenneth wished to know whether an ape would also see it in this way. I was studying chimpanzees at the time and he wanted me to show the cast to them and record their reactions.

Sadly, the chimps were not interested, but my curiosity was aroused and I asked him for the story behind the pebble. It seems that, in 1925, a South African schoolmaster had been exploring some caves at a site called Makapansgat. Primitive apemen called Australopithecines had been living in these caves about three million years ago and among their bones he came across a strange reddish-brown, water-worn cobble.

This smooth pebble was of a completely different stone from the rest of the cave and had clearly been brought to the site deliberately by the apemen. A search was made to find its source in a nearby river and it was established that the minimum distance involved was at least three miles.

Why did these primitive beings, halfway between ape and man, go to all the trouble of carrying this object over such a huge distance and then keep it inside their cave? The obvious answer is that they were reacting to the presence of the face on the pebble's surface. There is no suggestion that they sculpted the face; it is simply a freak, accidental resemblance. But even so, its transportation and retention make it by far the oldest artefact known on this planet – the world's first knick-knack!

Kenneth had hoped that my chimpanzees would show some reaction to the face and thus prove that a subhuman brain could respond to the image, but my failure to confirm this in no way reduced the pebble's importance. It simply meant that the apemen were more advanced in this respect than chimps. And it also suggested that 'art appreciation' was much more ancient than anyone had been able to prove previously.

The original pebble was placed in a museum in Johannesburg and I never imagined I would ever have the chance to see it, let alone hold it in my hand. But when we arranged to film some sequences for the new television series in South Africa, I asked whether it would be possible to have another cast made, so that I could return to the Makapan cave with it and talk about this most ancient of all art objects.

To my delight, the museum said that I could borrow the original pebble. It had never been allowed out of the museum before, but they would permit it to go back to the site of its original discovery, just for a few hours, providing it was accompanied by two of their scientific officials. We readily agreed to this and now, at last, here we are at the famous caves.

To heighten the dramatic effect, the producer, who is safely back in England, has decided that the pebble must be dramatically revealed at the end of a single, long tracking shot. According to his instructions, the camera will roam over the cave walls and along the cave ceiling and then discover me standing near the entrance. I will explain the significance of the pebble and then hold it up, saying: 'And here it is.' As I do so, the camera will close in on the pebble-face until it completely fills the screen. This may sound simple enough, but believe me, it is not.

The first problem is that a rail-track has to be laid down the whole length of the cave, curving this way and that as it follows the irregular shape of the cavern. We soon discover that, every time the camera trolley is pushed down this track, it subsides into the soft cave floor and the whole structure then has to be built up again, before we can try for another take.

Another problem is that, as the camera pans down from the roof of the cave to find my standing figure, there is an inevitable element of luck in locating my exact position. Many attempts to do this fail.

A third problem is that, in order to see the details of the face on the pebble I have to hold it at a very precise angle, so that the light shines on it in a special way. A few millimetres adrift and the pebble looks blank.

Yet another problem is that the museum officials have gently pointed out to us that we have not tucked our trouser-legs into our socks, as they have done. We look blankly at one another. They then explain (with that irritating cheerfulness born of superior knowledge) that there are some particularly nasty, jumping ticks around here, which love to leap onto bare flesh, run up your leg and lodge themselves in your pubic hair. Having established themselves in this snug, warm new home, they then start feeding on your blood and, in the process, generously inject you with Lyme disease. This is just what we want to hear when we are trying desperately to concentrate on all our other difficulties. As I am standing on a little mound of earth, I pretend to lob the famous Makapan pebble at them with the action of a baseball pitcher, and they look gratifyingly worried. But not half as worried as we are, as we belatedly stuff our trousers into our socks.

One final problem is that I have to remember my lines (while trying to detect crawling sensations on my pubic hairs), which are long and complicated (the lines not the hairs) and which have to be word perfect. Put these five hazards together and you have about as much chance of obtaining a perfect take as winning a lottery. After several hours of intense effort, we are beginning to wish that the producer who has demanded this impossible shot were here in person, not so that he could help us but so that we could strangle him.

In the end, after a full day's shooting, we do at last get the perfect shot and, now that it is 'in the can', we forgive him. We know that the viewing millions would never have noticed if there had been several cuts, chopping the shot up in such a way that we could have finished the whole task in half an hour. But we have to admit that there is a certain satisfaction in having successfully risen to this difficult challenge.

We are packing up to leave and thanking the officials for being so patient, but silently each of us is trying to calculate how long it will be before we can make a detailed inspection of our nether regions. On the long drive back to the hotel, we stop at a café ostensibly for a cold drink, but there follows an unseemly scramble for the toilets, where each cubicle is promptly witness to a contorted striptease. Happily, sighs of relief can be heard all around. (We are luckier than another producer on this series. John Macnish did indeed contract Lyme disease from ticks during a filming trip to West Africa.

Back in England this developed into meningitis and he was rushed into intensive care, where he nearly lost his life. So, although our synchronized pubic inspections did raise a few smiles, it was in truth no laughing matter.)

There is one more hazard to go before returning to England. I have foolishly suggested that it would be a good idea to hold a small crocodile in my hands while explaining the evolution of facial expressions. The simple point I want to make is that we have mobile faces and they do not. To do this we have to visit a crocodile breeding centre near the coast. It is run by one of those animal men who know their subjects so well that they can take risks others would be unwise to try. We accept his generous offer to allow us to enter the crocodile enclosures, but with some reservations.

The first enclosure contains Fred, who is introduced to us as a six-killer. This means that he ate six people before being caught and brought to the centre. I know enough about reptiles to be especially cautious because it is so hot here. Back in British zoos, crocs seem rather sluggish and slow-moving. That is because they are cooler there. Here, the intense heat gives them the metabolism that enables them to run at you like an express train. They need this speed to catch their prey and when it happens close to you it nearly scares you to death. We are walking past another enclosure, with only a low wire fence between us and a huge female croc. She waits until we are near and then hurtles herself towards us. We leap back and laugh nervously. And these are the animals we are supposed to go in with and film? I was once persuaded to feed a banana to an adult grizzly bear, by putting the fruit in my mouth and letting him take it out, but he was a tame bear and I trusted him. These are not tame crocs and I certainly do not trust them.

Our cheerful host is busy selecting a small croc that I can hold in my hands while I speak my piece to the camera. I could do it out here in safety, but for dramatic effect I must be seen to be inside the enclosure of the giant adults, so that the camera can pan up from the big ones to me holding a small one.

Croc Man now explains two things to make me more at ease. He and his assistant will be in the enclosure behind me, out of sight, and will each be armed with a small plank of wood. If one of the adults charges at me, they will hit it with their planks. Oh good. And the adults are unlikely to charge as long as I keep the young croc happy. If it gets miserable, it will let out a wailing sound and this will upset the adults, who are likely to rush to its aid. But the young ones hardly ever make a noise if they are held properly. Oh good.

We set up the camera, watched by some of the beadiest eyes I have ever seen. There is a huge male and several females. These are Nile Crocodiles, whose average length is 16 feet, with a maximum of 20 feet, and who weigh 500 pounds on average. I suddenly realize that one of the females is the monster that rushed us when we were walking past outside the wire fence. Perhaps she is all rushed out by now. Our host is explaining how we should run up to the end of the enclosure and jump over the wire fence if there is an incident.

At last we are ready to go. I have learned how to hold the young croc so that it cannot clamp its jaws onto my hand. And it is mercifully quiet. I speak my piece. For some strange reason I looked a little strained. I can't think why. Could I do it again, please? Sure, why not? And again? Now for the wide shot. Now for the close-up. Suddenly the little croc decides that enough is enough and lets out the most pitiful wail I have ever heard from the mouth of any young animal. It is enough to arouse the protective instincts of adult crocs for several miles around. That's it. The adults start moving, planks are waved and we all beat a hasty retreat.

Afterwards I tell Croc Man that I wasn't really too worried

because I was quite close to one of the fences and had calculated that I could easily vault over it if one of the adults decided to make a rush at me. 'Ah, yes,' he says. 'Well, I am glad you didn't, because *that* fence would have been a mistake. You would have found yourself in another enclosure, face to face with Fred the six-killer.'

When you sit in your library in England and write the scripts of television documentaries, you never stop to think of the practical consequences, but I made a mental note to omit all crocodiles from future scripts unless absolutely essential. However, having said that, there is a primeval magnificence about them. They have barely changed in two hundred million years. In temperament they are probably as near to dinosaurs as we will ever get. And sadly, like the dinosaurs, they will soon become extinct. For anyone living near them in Africa this will no doubt be a joyous day, but for the rest of us it will be a sad one.

A final word for Wes Craven fans – the feeding habits of crocs are the stuff of horror movies. Once they have grabbed your limb, they rotate themselves very fast, trying to twist it off. After they have gobbled up all they can, they may carry the rest to one of their larders – usually a large hole in the river-bank – and stuff what remains of you into it, alongside their prized store of other rotting body parts. If you are not dead by this stage, the experience must be a memorable one.

As we are preparing to board our jumbo jet to return to England, we are subjected to an extraordinary coincidence. No gambler would have put money on this. When we left England to fly to South Africa, we had to abandon the aircraft because a catering vehicle delivering our in-flight food accidentally rammed the side of the plane and damaged it. We were all taken off and had to spend the night at a Heathrow hotel, while another plane was made ready. Now, at Johannesburg, we are told that we will have to return to the city and spend an unscheduled night at a hotel because ... you've guessed it ... a catering vehicle delivering our in-flight food, accidentally rammed the side of the plane and damaged it. This is the kind of coincidence that will never, ever show up in any statistical prediction. The only explanation we can come up with is that, after the first accident, the London catering driver was sacked, flew out here to find a new job, and was hired for similar work at Johannesburg.

## NOTE

THE SIX-PART TELEVISION SERIES *THE HUMAN ANIMAL* WAS GIVEN ITS FIRST SCREENING ON BBC1 IN THE SUMMER OF 1994. BECAUSE OF ITS CONTENT, IT PROVED — AS I HAD FEARED FROM THE START — TO BE HIGHLY CONTROVERSIAL. DESPITE THE FACT THAT IT WAS OVER A QUARTER OF A CENTURY SINCE I HAD FIRST BEGUN REFERRING TO PEOPLE AS ANIMALS, THERE WERE MANY WHO REACTED WITH SHOCKED DISBELIEF, AS IF THIS WERE THE FIRST TIME SUCH A VIEW HAD BEEN PUBLICLY EXPRESSED. WITH DEEP RELIGIOUS CONVICTIONS, THEY CLUNG TO THEIR FAITH IN THE NOTION THAT HUMAN BEINGS ARE SOMEHOW ABOVE NATURE. WITH SUCH ARROGANCE, NO WONDER THE PLANET IS IN SUCH A MESS.

# TRAVELS FOR *THE HUMAN SEXES*

(1996)

THE SUCCESS OF *THE HUMAN ANIMAL* SERIES LED TO A REQUEST FROM 'THE LEARNING CHANNEL' IN AMERICA FOR A SEQUEL. THIS TIME I DECIDED TO TAKE A CLOSER LOOK AT ONE PARTICULAR ASPECT OF HUMAN BEHAVIOUR, NAMELY THE RELATIONSHIP BETWEEN THE SEXES. CLIVE BROMHALL, WHO HAD WORKED WITH ME ON *THE HUMAN ANIMAL*, BECAME THE SENIOR PRODUCER AND ONCE AGAIN WE SET OFF TO SCOUR THE WORLD FOR INTERESTING EXAMPLES. I WAS CONCERNED THAT, DESPITE THE GREAT ADVANCES TOWARDS SEXUAL EQUALITY IN THE WEST, WOMEN ELSEWHERE WERE STILL BEING FORCED TO PLAY A SUBORDINATE SOCIAL ROLE. I WANTED TO DEMONSTRATE HOW THIS WAS HAPPENING AND, ABOVE ALL, WHY IT WAS HAPPENING. A NATURAL DIVISION OF LABOUR DURING THE COURSE OF HUMAN EVOLUTION, LEADING TO A BALANCE OF POWER BETWEEN THE SEXES, IS PART OF OUR GENETIC INHERITANCE AND I WANTED TO INVESTIGATE HOW THIS HAD BEEN LOST IN SO MANY SOCIETIES. SOME OF THE SEQUENCES WE FILMED WERE UNSETTLING TO SAY THE LEAST, BUT THERE WERE OTHER TRIPS ABROAD THAT TOOK ME TO IDYLLIC PLACES WHERE, MIRACULOUSLY, PEOPLE SEEMED TO HAVE FOUND THE SECRET OF A HAPPY LIFESTYLE. ONE SUCH JOURNEY, TO THE SOUTH PACIFIC IN 1996, WAS PRECEDED BY A MOST UNEXPECTED ENCOUNTER.

## NO-NOS IN PARADISE

———— ◦◦◦◦ ————

THERE IS A FLEETING MOMENT as I arrive home from the airport after a foreign trip, when everything seems unreal. My study, where I spend so many hours writing, is viewed as if for the first time. I see it as others must see it when they visit me. The illusion passes in a matter of seconds. I quickly notice the pile of unanswered letters that made me feel guilty when I left and then, in an instant, I am back in my all-too-familiar workplace once more.

On this particular occasion, having flown in from giving a lecture in Holland, I am still in the unreal moment when the phone rings. The voice at the other end is also unreal. I assume it must be a joke. Several old friends of mine use disguised voices when calling up and this one is pretending to be Marlon Brando. My first guess is that it is David Attenborough, but I have never heard him do a Brando, so I am puzzled. I let the voice talk on, waiting for the moment when it can't keep up the mimicry any longer and collapses into laughter and familiar tones.

I am giving noncommittal answers, playing along with the game to see how far the charade will go. Then the voice says· 'I have been watching tapes of your last television series, *The Human Animal,* and I would like to meet you to discuss the banality of evil.' A tiny alarm bell starts to ring. 'The banality of evil'? This sounds like a quote, but it is not the kind of phrase David would use, nor any of my other, more jokey friends. A large part of my brain is still at 30,000 feet, but it is catching up with the rest of me fast. It is starting to occur to me that maybe this really is the man himself – the last of the Hollywood giants, arguably the greatest actor in the history of the cinema. I listen more attentively.

We arrange to meet in a few days' time at my son's London apartment. I still have a lurking suspicion that the whole thing is a hoax. But I can't figure out why, or who it could be. All the same, as we are supposed to be going out to dinner, I will wear a decent suit for the occasion, just in case. I am in the process of changing into it at my son's apartment when the doorbell rings. Whoever it is is not due for another half an hour yet. I potter out into the hallway in shirt sleeves and bare feet and peer at the TV security screen that tells me who is outside on the doorstep. Completely filling the small screen is the massive figure of the Godfather. There is no mistaking it, this is Don Corleone himself. I let him in and he subsides into the sofa, launching almost immediately into an intense debate on the future of the human species.

It is always disturbing to be faced with an iconic individual at close quarters. You have to strip off all the layers of prior knowledge before you can get at the real person. With actors this is especially difficult, because each layer is a different person. Before I can focus properly on what he is saying, I have to dispose of a whole cast of indelible characters, from Stanley Kowalski to Zapata, from Mark Antony to Napoleon, from Fletcher Christian to the mad Colonel Kurtz in *Apocalypse Now*. But I am getting there, and the man beneath them, as one might expect, is complex and fascinating.

We are talking so energetically that it is already time to go to dinner and I am still barefoot and in shirt sleeves. I was reading his autobiography just before he arrived, and I hand him the book with a request to sign it while I disappear to finish dressing. When I return I find that he has written in it: 'I hope you won't hold this drivel against me – what it really is – a pale mask as I hope you come to discover …' I can't think why he wants to deride his book in this way. It certainly doesn't deserve it. Perhaps it is because so much of it, inevitably, has to cover his acting roles and his showbiz life, and what he really cares about has largely been pushed back into the final pages of the lengthy text.

For some reason, the last thing he wants to talk about is his professional work. It gets only one brief mention in the four hours of non-stop conversation that follow. He is obsessed with unravelling and understanding human nature, and our discussions range so widely over different topics and cover so much ground that I find it hard to recall the details afterwards. What does stick in my mind, though, is the inner conflict of a man who, in his seventies now, is looking back on an amazing life and demanding some serious answers to questions about the causes of human violence. He has felt violence within himself and, even more, has experienced an intense hatred of violence. Somehow he needs to resolve this contradiction.

I offer what thoughts I can. In *The Naked Ape* I referred to man as the 'killer ape' and this has often been misconstrued by those who did not bother to read the full text. I was referring to the evolution of man the hunter, to man the killer of prey for food. I was not talking about man as a killer of other men. I have always argued that we are a remarkably peaceful, cooperative species unless we are put under unnatural pressures. When we lived in small tribes we rarely experienced those pressures. If primitive man had been as brutish as cartoons so often portray him, we would never have been able to spread across the globe with such rapidity. But our cooperative nature and our high intelligence were to write us a success story that was to be its own undoing. As we went from triumph to triumph, and our numbers grew, we soon found ourselves out of our depth. We had not become supermen, we were still biological specimens – naked apes in an alien environment of our own making.

There were no strangers in the small tribes when we were slowly evolving our human nature. Now, in huge super-tribes, we were surrounded by strangers, and their presence made it easier to treat them as non-humans and to prey upon them. Warfare became a warped new form of substitute hunting. And at a more personal level, men who were squashed under the weight of the overblown societies in which they were so often failing to express themselves, found the need to redirect their frustrations onto innocent bystanders. The man who had been humiliated at work would come home and redirect his anger onto those who could not defend themselves – wives, children, animals.

Onto this scene comes the man of honour who, when he witnesses the atrocities of war and those of domestic violence, erupts, smashing the heads of the thugs and torturers to stop them. Now our man of honour, our good man, our hero, has become a violent killer himself. And therein lies Brando's main dilemma.

There is no answer to this problem other than to make a careful study of how this chain of events came about and develop a true understanding of human nature. When we come to realize that most violent behaviour we see is *redirected* aggression, it may help us to handle it better. We may be able to avoid creating the situations that demand 'honourable' reactive violence. Man is not born violent, but he can easily be driven to violence, and the best we can do is to find out who is in the driving seat and why.

As our discussion flows on, I am surprised by how in tune I am with my host's outlook on life. Although there is one major difference between us (he is a genius and I am not), I find that we do have several things in common. We are about the same age; we both have an insatiable curiosity about the world in which we live; we both are serious observers of the minutiae of human actions; we both are, to quote from his book, 'still contemptuous of authority and of the kind of conformity that induces mediocrity'; we both love ice-cream and enjoy our food too much; and we both played the drums when we were teenagers. In fact, the only point of disagreement between us in the entire evening is over who is the world's greatest drummer – I favour Gene Krupa's driving beat, while he prefers the technical superiority of Buddy Rich.

(On the subject of drums, I have a none-too-original theory about young men who are passionate about drumming – I think it is a creative way of being violent. I recall the day when my father died at the age of forty-eight. I was only fourteen years old, and when my mother broke the news to me I disappeared into the stables and starting beating my drums furiously. After a while she came out to the stables and asked me to stop, because 'people will not understand'. That hadn't occurred to me. I was horrified and put down my drumsticks immediately. I had no idea why I had reacted in that way, but looking back on it now, I am sure that the skins I was beating so hard were the heads of the politicians and the generals who had ruined my father's health when they sent him out into the trenches, along with thousands of others in World War I, to do their dirty work for them, while they stayed safely back at HQ, sipping tea and calculating losses. It was fortunate for me that my drums provided me with a positive safety valve for my feelings, and I suspect they played a similar role, if for different reasons, for the teenage Marlon.)

He has chosen a good restaurant in Knightsbridge and I am delighted to see that he is knocking back Tequila – none of the precious, modern health-anxiety rituals for him; no delicate, self-denying sipping of spritzers or mineral water. Good for him. Towards the end of the meal I mention that I am about to depart for filming in the Society Islands in the South Pacific. As he happens to own one of them – Teti'aroa – I ask him about the local people. He obviously adores them and says that I will find them unbelievably generous and full of love. 'They are the happiest people I have ever known,' he says, beaming at the very mention of them.

We debate why this should be. My feeling is that it is a combination of a comparatively affluent environment, with abundant fruit and fish and a warm sun, and the small size of the island communities. As I have already been emphasizing, the human species evolved to live in very small communities and, for a million years, we must have been remarkably affluent, once we had learned how to hunt and enrich our primate diet with meat. It was only after we discovered the seductive efficiency of agriculture that our populations exploded and we were suddenly faced with societies too massive for our human nature. That was when our problems began.

The Polynesians, thanks to an accident of geography, have managed to retain our early advantages and to a large extent reflect the true nature of the human species before it became distorted into the angry face of urban humanity. And that is more that a metaphor – it does show in the face. In his book, Marlon has said of the Polynesian faces: 'What impressed me most was the serene expressions … They were happy faces, open maps of contentment.' I can't wait to get there, to record this, and to see them for myself. He is sure that I will react as he has done, and I believe him.

The dinner is over. We step outside the restaurant and night becomes day. There is a blinding white light and for a moment I think someone must have detonated a nuclear device. Then the blanket of light starts breaking up into separate points of brightness, and I realize that we are surrounded, like startled deer, by a dense circle of paparazzi-wolves. Word has somehow leaked out that the great Brando is in town and, all through dinner, they must have been gathering, waiting for their moment to pounce. As soon as we are out of the door, they are upon us. Needless to say, this has never happened to me before and I find it startling but rather fascinating. Marlon, on the other hand, has seen it many times and his reaction is very different. From the moment he arrived at the apartment he has been the epitome of courtesy and charming good humour. Now he is transformed. Reports on the mercurial nature of his personality are clearly not exaggerated. As we stride across the road to our waiting taxi I glance sideways at his face and it is a mask of glowering anger. I am walking next to Don Corleone. And I recall with some alarm that, in his autobiography, Marlon describes an incident in which he punches a photographer who is dogging him, breaking the man's jaw with a single blow. I try to dissipate the tension with a question: 'How did they find out?' I ask. 'One of the waiters,' he replies. 'They get paid for a tip-off. If I go back to that restaurant it will be to return their food to them in the form of projectile vomit.'

When we are safely inside the taxi, with cameras still flashing through the windows, he asks me what kind of car I am driving. I tell him that it is a Range Rover and he nods approval. 'Good, the boot will be big enough for me.' (I notice that his courtesy even extends to using the English term 'boot' rather than the American 'trunk'.) It seems that he is already anticipating the need for an escape in a second vehicle. My car is parked underneath the apartment and we will be able to transfer to that if we are pursued across London. And we are. A carload of photographers is following close behind as we travel down Park Lane. But the cab driver has a trick up his sleeve at Marble Arch and manages to ditch them. No boot-crouching needed tonight. Marlon tells me that he once had to travel over a hundred miles in a French boot when being chased by Gallic paparazzi. We say goodbye outside the apartment and he slips off into the night.

It has been an intriguing evening and the time has flown by.

Brando says he has no sense of time. He is not interested in time. Time means nothing to him. Once, he told me, he was buying drinks at a liquor store and had to pay by cheque. He did not know the date, so he said to the man behind the counter: 'It's the 12th?' 'No,' replied the man, 'it's the 5th.' 'Ah,' said Brando, 'the 5th of April, thank you.' 'No,' replied the man, 'the 5th of March.' 'Could you check the price of that bottle up there on the top shelf?' asked Brando. While the man climbed the ladder, Brando was able to sneak a look at the man's newspaper, lying on the counter, to find out what year it was.

---

Three months have passed and at last I am in French Polynesia in the South Pacific. Clive Bromhall, the film crew and I are coming in to land at Tahiti, the most famous of the Society Islands thanks to Paul Gauguin, but our goal is to move on quickly to the smaller islands. As with the Hawaiian and Fijian archipelagos, the main island of the group has become too developed. The trick when visiting any of these places is to use the comforts of the main island to catch up with sleep and then take off again for their unspoilt, less well-known neighbours. We will be heading for tiny Huahine and Moorea tomorrow, but tonight we will sample the delights of downtown Papeete. We find an Oriental restaurant and order an elaborate Chinese meal. As an aperitif I request a 'hot saki'. The waitress looks dubious. Do I really want it hot? Yes, please. I prefer it slightly warmed to bring out the flavour.

The saki arrives and, filling a small cup to the brim, I swallow the contents in a single gulp, as is my custom. Unfortunately, 'hot saki' here means something very different, as my tortured throat is about to discover. Heaven knows what this drink is, but it feels as though it is a mixture of pepper and million-proof alcohol. I am unable to speak. All I can do is croak and claw the air. I grab the glass of water that, thank heaven, has already been poured for me. Everyone is staring, wondering whether I am having a fit of some kind and will at any moment sprawl twitching and dying, across the large, round table. (Such an event is of particular concern to a TV producer. I recall the occasion when David Attenborough was surrounded by wild gorillas and a large female took his head in her jaws. David's producer groaned and was heard to mutter: 'Oh, no, we're only halfway through the series.' Luckily David survived, but it was clear where the producer's priorities lay. So I know my place and understand all too well my colleagues' concern.)

I am still in such pain that, without a word, I start grabbing the glasses of water poured for the others and downing one after another – such is the emergency that normal table manners are momentarily suspended. At last I try to speak and there is no voice there, just a wheezing gasp. I think my vocal cords have been prepared for a premature burial – the fire-water has embalmed them. Tomorrow I must speak in front of a camera, or this entire trip is wasted. Will I ever be able to talk again? Needless to say, after the initial shock, I am surrounded by a circle of helpless laughter which subsides at about the same rate as my discomfort.

We never do find out what the explosive concoction is, but it is clear that one is intended to drink it in tiny sips, not large gulps, and that in Tahitian restaurants 'hot' does not mean 'warm', but 'very, very, very strong'. The last time I exploded in a restaurant like that was half a century ago when, as a naïve teenager in a posh London eating-house, I liberally sprinkled powdery white sugar over my slice of melon, spooned up a large mouthful and discovered that the white sugar was in fact white pepper. On that occasion my reaction was so forceful that the entire table had to be reset. Both occasions remain vividly etched in my memory as set-piece embarrassments, but their huge entertainment value is undeniable.

The next day, with my tormented voice back in working order, we set off for Huahine. This island is truly, impossibly idyllic. My little hut looks out on a lagoon so perfect that it almost hurts. It is the kind of place that makes you wonder why on earth you would even consider living anywhere else. In fact, it is almost a relief to be bitten by a no-no fly and to discover that there are at least a few irritations here. If it weren't for the no-nos I think I might go AWOL from the rest of the world.

A serious word on the no-nos: these tiny, black, fast-moving insects have arrived here from the Marquesas, where they are a major pest. They were originally brought to the Marquesas from New Guinea by German trading ships in the early part of the twentieth century and have since spread to many of the islands. All attempts to eradicate them have failed. They breed in wet sand and each individual fly is capable of inflicting five thousand bites in a single hour. They have a range of about half a mile under their own power, but with a high wind can be blown much farther. Their bites itch so badly that it is almost impossible not to scratch them. Once the small blisters have been ruptured they easily become infected and fester. The best answer is smearing on lots of sticky goo and then, if bitten despite this (as I was), applying the maximum amount of self-control to prevent scratching.

It is hard to think about work in a place like this, but the next day we pile all our gear into a splendid old truck and set off to film in one of the small villages. The truck driver is a large woman with, as expected, a permanently beaming smile. The Polynesian face seems to require a special effort to form it into any kind of hostile grimace, but smiling comes easily. Even when completely relaxed it settles automatically into a broad, soft, happy expression. Sitting next to her, I enquire about her family. 'I've had nine children,' she replies, 'but I gave two of them away to my friend, because she didn't have any.' 'How did they feel about being given away?' 'Oh, they didn't mind at all. They knew I still loved them and they understood.' 'If that happened in England I think the children might feel rejected.' 'Not here. We all of us love all of the children.'

This last point is underlined by the fact that, when we reach the village and start work, she passes the time by wandering over to a group of toddlers, lying down in the grass with them and playing with them exactly as if they were her own. They accept her instantly, without any questioning, and a passer-by would never have guessed that they were anything other than a natural family playing together. There is a simple generosity of spirit here that, once you get used to it, makes the meanness of urban life seem aberrant and abnormal. There are no adoption papers, no litigations, no forms to fill in. Just a surfeit of love and sharing.

On the way back to the hotel I ask about the 'flower language' of the Polynesians. Is it still being used, or is it merely something for the tourist brochures? No, it is still very much in evidence. My truck driver explains: 'An unattached girl will wear a flower in her hair on the right side of her head. An attached girl wears it on the left side. It is easy to remember which is which because when your heart is taken you wear the flower above your heart.' After a pause, she adds: 'And if you hold the flower behind your head and wave it, it means follow me!' And she dissolves into girlish laughter. Men wear flowers in their hair too, but they sometimes cheat, switching them from left side to right side after they leave their house.

Unloading our gear, we are surprised to see in the hotel lobby what appears to be a pantomime dame busying 'herself' with the dusting and cleaning. Despite her huge frame, she is mincing about in a long dress with exaggeratedly feminine movements and gestures. We discover that she is a *mahu,* a traditional transvestite of a kind that is common throughout Polynesia. Apparently, in many families, one of the little boys is brought up as a girl, and lives out his life dressed as a girl and performing only women's tasks. There is no stigma attached to this. When they are adult, the *mahus* live together as couples and nobody would dream of belittling them or insulting them in any way. They are accepted as a normal part of social life.

This has a long history. It was first reported by Europeans in the eighteenth century. A British sailor, who had fallen for a lovely Polynesian dancing girl and had persuaded her to accompany him to his cabin, was shocked 'to find this supposed dancer, when stripped of her theatrical para- phernalia, a smart dapper lad'. Captain Bligh of the *Bounty* was one of the first to comment on the existence of *mahus.* Writing in 1792he remarked that they were 'as highly respected and esteemed as women'.

I am intrigued to know how the *mahu* tradition first began. It seems an odd cultural feature for such an uninhibited soci- ety. As far as I can tell, it dates back to the times when the local chieftains employed only male servants. Those delegated to care for the noble women were required to carry out only female duties, and to live in the female quarters. With regard to tribal taboos, they were treated as women rather than as men. It was a small step, then, to adopt female dress and habits, and the *mahu* class was born. Being a servant in the household of an important chieftain carried with it many social advantages. It bestowed social privileges and prestige, so that the *mahu* role was never associated with low status and was therefore never derided.

The next day we film the Huahine fruit-carrying contest in which the strongest of the local men each loads a huge pile of fruit onto a long stick, slings it over one shoulder and then sets off down the road and back in a mad dash, as a display of muscular manhood. Even this serious annual contest is accompanied by an inordinate amount of laughter and good humour. The laughter rises to a crescendo, however, when our cameraman, in order to capture the excitement of the race, leaps from our truck and runs down the road alongside the contestants. What appeals to the Polynesians is that he, like the fruit-carriers, had a heavy load on one of his shoulders – namely his large video camera. This makes him one of them, and they love it.

After the race is over there is a great gathering in a village hut to celebrate. We are all invited and have started to giggle along with everyone else, but for our own reasons. It appears that one of the two female members of our team has accidentally strayed into the changing room before the race, where the particular male runner who happens to represent our own hotel is about to dress for the race. At the moment she enters he is completely naked and although this means nothing to him, she beats a hasty, embarrassed retreat.

Unfortunately for her, one of the male members of our crew has overheard her confiding in her female friend that our hotel contestant is 'enormous'. Nothing odd about that. He is built like Lennox Lewis. But when asked 'How big?' she was heard to reply: 'Twelve inches.' As happens with film crews, this story has done the rounds in a matter of minutes and she is teased mercilessly at every opportunity. 'Big Boy', as the runner is soon christened, senses that something is going on, but instead of being insulted, thoroughly enjoys all the strange looks and giggles that follow, his face breaking into an even bigger smile than usual.

When it comes time to leave the hut, the village matriarch stands up without any warning and begins to sing a beautiful farewell to us. Then the whole village joins in and we just sit there feeling stupidly at peace with the world. When the song finally ends, every member of the village comes over and shakes hands warmly with each of us in turn. The men come last and when they reach the two female members of our crew they begin to embellish their farewell gestures. The first one adds a kiss on the hand, the next one a kiss on the cheek, the next adds several kisses, the next an embrace, the next a massive hug, and so on, each one wanting to outdo the others. When it is Big Boy's turn we all cheer and he glows with pride as he scoops up his admirers. It is all trivial fun, and yet it is done in such a way that, when it finally comes time to return to Tahiti, we all feel a bond of attachment to the islanders that goes far beyond anything we have experienced at a hundred other locations.

Now I know why, when Marlon Brando came here in 1962 to film *Mutiny on the Bounty*, he was bewitched by Polynesia, fell in love with his Polynesian leading lady and bought one of the islands.

One of the subjects of the television series we are making is human mating systems, including polygamy. I have argued that polygamy rarely works for human beings, who are fundamentally monogamous. We have already been filming this particular topic in Turkey, Egypt and West Africa, but we had not intended to cover it here in Polynesia. Then, at the last minute, we are told about a famous polygamist on Tahiti who has proved that, contrary to my assertion, this system can function successfully if handled in a special way. There is still time to include him if we work fast, so we try to find out more.

His name is Pierre Tarahu and he has eighteen wives, who have presented him with a total of sixty-seven offspring. Biologically he must therefore be counted as a major triumph, his genetic immortality safely assured. But how does he manage to organize this huge family? Elsewhere we have found that the relations between the wives usually become strained, tensions develop and disputes erupt. If Pierre has managed to beat this system, what is his secret?

The answer is that he does not make the mistake of thinking that polygamy must automatically involve a harem, with all the wives kept together. His solution is to do just the opposite – keep them well apart. Every time he can afford a new wife he builds two houses. Then he courts a girl, proposes to her, marries her and gives her both houses as a wedding present. One is for her to live in and the other for her to rent out. He visits her from time to time to make her pregnant, and she supports her family from the rent she receives from letting the second house. When he marries again, he repeats the process in another part of the island. By keeping his wives scattered widely across Tahiti he avoids the usual risks of bickering and jealousies between the women. Each one is happy rearing her family and collecting her rent and nobody seems to suffer. It appears to be the perfect system. Well, almost.

There are two snags. The first is that it is impossible for Pierre to keep a close eye on any of his women and there is the strong possibility that a few of the sixty-seven children are not his. With the harem system, despite its obvious weaknesses, the male overlord can feel much more certain that his wives are not straying. But in Polynesia, where, as we have already discovered, people are generous with one another's children, Pierre probably wouldn't mind too much if a little straying had occurred.

The second catch concerns male stamina. How does Pierre manage to support his huge house-building scheme, and how does he manage to satisfy the sexual demands of eighteen wives? The answer to the first question is surprising, unless you think in terms of life on a small island. Pierre has been able to afford to build his thirty-six houses because he has such an important job. He is the man who drives the service vehicle out across Tahiti's airport tarmac to collect the baggage of incoming flights. If Pierre lived in Paris, he might find that such a job left him a little short, if he wanted to use his take-home pay to build thirty-six Parisian houses, but on Tahiti it is a different matter.

The answer to the second question, concerning Pierre's physical stamina, is answered for us when we try to interview him. Sorry, he is too exhausted. So perhaps there is, after all, a flaw in even his wonderful scheme of things. Sexual exhaustion appears to be the no-no in his Paradise. Sadly we have to abandon our plan to film him and must now head for the airport and the flight home. As we taxi down the runway, we peer out of the window, trying to catch a glimpse of a weary figure, struggling with heavy suitcases. But he is nowhere to be seen. Perhaps his exertions have damaged his health to such an extent that he is away somewhere building two hospitals, one for himself and one for ...

## NOTE

THE QUOTE 'BANALITY OF EVIL' USED BY MARLON BRANDO COMES FROM THE (1963) TITLE OF A CONTROVERSIAL WORK BY THE AMERICAN POLITICAL PHILOSOPHER HANNAH ARENDT, *EICHMANN IN JERUSALEM, A REPORT ON THE BANALITY OF EVIL*, IN WHICH SHE POSTULATES THAT WE CANNOT PUT ALL THE BLAME FOR THE NAZI GENOCIDE ON A FEW LEADERS, POINTING OUT THAT HUGE NUMBERS OF 'ORDINARY' PEOPLE WERE ALSO INVOLVED IN THE EVIL.

THE FOUR-PART TELEVISION SERIES *THE HUMAN SEXES* RECEIVED ITS FIRST SHOWING IN THE AUTUMN OF 1997. THE LAUNCH THIS TIME WAS HELD IN GERMANY RATHER THAN ENGLAND, WHERE THE STORM OF CONTROVERSY THAT HAD ERUPTED IN 1994 OVER THE SCREENING OF *THE HUMAN ANIMAL* HAD APPARENTLY NOT FULLY ABATED.

# AROUND THE WORLD IN 92 DAYS

## (1998)

IN 1998, WITH MY SEVENTIETH BIRTHDAY RAPIDLY APPROACHING, I FELT IT WAS TIME TO EXPLORE AS MUCH OF THE WORLD AS POSSIBLE WHILE I COULD STILL APPRECIATE IT. RAMONA AND I DISCUSSED THE OPTIONS AND DECIDED TO CIRCLE THE GLOBE. WE BOOKED A SUITE ON THE *ARCADIA* MAIDEN WORLD CRUISE, LEAVING SOUTHAMPTON ON JANUARY 5TH AND TRAVELLING EAST, COVERING 37,000 MILES IN NINETY-TWO DAYS AND RETURNING TO SOUTHAMPTON ON APRIL 6TH AFTER VISITING TWENTY-ONE DIFFERENT COUNTRIES. IT WOULD COST A FORTUNE, BUT WOULD GIVE US AN AMAZING VARIETY OF EXPERIENCES IN A COMPARATIVELY SHORT PERIOD OF TIME. FRIENDS WARNED US THAT WE WOULD COME TO BLOWS IF WE WERE FORCED TO LIVE TOGETHER IN ONE CABIN FOR THREE MONTHS, EVEN IF IT WAS THE LARGEST THE *ARCADIA* HAS TO OFFER. WE IGNORED THIS AND BEGAN PACKING CLOTHES FOR ALL SEASONS IN WHAT WOULD RAPIDLY BECOME A MOUNTAIN OF SUITCASES.

WITH ENGLAND IN THE GRIPS OF FOUL WINTER WEATHER, WE WERE EAGER TO ESCAPE TO THE SUN AND HEADED TO THE SOUTH COAST AND SOUTHAMPTON DOCKS, TO EMBARK ON THE *ARCADIA*.

## DAY 1: SOUTHAMPTON

THE BAND OF THE Adjutant General's Corps plays 'D'ye Ken John Peel' and other rousing tallyho hunting songs from the quayside as we unpack our sixteen pieces of luggage. For the first time in our lives we are making a long journey abroad without having to worry about a baggage allowance. Air travel has made cautious packers of us all, whittling down our belongings to what will fit into a suitcase and some bulging hand luggage. But as we are going from Southampton to Southampton, via the rest of the world, we can indulge ourselves, buy a carload of extra bags and cases and throw in anything that might just, maybe, perhaps, be useful at one of our twenty-seven ports of call.

As we glide around our cabin, with the *Arcadia* lying firm and immobile at its Southampton berth, we are blissfully unaware of the fact that the ship has just fought its way through a force 12 gale, which technically qualifies as a hurricane, to struggle into port. We dawdle through an elegant dinner as we set off down the wonderfully calm straits towards the Isle of Wight. Then all hell breaks loose as we nose our way out into the Channel.

We spend the night being rolled from side to side. The following morning we give in to the elements and summon a doctor who is so pukkah in his spotless whites that he makes Dr Kildare look like a *Big Issue* seller. After we have gone through the inevitable 'I do enjoy your books drop your trousers' routine and had our seasickness injections, we are soon at peace again and able to enjoy the amazingly ferocious sea working itself into a lather outside our balcony.

It is strange having a balcony on a ship. On the few occasions we have been on a cruise ship before, we have boasted no more than a humble porthole. But this time we are being foolishly extravagant and have a massive terrace complete with a table, chairs and reclining seats, outside a long wall of French windows. It creates an odd sensation, as if we were in a large apartment building that had somehow drifted out to sea. The effect is intensified by the fact that we are up on 'A' deck, the equivalent of the eleventh floor in a building. So no matter how savage the sea becomes, it can never reach us. We may have splashed out on a suite, but it can never return the compliment. Even the forty-foot waves we will encounter on one memorable leg of our long journey cannot climb high enough to worry us. We feel quite invincible, but as one of our fellow passengers points out, the entertainments officer has been careful to omit the most popular film of the moment from our viewing schedule. *Titanic* will not be screened.

### DAYS 2 & 3: THE BAY OF BISCAY

WE DISCOVER THE delights of the ship's cinema, watching endless movies to pass the time until the gales will drop. By the end of the three-month voyage we will have seen an amazing total of seventy-three new feature films, from the very best, such as *The Full Monty* and *Mrs Brown*, to the very worst, like *Anaconda* and *Hercules*. After seeing so many movies on small television sets back at home, it is a luxuriating experience to have a huge screen and thundering sound again. Sinking back into the deep seats is a trip back to the fantasy world of childhood when a two-and-sevenpenny ticket was a magical escape from blackouts and air raids.

### DAY 4: MALAGA

ARRIVING LATE IN PORT after battling head-on winds, we barely have time to enjoy this famous southern Spanish city, but we are in luck. There is a horse-drawn cab waiting on the quayside. Nobody else seems interested in it, so we quickly hop aboard and set off at a gentle jog for an open carriage ride around the main streets. The city's principal claim to fame, of course, is that it was here, in the corner house of the largest square, that the great Pablo Picasso was born, in 1881. After reading the first volume of John Richardson's brilliant new biography of Don Pablo, I am determined to set eyes on the building that gave us the century's most brutally powerful artist.

When I mention Picasso's name, our carriage-driver nods his head and is soon pointing his whip at a tall building that has been gutted and is seemingly being extensively renovated. The heart has been ripped out of it, but perhaps all this building activity indicates that the good people of Malaga are about to honour their greatest son with a small museum in the house where he nearly died at birth. (The story goes that the midwife thought that little Pablo was stillborn and left his inert body lying on a table. It was only when his cigar-smoking uncle leant over and blew smoke in his face that the newborn infant let out a bellow of rage and was discovered to be alive.)

Picasso lived in this square (at No. 15, Plaza de la Merced) in Malaga for the first ten years of his life, and it was here that he made his first juvenile drawings and oil paintings. He was a pampered little boy, surrounded by doting women, and from the very beginning was fascinated by drawing. The first word he ever spoke was the Spanish for 'pencil'. Playing in this square, he used to make patterns in the dust. Looking down at its surface as we jog past today, I can picture that little boy hard at work, studiously developing a love of strong, sweeping lines that flow from the movements of his hand.

Boldly setting down the lines of a composition came so easily to Picasso in later life that he was able to create a confident new work in a matter of minutes. My favourite Picasso story concerns the time he went back to look at an old studio of his in Paris, and there, lying on a bench outside the gate, was an old tramp. Picasso recognized the man and asked what had happened to him. The old boy explained that he had fallen on hard times and now had nowhere to live. Picasso went over to a nearby rubbish-bin, pulled out a large piece of cardboard, did a quick drawing on it, signed it, and gave it to the tramp, saying: 'Here, buy yourself a house.'

When I was briefly the director of the Institute of Contemporary Arts in London, I arrived at the office one morning and nearly tripped over a wall in the entrance hall that had not been there the day before. I asked Roland Penrose, the ICA's chairman (and a lifelong friend of Picasso) why there was a large section of wall standing on the floor of the entrance. Was it some kind of surrealist object? No, he explained, it would soon be moved, but it was to be carefully guarded while it was here. It seems that Picasso had paid a brief visit to England in 1950 and that he and Roland had gone to see a scientist friend in his London laboratory. While Picasso was there he made a rapid pencil drawing on the whitewashed laboratory wall. This was the only 'mural' he ever made in England and was therefore of great historical interest. Unfortunately, the laboratory was now being torn down and so Roland had rescued the section of the wall in question and had arranged for it to be brought to the ICA's offices. Again, a quick Picasso scribble that was worth a fortune. No wonder waiters were always fighting over tablecloths where Picasso had doodled while dining.

In this sleepy little southern city it is hard to understand where Picasso's fire and urgent power came from. Perhaps they were a rebellious reaction to the softness of his childhood? When he was ten he moved north to a more lively world and never came south again. Strangely, he seemed to have nothing but resentment for this southern city of his childhood years. He once said that one of the few exciting memories he retained from it was learning to smoke with a cigarette shoved up one nostril – a trick taught to him by the local gypsies. When, many years later, the city fathers of Malaga paid the great man a visit to honour him on his ninetieth birthday, he snubbed them horribly by refusing to open his electronically controlled gates to let them into his estate.

Continuing our ride around the city, we find it difficult to see why he took against this pleasant, harmless place. Perhaps that was the key to it. It was too harmless, too quiet, too safe, too docile for his violent spirit. And there was also probably a reaction to social snobbery lodged in his child's mind, with unpleasant memories of the indignity of hand-outs from well-to-do relatives, who often helped out his impoverished art-teacher father. Even so, regardless of the maestro's rejection of Malaga, it remains the starting point of one of the greatest art biographies of the twentieth century, and I am glad to have had this chance, if only briefly, of absorbing its atmosphere before setting off for the long haul across the Mediterranean from west to east.

Now we are coming to the end of our short Spanish ride and it is time to return to the ship. Our horse is trotting along with that steady, pleasureless, businesslike gait so common in urban equines, but Ramona points out to me that he slows down significantly as we come close to the town bullring and speeds up cheerfully as we drive away from it. Poor creature, has he in the past been forced to enter the ring with the picadors, to face the bull, all padded up with a 'protective' covering (which is really there to conceal his wounds from sensitive eyes)? Or has he only smelled the blood of other injured horses there, and then deep in his equine brain lodged a lasting association between the bullring and pain?

How I hate bullfighting. I know that human beings evolved as hunters and that we are genetically programmed to include meat in our diet. I know that veganism is both unnatural and dangerous to the human digestive system. But if we must kill animals for food we should do so with regret and as painlessly as possible. In the bullring people actually take pleasure in killing animals, and that I cannot forgive. Spain has, to its eternal credit, given us the three greatest artists of the century – Picasso, Dali and Miró – but it has also, to its shame, continued to give us the debased spectacle of the bullfight. For me, this results in a love–hate feeling about Spain which has stayed with me for many years. So, with the uneasy sensation I get whenever I am near to a bullring, I am as glad to be leaving the country as I was to arrive.

As we shed a fistful of pesetas, sympathetically pat our long-suffering horse, and stroll back to the welcoming gangway, I notice the solitary figure of a leather-skinned old man, selling some sort of knick-knacks. On closer inspection these turn out to be cheap, decorated fans in the worst possible taste. 'No,' says Ramona firmly, but I insist on acquiring a box of four of them. This is madness. I would never in a million years consider buying such rubbish at home. So why have I done it? What on earth possessed me? Is it the fact that the forlornly dignified old man, reeking of peasant poverty, has clearly not made a single sale until the gullible Morris arrives on the scene, and I feel sorry for him? A little, perhaps, but there is another, unformulated reason. Unconsciously I am on a global treasure hunt, and this is my first trophy. Having no excess baggage worries, I am for once able to acquire local oddments without the air-traveller's usual inhibitions.

With twenty more countries to go before we arrive back in

Southampton, this uncontrollable urge could herald serious cabin-congestion. But it has all the appeal of those magical treasure hunts of youth, when as teenagers we set off in rival cars with a list of near-impossible objects (a pair of knickers, a road sign, a parasol) to be obtained without spending any money – the first car back at base, with everything on the list, being the winner. The dim memory of such childish pleasures is now threatening to push itself to the surface but I suspect, from Ramona's expression back in the cabin, as she sniffily opens and shuts my trashy Spanish fans, that my irrational trophy-collecting will experience some stiff opposition in the weeks ahead.

### DAYS 5 TO 8: THE MEDITERRANEAN

WE ARE ENJOYING a wonderfully smooth crossing of the Med. This is what cruising is all about. At first, out of habit, we try to fill every minute of the day. Then, gradually, we develop the knack of purposely doing nothing for long spells of time, allowing the brain to go off-line. It is a strange, semi-meditative sensation – not entirely unpleasant, once you get used to it.

### DAY 9: ASHDOD AND THE HOLY LAND

As WE ALL KNOW, Israel is full of suicide bombers wearing anoraks lined with sticks of dynamite. Our Jewish guide spends a great deal of time trying to dispel this notion and extolling the virtues of his country as the ultimate holiday resort. He spends even more time bewailing the high taxes, the defence budget and the need to serve periods in the military all through life until the age of sixty. He says he was told his rifle was his wife. He also explains that there are no underground trains in Israeli cities because builders are afraid of breaking into Mossad HQ. He then feels the need to explain that this is a joke. Talking about recent wars, to appease British tourists he says the Israelis only tried to destroy British weapons, not to hurt the British soldiers.

Ancient Jerusalem – the tiny walled city – is a delight. Divided up like postwar Berlin, it has four ruling quarters, one Armenian, one Catholic, one Moslem and one Jewish. We are taken to the Wailing Wall in the Jewish section. As we pass through the electronic checkpoint our guide shouts out to us: 'Leave your grenades here before you go in.' The police guards fail to laugh at this. At the Wall we are told to separate into males and females if we wish to wail. And if we are male we must put on little round hats that are stacked up at the entrance. Not having anything to wail about, I skip this and spend the time photographing a non-wailing cat that is busy washing its private parts. In the distance, men in black give the impression of rhythmically banging their heads against the stone wall. Before they leave the Wall, they stuff a written message to the Almighty into the cracks between the stones. If they ask nicely, their requests are granted. Our guide explains: 'We are told not to ask for lottery numbers.' Apparently the only reply from the Almighty to such a request is 'Buy a ticket'. Nowadays it is possible to send faxes to the Wall, and six hundred arrive each day from all over the world. So you can be a pilgrim without leaving your office.

The Golden Gate to the Old City of Jerusalem is closed. This was done by Moslems to prevent the Messiah from re-entering. And to make sure, they built a Moslem cemetery in front of the closed gate. No Messiah worth his salt would tread on such a place. So that takes care of the Second Coming.

There are now seventy thousand Jewish graves on the Mount of Olives, including Robert Maxwell's, but we skip that too. Nearby at the Garden of Gethsemane, where Christ was arrested and taken off to be tried and executed, I notice that stigmata are starting to show up on the palms of my hands. Very clever – how do they do that? I suspect they put small rough spots on the railings. I bet it scares the life out of the devout (unless they happen to know the truth, namely that crucifixion nails were driven through the victim's wrists and not his palms).

Railed off, inside the Garden of Gethsemane, are some aged olive trees. They are so gnarled that one feels that they must be old enough to have been here when Christ was lingering in the garden after the Last Supper, perhaps leaning up against one of their trunks. I check my guidebook to see how old they are supposed to be. To my surprise it says: 'For whatever it's worth, the olive trees have been carbon dated and are as old as the saviour.' Even hard-nosed botanists agree that olive trees can grow to 'over 1,500 years', so I suppose it is possible that this dating is accurate. I look at these twisted trunks with new respect. It occurs to me that, if you are a clever tree, it is a good idea to have a trunk that is too twisted to turn into a plank of wood. If you are a stupid tree – as thick as two planks – you soon feel the axe.

When we stop for lunch, the hotel restaurant is like something out of Stalin's Moscow. The atmosphere is strained and what signs of happiness there are seem to be strangely forced. The small band forlornly plays Topol's 'If I Were a Rich Man'. This is not a country at ease with itself, but I suppose that is to be expected. There must be so many inner conflicts eating away at the people who live here. What Woody Allen is to comedy, the Israelis are to real life – and an anxiety-ridden, crisis-torn life at that.

At Bethlehem we are taken in to see the manger where Christ was born. It is not in a stable but in a small cave which is now beneath a church. Even for a non-believer like myself, it has to be admitted that this cramped little space does possess a very powerful, eerie atmosphere. The air is suffused with the heavy pheromones of endless devotion.

We are told that literally millions of Christian pilgrims will be descending on these holy places on December 31st, 1999, to see in the new millennium. What do they expect to witness on that totally artificial date? If Christ was going to return two thousand years after his birth, he would have appeared in 1994, because scholars have now agreed that he was actually born in the year 6 BC. If he was going to return two thousand years after his death, he would not show up until 2030, because he was thirty-six when he was crucified. Either way, the year 2000 has no religious significance whatever and is best ignored, unless of course you happen to be Bill Gates.

On the way back to the ship we are given an unexpected treat – a ten-minute stop at a Tank Museum, with row after row of defunct tanks from every conceivable theatre of war. Only three elderly men get out of the bus to take a closer look. Tanks for the memory.

## DAY 10: PORT SAID

THE HARBOUR BUILDING here is magnificent. In most ports today the main visual impact on arrival is of ugly commerce – great walls of huge metal boxes, as if someone were trying to build a pyramid out of containers but lost the plans. But Port Said, despite its sleazy naval reputation for sexually explicit nightclub acts, has managed to keep its antique splendour and offer the sea-visitor a harbour façade as elegant as it is welcoming. If only the countless knick-knacks spread out on the ground all around it, and so insistently offered for sale, were as appealing as the building itself.

A Mr Walli takes us around this notorious, bustling Egyptian port in his horse-drawn carriage. We fix the price with him beforehand, but at the end there is the inevitable debate about how much we should pay the horse. Under the stress of seeing two well-fed Morrises climbing on board, the poor animal had developed a serious attack of diarrhoea, so we pay up.

Back on board there is local entertainment provided by an Egyptian magician called the Gulli Gulli Man. As he makes his entrance, our first glimpse of him does not inspire confidence in the performance to come. David Copperfield he is not. A wizened little man carrying a battered old suitcase, he patters across to the centre of the large stage where a small, simple table has been positioned. Upon it he places the suitcase, opens it and starts to perform rather routine card tricks. So far, so bad. But gradually something strange begins to happen. His little tricks and sleight of hand develop a rhythm and a mounting complexity until he is doing things that seem increasingly impossible. Every so often he says 'Gulli, gulli, gulli', sounding rather like an excited turkey, at points where other magicians might intone 'abracadabra'. Suddenly day-old chicks are appearing from all over the place. And then, in a finale that I still find completely mystifying, he opens his mouth and out pops another live chick, dry and fluffy and chirpy. Despite the fact that I am sitting very close to him, I have no idea how he does this. He has just been uttering 'Gulli, gulli, gulli', so where was the chick then? I know I am deliberately naïve when it comes to magicians' secrets, because I don't want to spoil the magic, but this is so audaciously simple and yet so incomprehensible to me, that it impresses me more than all the modern, high-tech effects of the great international performers. And as the little Egyptian shuts his sad suitcase and shuffles off, I have the feeling we have witnessed the kind of show that has been presented on street-corners here in Egypt since the days of the Pharaohs. Probably using the same suitcase.

## DAY 11: SUEZ

PASSING THROUGH THE Suez Canal is about as exciting as driving down an aquatic motorway, with long stretches of featureless shoulder-landscape gliding monotonously past the balcony, the tedium broken only by the occasional Egyptian army nerve-centre – usually with three men and a dog detailed to defend the populace against the might of the distant Israelis, should they ever decide to retake the barren Sinai. The oil-streaked water contains many mercifully unidentifiable floating objects. The only recognizable piece of flotsam is a dead goat whose final act was presumably taking a drink of the polluted water from the edge of the canal. Now its soft corpse flops along in the wakes of tankers, awaiting a vacationing Damien Hirst with a long boat-hook.

The desert that threatens to silt up the canal whenever high winds whip up a sandstorm is a pale, dingy dirt-brown instead of the romantic yellow-ochre of the travel posters. The corrugated hills rearing up on the horizon are a reminder that this is the wilderness into which biblical figures retreated to solve the trickier philosophical problems of their day.

## DAY 12: SHARM EL SHEIKH

ALTHOUGH IT IS technically in Egypt, Sharm el Sheikh feels much more like a Middle East seaside resort. There are no ancient temples or tombs here. Until recently it was no more than a small fishing village, but then it was discovered to have the best coral reefs in the northern hemisphere and everyone came rushing. Huge hotels sprang up and now there is this flourishing tourist resort and dive centre at the very point where two huge continents meet (turn left for Africa, turn right for Asia).

In the short time we have available, we have decided to abandon the resort and head inland to see one of the world's most remote treasures – St Catherine's Monastery – which is 137 miles inland from here. It has several claims to fame. It is one of the oldest monasteries in the world. Hermits were active there as long ago as the third century, and the fortified monastery was built during the sixth. It is the only ancient monastery never to have been plundered. When things were hotting up in the seventh century, they asked the Prophet Mohammed to give them a note saying 'excused wars', and he did. They still keep a copy of it (the *ahtiname,* or immunity covenant) in their monastery library. The Middle East being what it is, you never know when you might need it.

About a thousand years ago, some bright spark had the clever idea of building a small mosque inside the Christian monastery walls, which made it even more difficult for Moslem hordes to desecrate the place. As a result of all this special protection, St Catherine's has the most amazing library in existence – 5,000 books and 4,500 manuscripts of unbelievable rarity. It also has a huge collection of over 2,000 wonderful early icons, dating from the sixth century.

There really is nothing quite like this place anywhere else in the world. And, of course, it was here that Moses had that intimate talk with God on top of the nearby Mt Sinai. If you are up to the climb, it is apparently only 3,700 steps from the monastery up to the summit. Once there, you can (our guide assures us) stand on the actual spot where the great event occurred. To top everything, the monastery building sits on the exact spot where Moses encountered the famous Burning Bush. Sadly, the first bush has long since vanished, but we have been told that there is a new one, grown from a cutting taken from the original, that is on display in the centre of the monastery. An irreverent thought comes to mind – will there be a label on it saying 'no smoking'?

We strike out for the interior. The Sinai Desert is as bleak as it gets. At first glance it seems that nothing could survive on this never-ending, rumpled yellow-brown carpet of barren rock, sand and soil. But the Bedouin are here, with their goats, sheep and camels, somehow clinging to life, and there are still a few gazelles and oryx to be found wild. Hunting has always been the premier sport of the region, with peregrine falcons fetching the equivalent of £7,000 apiece, so the environment is doubly hostile. Ostriches once lived here but are now extinct in the entire Sinai Desert, although, as we will discover, ostrich eggs appear in the hanging ceiling trappings of the sixth-century Church at the Monastery. It will take us three hours to reach St Catherine's, through this interminable lunar landscape, but imagine how long it must have taken before the advent of modern roads and high-speed buses. We are heading for the spot where Moses took his tablets. Unfortunately, Ramona has forgotten to take hers.

We pass a number of Bedouin tribesmen. Apparently their camels are allowed to wander freely, finding food for themselves, but they always return to the home camp eventually and rejoin their owners. Sometimes, when out and about, unsaddled, they find themselves attended by helpful, tick-eating birds. At the roadside, two large black crows are sitting on a resting camel's back.

We are told that the temperature here in the deserts of Arabia rises to over 120 degrees Fahrenheit in the summer. Perhaps this explains why the Burning Bush burst into flames. Our Egyptian guide informs us that the biggest problem for the American soldiers during the Gulf War was preventing their chocolate bars from melting in the fierce desert heat. Egyptian soldiers, it seems, are so poor that they never have to face this challenge.

Finally we arrive at the monastery and it is immediately obvious that the long trip has been worthwhile. This tiny walled gem, like a little fortress in the middle of nowhere, has a fairy-tale quality. Its fortified walls are 10 feet thick and 28 feet high. At its heart stands the Church of St Catherine, containing her remains. As a child I used to enjoy seeing Catherine Wheel fireworks going around and around on Bonfire Night; I little realized that they represented the hideous form of torture to which St Catherine was subjected before being beheaded.

The icons on the walls are as magnificent as we expected. We soon discover that there is now an eleventh commandment here: thou shalt not use your cameras inside the church. One elderly Australian pretends he has not heard this rule and quietly sneaks a few moments, switching on his video camera in the centre of the church when he thinks nobody is looking. But in an instant, towering, black-bearded monks in black robes and black pillbox hats angrily descend upon him and he reluctantly puts it away. Grumpy, he offers them no apology.

I ponder the question of how desecration by camera works. After all, there is a monastery gift shop (horribly incongruous here) selling calendars, books and postcards, with plenty of photographs of the inside of the church, so what is the big deal about visitors discreetly taking a few shots? I suspect it is simply a matter of making us feel a little less important.

The isolated cats of this remote monastery, over a hundred miles from the nearest town, are white with small patches of tabby, black and ginger on their extremities. One of them has odd eyes – one amber and one blue – like the cats of Lake Van in Turkey, a thousand miles to the north. They do not look very well cared for. If I were one of the fifteen monks who spend their lives here I would want to pamper my monastery cats a little and enjoy their company. But these stern-faced men seem positively to relish the austerity of their world. Presumably the deal is that they get a better time in the next one.

The monastery charnel-house looks like a dark corner of a nightmare pick-'n'-mix candy store, with bones and skulls heaped up in great wire baskets. The reason they are in here is that the monastery graveyard is so small. When a new monk dies they have to dig up an old one to make room for him. The old monk's skull is added to the skull-cage, his limbs, hands and feet are placed in their respective cages, and there he stays, scattered around in the different sections, for all to see. I find it strange that they would want to allow casual visitors like me to see these remains, as it is much more intrusive than a few video-shots of the church interior. After a quick glance round, I turn and head for the door, watched accusingly by a hundred pairs of eye-sockets.

Outside the Ossuary building I pass the time by photographing a camel, only to be accosted by an Arab who comes running up and demands immediate payment for permission to take the picture. Just when the devoutly pious atmosphere of this place was beginning to get through to me, I am back in the commercial world with a bump.

On the seemingly endless journey back to the ship, a smart silver Mercedes shoots past the window of the bus at high speed, going in the opposite direction. Mysteriously, the car is upside-down and rolling over as it passes us. There is no bang. It has hit nothing. So what is it doing? Another mystery in this desert of mysteries.

### DAY 13: Aqaba

WE ADORE JORDAN. It is our favourite Middle Eastern culture, with people so at ease with themselves that they are friendly without trying. If we had to live in the Middle East this would be the place. The country has only this one port and we devote our time to exploring its shops. They are a hoot, with every weird form of merchandise known to man, from stuffed batfish to Yemeni daggers; and from masses of ethnic jewellery to endless bottles filled with multi-coloured sand. We foolishly buy rather too much.

The main attraction of the *Arcadia*'s brief stopover in Aqaba is the chance it gives of visiting the legendary lost city of Petra. It is only about sixty miles north of here, and is reached by a dramatic drive through the great emptiness of the desert wilderness known as the Wadi Rum. We would be the first to grab this opportunity had we not already made the trek on a previous trip to Jordan. Petra is so breathtaking that we might well have repeated the experience, but our memory of what happened to us there is still painfully sharp.

The day of our earlier visit to Petra had begun well enough, with a long horseback ride down the winding ravine that leads to the hidden valley of the ancient city. It had lain abandoned for 1,450 years, until it was rediscovered in 1812 by an astonished Swiss explorer. This deep gorge, cut into the soft rocks by a long-dead river, is known as the Sik. It is so narrow that no modern form of traffic can travel through it. In some places it is even difficult for two horses to pass one another. But in reality this is a great advantage because it forces the visitor to experience the journey at a more leisurely pace. From the back of a docile, clip-clopping horse one can look up at the tall, rocky walls of this deep cleft in the landscape, and imagine oneself arriving here 2,300 years ago, when Petra was a thriving way-station for the spice trade. Caravans of camels stopped here for its precious water, so rare in the centre of this parched desert landscape. They paid tolls and the city grew rich.

Neither Ramona nor I was particularly experienced with horses, but in such a confined, rocky space, there was little that could happen to us – or so we thought. The 1¼ mile journey down the 160-foot deep ravine was uneventful. For most of its length it is a chasm so overhung that it is almost a tunnel, but then, without warning, at its inner end it suddenly opens out into a wide, steep-sided, rock-walled valley. This is the Valley of Moses, where he was supposed to have struck a rock so that water gushed out. You have to be a great leader to know how to take credit for a natural spring.

As we emerged from the narrow gorge, there, opposite, was the amazing sight of a massive classical façade, deep red in colour and ninety feet high, cut into the living rock-face. We recognized it immediately as the place where, in the movies, Indiana Jones finally catches up with the Holy Grail. Romantically known as the Pharaoh's Treasury, it has a sophisticated presence, here in the back of beyond, that stuns everyone who sets eyes on it.

This moment alone would have been enough reason for making the long journey, but then, turning right, we saw that this is only one of a whole series of such façades. Scattered down the valley, there was an astonishing array of silent, rock-hewn palaces, temples and tombs, as though a whole Hellenistic city had been carved into the steep valley walls.

Riding farther down, we dismounted and were allowed to explore. In the complete absence of any modern forms of transport, we were overcome by a feeling of having being transported back in time, a sensation that few other sites in the world can create quite so completely. I was fascinated by the colours of the sandstone rocks – red, purple and yellow in thin veins and layers, so that small fragments of it looked almost edible. At one point, cut into this rock, there was a long stairway rising up and up to a high platform – a sacred sanctuary, 45 by 20 feet, that was once completely covered in gold and was thought to be used for sacrifices.

Exploring one ruin after another, I eventually disappeared into a cave. When I returned I realized immediately that all was not well. Several Jordanians were surrounding Ramona in an agitated manner. As I approached I saw that she was smiling at me in a strange, unnatural way. There had been an accident. She had been standing near her horse, ready to mount it again, when a stinging insect had bitten it and, in sudden pain, it had kicked out and smashed its hoof into her leg. Looking down I was startled to see blood pouring from a large gash and a piece of her flesh hanging down in a way that signalled an urgent ride in an ambulance. 'It wasn't the horse's fault,' she kept saying, because the guides were so angry at what had happened. All I could think about was that there was no way we could get an ambulance down here and that she was losing a lot of blood. It was impossible for her to remount the horse and ride back, and I was now becoming seriously worried.

To the rescue came an elderly Arab with a tiny chariot, just big enough for the two of us to squeeze in behind him. He had used it to bring two infirm visitors down the gorge, but they kindly agreed to wait while he rushed us back up it, to find the local doctor's surgery. We climbed in, with Ramona in considerable pain. The driver cracked his whip and the little horse took off at a gallop, bumping and swaying its way up the ravine, almost touching the rocky sides. He shouted at walkers to get out of the way and they did their best to flatten themselves against the walls. Some scattered too late and we almost knocked them over, but all my thoughts were focused on Ramona's acute discomfort.

Halfway up the ravine, to our surprise, the driver suddenly stopped. He had seen a woman friend of his struggling to make the long walk. As she was clearly at least eight months pregnant, probably with twins, he offered her a lift and she clambered gratefully aboard, even though there was not an inch of space to spare. Huddled together with a proximity almost as intimate as if we were midwives attending her birth, we sped through to the end of the gorge and then on into the nearby village. There we found a doctor who proceeded to douse Ramona's leg with disinfectant and sew up her wound with thick brown twine. Local anaesthetics did not appear to have reached this remote part of the world and I was astonished, yet again, at the stoical way in which women endure such agonizing treatment. Had it been me, I would probably have solved the problem, in a typically male fashion, by passing out cold.

As we were leaving the doctor's surgery we noticed a large Arab sitting in the waiting room, his foot covered in blood. 'You poor thing,' said Ramona. 'What happened to you?' The Arab explained to the doctor, who translated for us: 'He says he was run over by a small chariot.' We did love Petra, but once is enough.

### DAYS 14 & 15: RED SEA

W E PUSH OUR WAY DOWN the Red Sea with the air growing hotter and more humid by the hour, heading for Bombay. The first fortnight of our three-month odyssey is over.

### DAY 16: ARABIAN SEA

I WAKE UP at 6 am to find a fax shoved under the door. It is from son Jason in England and contains some startling news. It is startling because his teenage rebellion took the form of being extremely sensible, in contrast to the erratic lifestyle of his parents, and it seems that he has now, at last, thrown his usual caution to the wind. The fax reads as follows:

Free from parental control at last. Let's go wild! Decide that best form of rebellion would be to throw away all my money by becoming a racehorse owner, but which horse? Phone call out of the blue from point-to-point trainer Jenny Pidgeon. Ask her about my favourite pointer, Wild Illusion. Such is my enthusiasm that she offers me the lease on the horse for the season. What an opportunity. Must be fate.

Take the day off work to visit Jenny and see Wild Illusion on the gallops. Freezing cold, standing on top of a mound for an hour as the horse canters up the gallop four times. Annie and Matilda [Jason's wife and six-week-old daughter] sensibly sleep in the car. Horse looks a picture of health. Same can't be said of his prospective new owners (me freezing, Annie with a sore throat). We get on well with Jenny, although she is a very forceful lady – makes Lady Thatcher look like a shrinking violet.

Back home, having serious second thoughts and get the calculator out to work out all the potential costs that will be involved. Can hear voice of doom urging caution. Annie says there's no choice, we've got to do it, sod the expense, think of the fun. God I love her, what a wonderful woman.

We are now the proud owners of Wild Illusion. This news is not met with the euphoria that I expected among friends and colleagues. The point-to-point cognoscenti seem to relish reminding me that the horse is now fourteen (old for a racehorse, I admit, but like fine wine and my parents, he could get better with age) and over the hill. Among the comments are: 'that old has-been', 'he's past it', 'his best days are long gone' and 'hasn't he got a broken leg?' Oh, did I forget to mention that he broke a bone in his hind leg last year and nobody can be 100 per cent certain that he's fully recovered, especially given his age. Still, he's got lovely big ears! Sign of honesty.

Talk to Jenny to seek reassurance. She says that Wild Illusion was coughing some time ago (funny thing is she didn't mention that before I leased the horse, obviously slipped her mind, easily done) but she is hopeful that all is now well. She adds that the horse may run at the weekend. We therefore need to design our colours a.s.a.p. as very little time to have them made before Saturday. Get the crayons out. Seek inspiration. Decide against using our previous colours. Instead, go for 'yellow, red hoop, royal blue sleeves, royal blue cap with a yellow diamond'. Nice, bright combination of Oxford United colours and Annie's favourite colour – red. Jenny not impressed when I tell her.

Receive entries for the weekend. Horse needs firm ground and it hasn't stopped raining since you left. Distant Ipswich is the only option, but it looks a very competitive race. Five or six other horses in the race of a similar ability and they're not fourteen-year-olds. Decide that we should be happy if we are placed. In fact, should be very happy if we just manage to *find* the place.

Pre-match nerves. Terrible diarrhoea. Matilda also fractious, clearly equally excited about tomorrow. Cock-up with our set of colours as the bloke making them clearly thinks our jockey is the Hunchback of Notre Dame – has made huge shoulders and only long enough to go halfway down his body. Will have to race in previous colours – 'blue, yellow cuffs, red sleeves'. Same colours as ours, just a different combination. Must be a bad omen. Doesn't augur well for tomorrow. Jenny sounds very nervous on phone. Starts saying things like 'Just want the horse to come back in one piece'. Also tells us that the horse ended up in a ditch out on the gallops today and was lucky not to be injured. Lost a shoe and needed to be replated.

Set off for sunny Suffolk before dawn. Navigate by the stars. Arrive at the course – pools of water everywhere. Meet Jenny, who is concerned the ground will be too soft. Still, Wild Illusion looks magnificent, a beautiful chestnut with a white stripe down his face. Look at the race-card comment – 'won 24 of 44 races, useful but not as good as he was, best on a right-handed track'. All confidence evaporates – the course is left-handed and Jenny starts worrying that he may have deteriorated.

Watch the first race (we are in the third) at the last fence. Horse and jockey take a crashing fall right in front of us. Annie and I gasp. Matilda blissfully asleep. Declarations come through for our race. All the main dangers run – nine runners in total and six of the others are real threats. One in particular – Stormhill Pilgrim – has excellent form, is owned by the leading point-to-point owner in the country and has come all the way from the South Coast. The top East Anglian horse is also present. Both are very strongly fancied.

Meet our jockey, Richard White. Nice guy and good jockey, but hasn't ridden a winner for twenty months and has been off the course for a year due to an injury. Doesn't inspire confidence. Enter parade ring nervously. Wild Illusion jig-jogging about like a two-year-old. He looks fantastic, but all the others look fit as well. Try to appear relaxed. Fail. Horses canter to the start.

Annie insists we have a bet. There has been a huge gamble on Stormhill Pilgrim (7/2 in to 6/4). Wild Illusion is 2/1 second-favourite. Was going to put £20 on him but consider these odds to be an insult to such a grand old campaigner with a better than 50 per cent strike rate, so increase my bet to £200. Get 9/4. Immediately regret this foolish act of bravado. Matilda momentarily stirs from her slumber and looks at me disapprovingly. Castigated by my own six-week-old daughter. Feel very guilty about squandering her inheritance in such a reckless manner. Still, it could be worse, I tell Tilly, at least I'm not blowing the lot on an around-the-world cruise of a lifetime.

Reassured, Matilda falls back asleep as the race begins. Stays asleep for the entire race as Wild Illusion romps to victory. Annie is presented with a huge trophy and is photographed balancing it on Tilly's head before we spend the evening drinking port out of it with friends. Matilda is also overcome with the excitement of the day and smiles at her mother for the first time.

I show the fax to Ramona and expect her to be upset. Jason is facing the new responsibility of becoming a family man and, as everyone knows, owning a racehorse is just an elegant way of losing money. Most mothers would be horrified. But she surprises me, as she has done so many times in the past. 'Good for him!' she says. No wonder he has always found youthful rebellion so elusive.

## DAY 20: BOMBAY

BECAUSE THE French President, Monsieur Chirac, is making a state visit to the city, the *Arcadia* is forced to give up its berth to a French aircraft-carrier, without which support, apparently, the President will not set foot on foreign soil. I am not surprised that Chirac has embraced the pageantry of presidential pomp. I interviewed him once in Paris for a BBC television programme, before he was President, and found him refreshingly humorous and sharp-witted for a politician. When I asked him what kind of dog he owned, he replied with mock exaggeration: 'I a*dore* my labra*dor*,' adding disarmingly that he had one because: 'If you want to get ahead in politics you *must* have a labrador. You *have* to have a dog, and *no* other breed will do.' Here, I thought, is a man who treats political displays in the manner they deserve – as amusing games. And I suspect that, now he is President, he enjoys playing even bigger games, complete with carrier-sized toys.

All this is no comfort to us today. As a result of Chirac's desire to contemplate his naval forces, we have to wait for ages and then make a two-mile trip by tender to reach the shore from our anchorage. Strong anti-French feeling is expressed by all on board. I rehearse the most obscene French insults I can find in my *World Guide to Gestures*, but sadly the French warships all appear to be deserted as we chug past them.

When we step onto dry land we are each dabbed with red pigment to give us the familiar Bindi spot on the centre of the forehead. This is the sixth centre of spiritual energy, the source of memory, and has nothing to do with the married state. On us, it simply gives the impression that we have been shot by a Hollywood sniper.

Bombay suffers, not merely from overpopulation, but from something approaching human infestation. Two and a half million passengers a day crowd into the city trains. Each train is designed to hold two thousand, but five thousand squeeze in. An average of four are killed per day – falling off or under the moving coaches.

We are bussed through near gridlock to a Jain temple, seemingly decorated by Disney on a bad day, with its twenty-four gods and its three sacred symbols: the swastika, with its four arms representing the four stages of life (youth, marriage, detachment and spirit); its three dots, representing fate, action and knowledge; and its half-moon, representing salvation.

The Jains are the strictest veggies in the world, refusing to eat not only any kind of animal food but also any plant food that grows underground. This is because uprooting such plants might infringe the rights of countless microbes in the soil. For this extreme sect, even bacteria must be treated with respect.

Flying insects also have to be protected, so the devout Jains wear face masks. They cannot ride on animals because it exploits them, nor can they use any mechanical devices, any power sources such as electricity, or anything that stems from material advancement, since all such progress is against nature.

The most extreme Jains will not wear any clothing, even in public. They walk about totally naked. And they never wash their bodies, in case this might kill off microbes on their skin. Intriguingly, the grateful microbes respond by setting up a natural life cycle on their skin that protects these ultra-Jains from any body odour.

At the Hanging Gardens of Bombay we are shown the sinister Towers of Silence over which large, stiff-winged birds are circling. Mercifully we are not allowed inside because this is the place where a sect called the Parsees lay out their dead so that the flesh can be cleaned from their bones by the ever-helpful vultures.

At the Prince of Wales Museum we are shown early Mogul miniatures notable for their vivid colours. It is explained to us that the intense yellow tints were obtained from the urine of 'jaundiced cattle' and that if a darker yellow was required the cattle were specially fed on mangoes. Ordinary cattle pass water; sacred cattle pass water-colours.

Bombay is a city of cruel contrasts, with the very rich paying £500 a square foot for land in the posh districts, while Dobhi Wallas will do all your laundry for £10 a month, and families of penniless beggars sleep in the exhaust fumes of the traffic-jammed gutters.

There are no fewer than 270 cinemas in this aching city, where 900 conveyer-belt films are made each year in the vast Bollywood studios. The huge hoardings advertising these films are all laboriously hand-painted *in situ* by vertigo-free sky-artists. There is now great concern that, since the city was formally given back its old, pre-colonial name of Mumbai in 1996, Bollywood may have to be rechristened Mollywood. It just doesn't have the same ring to it.

At dinner tonight, on a nearby table, someone is celebrating a birthday with a candle-lit, sickly-sweet cake, tall glasses of fizzy champagne, and a bevy of Goanese waiters doing their best with an enthusiastic rendition of 'Happy Birthday to You'. Ramona gives me a dirty look because it also happens to be my birthday – my seventieth – and I have forbidden any mention of it. In fact, it is no accident that the timing of this long trip abroad coincides with this personal milestone. Our absence abroad makes any family celebrations at home impossible. Perhaps I am odd in hating birthdays. I have always thought that they should be times for quiet commiseration, not for rejoicing. Who on earth wants to be a year older and nearer to death? Life is rushing past far too quickly for me and I certainly don't want a stale ritual to remind me of this fact. My mother was eighty-five before she would admit to being 'over thirty-nine', and even when she was approaching her ninety-ninth birthday she was still pretending to be a few years younger.

Whatever sentimental rubbish is trotted out to placate the elderly, the hard truth is that young is always better than old. So to hell with birthdays.

## DAY 26: SINGAPORE

As WE OPEN THE DOOR to the cabin balcony, we are hit by an invisible slab of damp heat. It is almost the end of the monsoon season, but not quite. Heavy clouds hover over the giant statue of the Merlion (Singapore's emblem – a mermaid with a lion's head) as we set off for downtown. The city centre now looks just like skyscraping Dallas and at ground level there is an endless maze of shopping malls, each more pretentious than the last. Acres of exclusive designer-clothes and expensive scents, but not a street-café or a news-stand in sight. There are strange activities here. A huge banner outside an exhibition centre proclaims, in English, 'First Discus Competition and Goldfish Show'.

On this amazingly decorous and sanitized island, where public cleanliness is almost a religion, where you can be fined for lighting a cigarette in a taxi, where no pet animal seems to venture onto the streets, and where grass verges appear to be trimmed with electric razors, the inhabitants live a safe, cheerful and slightly unreal existence.

Singapore's most notorious law is the 'Prohibition of Imports (Chewing Gum) Order', introduced in 1992, which makes the possession of chewing-gum a criminal offence. Anyone who has ever stepped onto a freshly discarded piece of gum in the street and then entered a building and tried to walk across a thick carpet will have some sympathy for this restriction, but the penalties do seem a little steep: 10,000 Singapore dollars ($6,000 or £3,700) or twelve months in jail for the first offence; double that for the second.

This draconian law was apparently introduced because somebody once stuck their piece of discarded gum on the electronic door of a Singapore commuter train. The doors jammed, the train stalled, and the entire commuter system descended into chaos. Thousands of workers arrived late at their jobs and their bosses refused to believe their excuse. Since everything in Singapore must run like clockwork, there was an immediate demand for a complete prohibition of chewing gum. So, today, if you feel an uncontrollable urge for a quick chew you have no choice but to cross the border into Malaysia, where anything goes.

They claim there is no drug problem in Singapore because if you are found using any illegal drug, you don't get twelve months, you are put to death. No half measures here. This is a tidy, orderly place.

Our guide tells us that in Singapore young couples are given a large tax deduction if they have a third child. Most local women do not want to do this because it interferes with their careers, which are more important to them, she explains, than rearing children. Very old people have to be supported financially by their children and if they are not, they sue their children for maintenance money. Ramona and I look at one another and nod, making a mental note to move here in a few years' time.

I ask if anyone has seen the elusive Singapura Cat and am told that the breed is now almost gone, having interbred with other cats for years. When I suggest plaintively that perhaps I may see one roaming the streets, I am gently informed that Singapore does not have stray cats or dogs wandering the streets and that recently all such animals were rounded up and exterminated as part of the government's public cleanliness campaign. It is doubtful if any Singapuras still exist on the loose, I am told, although there are a few carefully kept pedigree examples, some of which were recently shown on local television.

When I point out that as recently as 1991 the Singapore Tourist Board started a special campaign to promote the Singapura as 'Kucinta, the Love Cat of Singapore' and that bronze statues of the breed were to be installed on the banks of the river where it was supposed to have originated, I am told that, despite the Tourist Board's best efforts, the campaign failed and was abandoned. The reason was simply that the country already had a dramatic symbol in the shape of the 'Merlion', and a second animal emblem was surplus to requirements.

But what about the bronze statues of the Singapura? Yes, they are still there, a relic of the abortive campaign, and I am given directions to their location overlooking the Singapore River. They are positioned at one end of the Cavenagh Bridge, a famous city feature spanning the river near to the spot where the colony founder, Sir Stamford Raffles, first set foot, in the nineteenth century. Approaching the bridge I can see no sign of any feline statues. Crossing it, I finally catch sight of them. They are tiny – little more than life-size – and consist of a mother cat watching her two kittens playing by the water's edge. Hardly the monumental celebration I have been anticipating, but at least they will serve as a permanent reminder of a unique feline.

We take tea in the billiards room of the Raffles Hotel, heaping plates with scones, cream and jam, currant cakes, cream cakes, thin cucumber sandwiches and other assorted remnants of British rule. Finally we order hideously, luminescently, blindingly pink Singapore Slings and nonchalantly suck them dry as if we did this every day. Fortified, I rush around the seventy shops in the hotel mall (even the hotels have malls) looking for No. 32, Exotica, which sells Chinese antiquities. Fortunately it is closed, because it contains treasures beyond my wildest dreams, including a near life-size terracotta Han horse.

Singapore is a small oasis of earnestly sustained luxury in a geographical region where it is more common to find primitive poverty accepted with a quiet resignation. One gets the feeling that, here, even fun is hard work. Hurry, hurry, says the bold poster, and win free tickets to visit London, home of the Spice Girls.

At the quayside, an acrobatic dragon dance sees us off through the busiest waterway in the world, as we head up north towards the more backward charms of Kuantan.

## DAY 27: KUANTAN, MALAYSIA

THERE IS SOMETHING about Malaysia that sets it apart from the rest of Asia. Both the landscape and the people seem to be a cross between India and China and yet they have their own special nature. They also have their own unique ball game called Sepak Takraw, played by two teams of three players who must use the sides of their feet to hit an open-wicker ball up into the air and keep it there.

They appear to enjoy unusual competitions: we are shown competitive top-spinning (the record spin, we are told, lasted one and three-quarters hours) and competitive kite-flying, not to mention competitive dancing based on the martial arts.

They have stylish, conical coolie hats and I decide to buy one. After a great deal of encouragement I persuade them to climb up and bring down the most carefully crafted one, unpainted and subtly sculptured – more austere than the coloured tourist ones and much, much more authentic. I ask the price but they are reluctant to quote one. I ask again, and then, with extreme embarrassment, they enquire why I wish to buy a Malayan lampshade to put on my head.

On the roadside I spot a wild boar, water buffalo, a goat with a mynah bird sitting on its back, and a cat with a kinky tail. The forty thousand wild Malay tigers have now been hunted down to a mere four hundred and will soon vanish altogether. Like everywhere else in the world, agricultural man has triumphed and tamed the landscape into regi-mented submission.

### DAY 29: DA NANG, VIETNAM

THE BIG SURPRISE about Vietnam is how beautiful it is. Succulent green countryside lies below soaring, forest-covered mountains, their peaks wrapped in white cloud-scarves. It is hard to imagine how the Chinese and American military, in their arrogant war-games, back in the napalmy days of the late sixties and early seventies, could have brought themselves to unload thousands of tons of destruction on these modest people and their lovely landscapes.

Although Vietnam is now officially a Communist state, there is little sign of it apart from a few hammer-and-sickle posters. The long-suffering and remarkably forgiving inhabitants have simply reverted to their quietly relaxed habits, slipping back into a way of life that they have probably been practising for centuries – from long before a mixed bag of foreign powers tried to interfere with them.

At a Buddhist shrine in the old imperial capital of Hue, there is a 1963 eggshell-blue Austin car on display. It is the most incongruous object one can imagine in such a solemn, formal setting. But there is a photograph on its rust-pocked bonnet that explains its presence. It shows the Buddhist monk who owned the car and who drove it to Government headquarters one summer day in 1963, got out of it, calmly poured petrol over his body and set fire to himself. The picture shows him serenely burning to death alongside this battered old Austin, and his now famous action, in protest against Government policy, has transformed the car into a sacred object.

Vietnamese teenagers giggle and point when they see Ramona. At first this seems rude, but then they pluck up courage and ask permission to be photographed with her. When we agree they rush across and hug her tight while their friends click their cameras. It appears they are in awe of her long blonde hair, and their childlike reaction reflects the new mood of young Vietnam, as if it were a newborn country, forgetting its nightmare past and starting out afresh on its history.

### DAY 31: HONG KONG

So this is Communist China! Nothing seems to have changed. Downtown HK makes Manhattan and Singapore look like hick villages. There are so many thousands upon thousands of expensive shops that it is impossible to see more than a minute fraction of them even after endless hours of seriously motivated walking. In one shop I see a fifteenth-century Tibetan painting I like and enquire about the price. It is only 3.6 million, I am told. In British money that is approximately £300,000. I tell them I will think about it. I then ask about the Haniwa pottery horse. That is more reasonable, a mere £76,000.

The Red Lips Bar (No Cover Charge) is still cheerfully plying its trade, although it's not clear what the Masters of Tiananmen Square think of its displays. The massive sign for The Swank Shop above the Ocean Terminal looms into view outside our balcony, but from where Ramona is watching the first letter 'S' is unfortunately obscured.

The local Racecourse takes over 85,000 racegoers and is said to be technically the most advanced in the world, but we have no time to pay it a visit. It must be the only racetrack in the world with its own football club. The last time we were here my young son dragged me off to see a match between Racecourse United and a club with the unbelievable name of Hopeless FC. One can imagine the ridiculous conversations: 'Who do you play for?' 'I'm Hopeless.' 'Yes, but who do you play for?' And so on.

## DAY 34: MANILA, THE PHILIPPINES

MANILA IS STILL SMOG-BOUND, following El Niño, but is no worse than Los Angeles on a bad day. Back in November and December, the air was so smoky that more than a thousand horses died of respiratory failure in Manila alone. The fumes from the constant traffic chaos add to the fetid fragrance of the atmosphere in downtown Manila. The streets are full of converted US Army Jeeps, enlarged and highly decorated and now called Jeepneys, which act as minibuses for twelve people. Somehow about forty manage to cram in.

We are shown around the presidential palace, which is totally panelled in dark wood and lacks any joy or sense of humanity, despite florid declarations on the walls stating that the poorer the people the more important they are. A major exhibit is an elegant two-tone shoe, sitting incongruously in a massive display cabinet. It is explained to us that this was all that was found of one of the earlier Presidents when his plane crashed. We are then shown the rocking chair in which another President had a heart attack. A third one apparently had a heart attack when making a speech, and yet another keeled over with TB. The manner of dying is strangely significant to our guide, who finds it all quaintly amusing. There is a unified groan from our little group at the announcement that Imelda Marcos's famous collection of two thousand shoes is now stored in a basement and is not on view, as she is being sued. The connection between hiding the shoes and her impending court case is not made clear.

The Philippines is a beautiful collection of over seven thousand fabulous islands, but all we see is dirty, suffocating, gridlocked, downtown Manila. The highlight of a solitary stroll I take around the port, later on, is the offer of a Lady Boss for one hour – apparently a very friendly Filipino who will make me extremely happy. Despite the fact that her agent walks at least half a mile with me, thrusting at me an unbelievably grubby, dog-eared card, embossed with her name and address, I manage to resist his generous invitation.

## DAY 36: BRUNEI

THE PALACE OF THE SULTAN, the second-richest man in the world, cost $600 million to build and has 1,788 rooms, 44 staircases, 18 lifts, 260 toilets, 13 acres of Italian marble floors and dining rooms to seat 7,000. His personal income is $5 million a day. He has a personal fleet of 350 cars in his underground garage and, at his coronation, he had a solid gold forearm and hand made to prop up his chin during the lengthy ceremony. The Sultan's personal fortune is estimated to be $37,000,000,000 and is exceeded only by that of the boyish American computer-nerd, Bill Gates.

Despite his addiction to displays of personal opulence, the Sultan is apparently a benign and generous ruler. The few hundred thousand Bruneians under his protection pay no income tax or death duties. If they wish to study at university he pays their way and gives them scholar-ships. Medical treatment in the high-tech hospital costs 30 Brunei dollars (equivalent to about $16 or £10). On his birthday recently he gave every citizen a free satellite TV.

The 30,000 fishing-village people who live in little huts on stilts in the harbour are all presented with free houses by the Sultan, who personally hands them the keys. Most of them immediately rent the houses and go back to their hovels, where they feel at home. But despite external appearances, including stinking, garbage-strewn mud a few feet beneath the floorboards, these are amazingly cosy hovels complete with air-conditioning, electricity, hot and cold water and colour TV.

The Sultan has two wives – the first is his cousin and the second was an air-hostess. He wisely keeps them in two separate palaces, with a twenty-minute helicopter ride between them. If you see a jumbo jet flying low over Brunei, you know that it is the Sultan out for a spin at the controls of one of his personal fun-craft. Nobody else is allowed to fly that low.

Other restrictions in Brunei include not wearing yellow in public, not driving a car with darkened windows and not pointing with your finger. Yellow is the royal colour and is unofficially reserved for members of the royal clan. Dark car-windows are a sign of status – the higher your status, the darker your windows can be. A middle-class Bruneian was recently fined $70 for driving a car with windows that were too dark for his rank. And if you want to point at something, you must use your thumb, or it is considered impolite. Politeness is a major factor in local society. To lose your temper is to lose face and that is the worst fate that can befall a citizen of the 'Land of Peace'.

## DAY 39: SURABAYA, JAVA

INDONESIAN CURRENCY has suffered a catastrophic collapse. This has an amazing impact on our tourist shopping. Six yards of high-quality dress material costs all of 62 pence! Superb leather briefcases with digital locking are on offer at £5. Just as well we have very little time to shop. Java boasts over half the population of Indonesia although it covers only seven per cent of the total land area. And most of the population seem to be teeming all over the dock as we arrive. In the city there are thousands of tricycle rickshaws. They are of two types: blue for daytime and white for night-time. We point out that there are both blue and white ones on the streets, but it is explained to us that the Latin–Asian spirit of the Javanese is highly flexible where rules are concerned. This is brought home to us every time our driver ignores a red light in the city centre. Each time he manages to avoid a collision with angry transecting traffic we all give him a round of applause.

Although the Javanese are allowed four wives, the extra wives get no government allowances or social security, so monogamy is the rule. To be a *real man*, we are told, a Javanese must have: (1) a house; (2) a horse (now replaced by a Mitsubishi); (3) a wife; (4) a cock. They are very big on cocks and every upper-class house must have a caged cockerel on display as a status symbol. They are also big on bulls and stage regular bullfights, but here the bulls do not fight matadors, they fight one another. In the dry season, from August onwards, dramatic bull races are also staged, with the grand finals coming at the end of September. Java is lucky to have escaped the El Niño forest-burning smoke-clouds.

This land of three hundred languages has suffered repeated intrusions: they have been Moslemized, Christianized, Hinduized, Nipponized, Communized, Netherlandized and Anglicized. Each time they have smiled and said 'yes', but inside have always meant 'no'. So they have been able to take the best from each influence and discard the rest, remaining essentially Javanese to the end.

## DAY 40: BALI

BALI IS AT SERIOUS RISK of becoming a tourist pastiche of itself. The startling religious intensity of the old dance rituals has declined into comic pantomime. The road system has been modernized to accommodate the huge tourist buses, and in place of the old dirt tracks there are now stretches of dual carriageway. Hordes of frantic memento-sellers descend on each bus as it draws to a halt, like hunting dogs around a wounded buffalo, screaming, pushing, blocking the paths of visitors and refusing all rejections.

Fighting cocks are everywhere in their little wicker cages, awaiting their big days. Our guide makes the alarming statement that 'when Balinese men have nothing else to do they can be seen sitting in front of their houses massaging their cocks'.

Revisiting Bali today, Ramona and I are in a state of conflict. It is always exciting to come to this remarkable island, but we have powerful memories of our last visit here, twenty years earlier. Then, the impact was extraordinary and we regret having those recollections blurred by what we are seeing today.

I remember well the shock, back in the seventies, of arriving at a Balinese monkey temple to find a large notice proclaiming in English: '*Attention*. To maintain the religious purity and cleanliness of this temple: Women during menstruation should not enter the temple.' It didn't seem to matter that the monkeys which were scampering all over the temple ruins were urinating and defecating everywhere. Nor did it seem to matter that some of the female monkeys were undoubtedly menstruating. *Their* body fluids, presumably, were sacred and were therefore excused.

Almost everything in Bali on that earlier visit seemed to be sacred. Even the dancing was suffused with religious zeal. On one occasion, an Italian photographer decided to move up into the area where the dancers were enacting an ancient legend, and was promptly booed by the rest of the audience – not because she was blocking their view, which she wasn't, but because her treatment of the dance ritual as mere entertainment seemed somehow sacrilegious, as if somebody has walked up and shoved a lens into the Pope's face during mass. None of the people who booed were Hindus, but they all felt a deep respect for the musical ceremonies they were privileged to watch. It is that respect that seems to have vanished and with it much of the emotional impact of the performances.

There was, however, one completely non-sacred moment

that I also recall, with great embarrassment, from our earlier trip. On that visit our son, Jason, was with us. He was ten years old at the time and, as any father knows, ten is the age for fanatical hobbies. It is too old for toys and too young for girls, so all a young boy's emotional intensity is funnelled into pastimes. With Jason it was sports – any kind of sports – and as a good father I was expected to participate. One form of sporting torture I had so far managed to avoid was golf. Being left-handed I could never get the grip right.

Now you might think that, on this sacred tropical paradise of Bali, there would be little risk of exposure to that hateful game but, unfortunately for me, Jason had managed to locate a golf-course on his much-thumbed map of the island. There being no other sport available to him here, he demanded that we launch into our first game of golf without delay.

For a ten-year-old, the concept of 'without delay' means 'now!' Being unprepared for this demand I had no ready excuses to offer and it was too late to develop a convincing limp. But it occurred to me that, if I had to make a fool of myself on a golf-course, it would be better to do it here where nobody understood the game, than at home, where everybody took it so seriously. So off we went in search of what to my mind must be some scrubby little dump. Bali was so exquisitely beautiful that I could not imagine them wasting space on a golf-course, unless it was near a sewage farm or a rubbish tip.

When we arrived at the entrance my heart sank. It was exotically beautiful, like some glorious tropical garden through which a brilliant landscaper had cut a swathe of immaculate fairways. I had been completely wrong. This was clearly where the élite of Bali's social world came to demonstrate their prowess. This was the exclusive playground of rich landowners, titled jet-setters and distinguished diplomats. What a nightmare.

We hired sets of clubs and were about to carry them out to start the first hole, when there was a great commotion. What had we been thinking of! We had already done the unpardonable – we had picked up our heavy golf-bags. Such a lowly, demeaning act was unspeakable. From the depths of the clubhouse there emerged two exquisitely beautiful young Balinese girls in full costume. These were our caddies (ye gods, we had caddies!) and were horrified to think that we had been forced to lower ourselves by carrying our clubs for all of five seconds.

I was starting to panic, but it was too late to turn back now. We strode out onto the first tee. I did my best to look as though I had done this a thousand times before. I set up my ball and gazed knowingly down the fairway. There was a sudden chattering sound, as if a flock of huge starlings had been disturbed in the nearby foliage. The birds in question turned out to be seventeen Balinese gardeners who had been tending the lush vegetation around the clubhouse. They came scampering out of the undergrowth in a state of great excitement and proceeded to squat in a long line to my right. At first I thought they must have been frightened into the open by the arrival of a fierce animal. Then the awful truth dawned on me: they had gathered to watch me tee off.

Worse was to come. I heard a noise behind me and saw some big glass doors being rolled back. Out of the clubhouse strolled a bevy of senior club members, beautifully attired and carrying assorted cocktails. They assembled behind me in a silent body, expert and critical, awaiting my first drive with intense interest. Clearly, any visiting Englishman who took the trouble to visit this golf-course must be at least approaching championship status, and they did not want to miss a thing.

There was now no escape. I did my best to transmute myself into an earthworm and burrow rapidly down into the green turf, but to no avail. Surrounded by the eager eyes of caddies, gardeners and lofty club members, I had no choice but to strike a blow for England. I stared down at the horrid little white ball and took an almighty swing. Staring down the fairway I could see nothing. Could I have blasted it out of sight? No, I had missed it completely. It had not moved even one millimetre. A soft murmur went through the watching crowd, which was growing by the minute. Brazenly, I announced that my club was satisfactory and I would now begin.

I took a second huge swing and this time something did fly down the fairway – I followed it with my eyes and saw it drop. It was a large clod of earth. More murmuring. The ball still had not moved. Hurriedly, a third swing, and this time I did hit it. But my joy was short-lived. There was a high-pitched scream from my right. I had sliced the ball terribly and was just in time to see it skim over the heads of the long row of Balinese gardeners. They ducked, like a line of synchronized chorus boys, and I think all but one of them managed to avoid it. My fourth swing was, at last, a success and my ball flew straight down the middle of the fairway – all of ten yards. Young Jason, needless to say, struck his ball well with his first swing, and with great relief we sauntered off as a buzz of heated discussion arose behind us. Mercifully, I could not pick out the words.

The rest of the round of golf was comparatively uneventful, although Jason's relationship with the caddies deteriorated rapidly. It soon became clear that, since I was senior to Jason, my card had to be marked in such a way that I would win. It was unthinkable in Bali for a senior man to be beaten by a junior. Had this happened, I would probably have had to build a cremation tower for myself, light it and jump on. But Jason's sense of British fair play was totally outraged. 'They're cheating. They're letting you win,' he kept hissing at me. I

reassured him that I would ignore this, but he wanted to keep
the cards to prove how well he had done and was having none
of it. All in all, not one of my happier sporting occasions, and
the rekindled memory generated a great relief that I would not
have to play golf on Bali on this second visit.

## DAY 44: PERTH

AFTER THE FESTERING BEAUTY, poverty and urban chaos of
Asia, Australia is unnervingly neat and orderly, as if whole
cities have been sent to the dry-cleaners. Freemantle is like a
filmset for a Victorian drama and Perth is too tidy to be true.
We are shown the houses of the rich and infamous along the
Black Swan River; one was sold recently for 35 million
Australian dollars – about £14 million sterling. We are offered
Matilda Bay Bitter – a local brew named after the wife of the
first Surveyor General of Australia, a man by the name of John
Septimus Rowe.

We are warned that the water is full of jellyfish, but the good
news is that they do not sting. There are so many of them,
however, that they find their way into the women's swimsuits.
This thought seems to horrify our guide. He exclaims:
'Imagine that, girls! Yuck-*oh*!'

There are white parrots in the trees and black swans on the
river. And the crows have a stridently raucous vocabulary all
their own. Every element of the natural world is slightly
different here, and all the more fascinating for it.

Lunch in a downtown restaurant consists of Popeye Salad
followed by a coronary-sized confection known as 'Snowy
Mountain Dream'. The signs as we enter this culturally
conscious establishment read: 'Me belly thinks me throat is
cut'; 'I could chew the arse out of a ragdoll'; 'Still the worms';
'I'm as dry as a pom's towel'; and 'Fill up me hole'. Equally

edifying is the sign we notice as we leave, which announces: 'I'm as full as a fairy's phone book'. Outside there is a card which asks the question: 'Why is beer better than a woman?' The only printable answer is that beer is *always* wet. And I was foolish enough to think Dame Edna and Sir Les Patterson were caricatures.

## DAY 48: ADELAIDE

OFFERED A 'DAY AT THE RACES' as a special tour, we are happily back in the world of Trifectors, Quinellas, Doubles, Punters Pools and Fourtrellas. At the Victoria Racetrack a small marquee has been prepared for us with unlimited food, unlimited booze and a professional tipster in the form of the racing editor of the local newspaper. (He also has a horse of his own running at 25 to 1, and we all feel obliged to bet on it despite the fact that it is an outsider. It comes fourth.) We are photographed with a 51-year-old jockey who has won 1,578 races and is a sure thing in the seventh. He makes a welcoming speech, thanking Lester Piggott for being older than he is, and we all feel obliged to bet on him. He comes fourth.

An eccentric lady in our party never comes fourth. Before each race she disappears towards the bookies to place her bet. After each race she returns waving a wad of Australian dollars, announcing loudly to everyone: 'I've won, I've won!' Since none of us knows anything about the local form and we are systematically losing race after race, we find this increasingly odd until someone points out that the wad of notes she waves each time is always crisply mint, like the currency we were all issued on the *Arcadia*. As anybody who has ever been lucky enough to win at the races knows, the notes the bookies count out for you are always grubby and crumpled. So we draw our own conclusions. But the mystery remains as to how anyone would gain pleasure from such a peculiar charade.

The Punters Pool is a special Adelaide attraction in which you pay $20 and leave the betting to a group of local experts. Operating from a small grandstand with a big board of complicated figures, they build up a pot of about $6,000 and then set about investing it, making regular announcements to their eagerly watching shareholders. At the end of the afternoon they tell us that they have won the Fourtrella. We read in the local turf paper that the Fourtrella roll-over jackpot is today worth $500,000 and we start contemplating how we will spend this huge sum of money, but when we go to collect our winnings it turns out that our $20 investment only pays each of us $5.

Despite our punting disappointments we have an idyllic day at one of the most charming racetracks we have ever visited, in one of the most elegant cities on earth. And it is a small world. At the races a woman introduces herself and says she has played bridge with our small son at the Bridge Club in Oxford, and also at my mother's house. She is astonished to learn that Jason Morris is now an official of the British Horse-racing Board, because in addition to playing bridge she and her husband are also breeders and trainers of racehorses at Garsington near Oxford. And here we are on the other side of the world. What are the odds on that?

As the ship leaves the quayside the Adelaide band plays 'Waltzing Matilda' and the ship's restaurant serves up an Aussie menu of Beer Soup and Emu Stew.

## DAY 51: SYDNEY

SYDNEY HAS BECOME the Manhattan of the southern hemisphere. Just outside the exploding city, feverish work is taking place to complete the vast Olympics Centre for the next Games. Inside the city it proves difficult to find a CD of Aussie music. There are acres of didgeridoo recordings with face-painted Native Australians on their covers, songs of the humpback whale and sounds of the rain forest, but nowhere can I find 'Waltzing Matilda' for my granddaughter.

It's a sad comment that the only Native Australian we encounter in the flesh is a fully tribally decorated one with an alarmingly hairy back and a massive curly beard, wearing only a loincloth, and playing – yes – a didgeridoo while tourists place coins on a small piece of cloth he has spread on the ground in front of him. He looks exactly like the one pictured on the CD covers. If he is indeed the same one, and if he has a contract with a major recording company, then someone should tell him he needs a better agent.

## DAY 54: New Caledonia

THE SEA IS TOO ROUGH to land at the Isle of Pines and the political scene is too rough to land on the main island, so we have to spend the day cruising around the primeval coastline, our snorkels frustratingly dry and useless in our bags. A bad start to our crossing of the Pacific. El Niño still lurks here.

## DAY 56: Lautoka, Fiji

THROWING OPEN THE cabin curtains and stumbling out onto the balcony at 7 am, in pyjamas and with one eye still closed, I am confronted with a huge choir of rigidly erect Fijians singing something that started life, long ago, as a Christian hymn. A different kind of El Niño lurks here, courtesy of some meddling missionaries of an earlier century. How sad to see the glorious, funny, sexy, childlike Fijians roped into the boring rituals of devout, humourless, God-smacked Europeans. Why on earth didn't the local inhabitants eat the lot of them when they first landed on the shores of these generous, densely green islands? Later in the day, I purchase a tourist knick-knack in the form of a traditional cannibal fork – the only tangible survival of their missed opportunity.

At a tourist resort we are waited on by huge-bodied Fijian servants. It's depressing to see that these lovely giants have changed from head-hunters to head-waiters in just a few generations. But at least they have retained a sense of humour about it. On an earlier visit to Fiji, during a trip to the interior of the main island, I was asked to dance with one of the village girls. When I declined, they said: 'Either you dance with her, or we have you for lunch.'

On that earlier trip I had a brush with death. I was walking barefoot down a sandy beach when Ramona shouted 'Stop!' and pointed at my leg. Freezing in my tracks, I looked down and saw that my foot was poised six inches above a stranded sea snake. Had I had taken one more step, I would have trodden on it. If it had bitten me I would have felt little pain, but would probably have been dead within a few days. Although it was not a large specimen, the venom of sea snakes is up to fifty times more potent than that of king cobras, so I would have stood little chance.

Ramona and I had written a book about snakes back in the sixties and I remembered all too well the details of how you die from a sea-snake bite: ascending paralysis, beginning with the legs and ending with lockjaw; nausea, vomiting, muscle-twitchings, spasms, writhings, convulsions, unconsciousness and death. In the ocean, where sea snakes spend nearly all their time, they keep out of your way and are safe enough. But they tend to get tangled up in fishermen's nets, then drop out and lie rather pathetically on the ground. Before they can find their way back into the sea, they get trodden on and automatically react to the pain by striking out.

Ramona had saved my life and I was immensely grateful to her. When I thanked her, she replied, with her usual sense of priorities: 'The poor little thing. I thought you were going to hurt it.' She then insisted that we catch it up and release it back into the sea, so that it would not be killed by some foul snake-hater. We managed this operation with some difficulty and watched it swim elegantly back into its natural domain. Ramona loves serpents of all kinds. In fact she leaps to the defence of any persecuted animal, and since nothing has been so savagely or irrationally persecuted as snakes, they receive her special attention whenever she encounters one in trouble. Saving this one from being squashed by the clumsy foot of her husband has made her day.

### DAYS 62 AND 63: OAHU, HAWAIIAN ISLANDS

THE TRICK HERE is to find a genuine Hawaiian. There are thousands of Americans, hordes of Chinese, countless Japanese and crowds of tourists, but no sign of any native Hawaiians. Where have they all gone? Wandering through the endless walkways of the world's largest shopping centre in downtown Honolulu, we might be anywhere in the world, from Rodeo Drive to the Champs-Elysées. It's designer-world gone mad – not a bit like the posters showing dusky maidens dancing in grass skirts. One whole shop is devoted to baseball memorabilia, another solely to kite-flying, and another to motor-racing. This island may be advertised as a tropical paradise, but in the last few decades it has rapidly become a Pacific Miami complete with urban traffic jams and urban crime.

In fact, violent crime is not far away. After dinner at Kengo's seafood restaurant, we are strolling back to the ship when police swoop through the door of a nightclub as we are passing. We later discover that a gang had attacked the club's huge bouncer and he had retaliated by picking up a heavy metal ashtray and slamming one of his tormentors on the head. After this triumph, he had rushed after a second attacker and beaten him to a pulp. He had then leaped into a taxi and vanished into the night. As his first victim lay dying on the floor, the club staff had called the police but, like us, the cops arrived just too late to see the action.

The meal at Kengo's was itself memorable and has at last provided the answer to the difficult question of where all the native Hawaiians have gone. They have gone to Kengo's. They have gone there to stuff themselves with the all-you-can-eat buffet to keep their vast frames at full weight. Their bodies are now so huge that all the males could be sumo champions without even trying. In fact, it just so happens that the present Grand Champion in Japan, who weighs 500 pounds (ie, 35 stone) did indeed come from a village only a few miles down the road. After a single dinner here I could already feel the crouching sumo foot-stamp and salt-throwing arm-swing overtaking me.

For what it's worth, my little dinner was as follows: clam chowder, one and a half lobsters, octopus salad, roast rib of beef, Korean spare-ribs, chicken teriyaki, strawberries, pineapple and orange, washed down with two Mai-tais. This was modest compared with the heaped plates of the families of gigantic Hawaiians who filled the restaurant with shouts, laughter and the sound of enormous crab-legs being cracked open. One female Hawaiian had to rest her massive buttocks on our table in order to squeeze past us. The joy of uninhibited gluttony filled the air.

The following day, I decide to take a submarine trip to enjoy the company of puffer-fish, unicorn fish, trigger fish and needlefish. On the way to the harbour, our guide asks us a trick question. Do we know the name of the national fish of Hawaii? We are all supposed to say 'no', and she will tell us that it is 'Humu-humu-nuku-nuku-apo'aa' and then we are supposed to say it after her, get hopelessly muddled and have a good laugh. My problem is that, having studied tropical marine fish for many years, I not only know how to say it, but can say it very fast. So what do I do? If I pretend not to know the answer I am being phoney. If I shout it out, I am showing off.

As I am sitting at the front of the bus I compromise by saying it so softly that only she can hear me. This completely throws her and I feel rotten about it. I should have kept my mouth shut. But soon we are deep under the waves, peering out of the little portholes of the submarine and, in my case, wishing I had gills so that I could explore this vast, beautiful world for days on end. Why is it that movement in water is so much more graceful than movement on land?

After the short underwater trip, we are on a catamaran in Honolulu Bay, on our way back to the harbour, when there is a shout of excited disbelief as an adult humpbacked whale, even bigger than a Kengo's diner, leaps completely clear of the water, right in front of us. It smashes back sideways into the water, like a crashing jumbo jet. Totally unexpected, it is an all-too-brief moment, but leaves an indelible image in the memory. In cold zoological terms, it's only a big mammal in the breeding season and yet somehow it is the most remarkable natural sight on the planet.

As we sail from Honolulu, dusk is falling and reveals what look like several streams of molten lava pouring down the steep valleys of the dark volcanic mountains that rise up right behind the city. Viewed through binoculars, these burning lava-flows turn out to be brilliantly lit, expensive housing estates that have crept up the slopes as building land becomes more and more difficult to find. If we return in ten years' time I suspect that they will have all joined up into one vast urban glow.

### DAY 68: SAN FRANCISCO

OUR FIRST SIGHT of the United States, as dawn breaks, is the forlornly defunct Alcatraz prison on its craggy little island. As we dock, the dingy waters of the quayside are alive with gulls, pelicans, cormorants and a whole family of seals.

Knowing the hilly delights of this great city well from previous visits, we decide to explore farther south during our short stopover, and board a tour coach that is making the long trek down to Monterey and Carmel. As an unscheduled bonus, before the coach leaves, we are able to enjoy a brief moment of social drama. There is always one couple who rise early, rush down the gangplank as soon as it is open and then stand eagerly awaiting the arrival of the bus. The instant its door is opened, they pile on and grab the front seat so that they can enjoy the forward view as we drive along. Such couples are always well groomed and finely equipped for the journey, oozing a smug air of well-organized living. The rest of us arrive up to an hour later, stumbling and mumbling our way onto the coach and collapse into its rear seats. Smug couple sit brightly alert, waiting for the bus to leave. But on this occasion all is not well. Opposite them, in the other front seat, is a disabled woman who has been given this as a specially reserved place. But now the tough American lady who is to be our guide arrives and insists that the disabled woman is in her official seat next to the driver and that, sadly, she must be moved. However, as the poor woman must have a front seat, this means that the smug couple must make way for her. They refuse, saying they rose early especially to secure their seat and they are not going anywhere. Tough lady gets off the bus and discusses the impasse with P & O officials. She is not being difficult. She has to be able to communicate with the driver and must therefore sit immediately behind him. Either that, or the trip is off.

Much heated argument follows, but the smug couple are clearly losing ground as they are competing with a woman with a serious disability. Eventually, with stiffly angry bodies, they retreat to a rear seat demanding to see a senior tour official. One is fetched and she rather cleverly explains to them that if only they had applied to reserve their front seats, they would have been warned of the problem and this unpleasantness could have been avoided. Having no idea that such reservations could be made, they are nonplussed by this information and sit sullenly silent, defeated by the system. How huge these tiny social problems can become if you take life too seriously.

We set off and travel along the stunningly dramatic coastline of California. For some reason, our American guide is at pains to regale us with a joke about President Clinton and the Virgin Mary, which is in such bad taste that it's almost funny. We drive pass endless artichoke and strawberry farms, pausing at the coast to watch a colony of sea lions and meet some fearlessly friendly marmots. At Monterey we visit the amazing aquarium to see the largest sheet of glass in the world, behind which swims the most amazing fish in the world, the 14-foot tall, two-ton sunfish. Not to mention sharks, tuna and turtles. Another tank, the kelp tank, is no less than 30 feet deep. In smaller displays there are sea otters, cuttlefish, huge jellyfish, nautilus and a giant octopus. The aquarium has a strange history. The daughter of the boss of Hewlitt Packard Computers was asked by her doting dad what she would like for her birthday. She said she wanted an aquarium, but instead of a little tank with a few guppies, she got this place.

The only bad moment for us is when I am paying to enter the building and ask for the reduced 'seniors' tickets. I expect a cynical smile or, at the very least, a query and a demand for documentary proof of advanced age, but to my dismay I am given these tickets without a murmur. So much for feeling young.

## DAY 73: ACAPULCO

'COME FLY WITH ME,' sang Sinatra, 'Down to Acapulco Bay,' and he was good to his word. His clifftop villa here is the ultimate stud-pad. This is the city of high-status males, from John Wayne in the old days to Sylvester Stallone today. Their multimillion-dollar properties are perched high around this vast bay which looks remarkably like Rio and which embodies the same disgusting contrasts between local poverty and imported wealth. There are echoes of Las Vegas in the outrageous extremes of the hotels and restaurants. Las Brisas is the only hotel in the world that provides a personal swimming pool for each room; there are 250 rooms and 250 pools. The Mayan Palace has the world's longest swimming pool – it is no less than a thousand metres in length – over half a mile.

In downtown Acapulco, the restaurants are hymns to comic architecture with cactus-shaped pillars and sombrero roofs. This is a city lazily devoted to a shallow hedonism and yet, despite everything, it has a seductive air that is hard to resist. By the end of the day I am sufficiently filleted by margaritas and pina coladas to be talked into buying the largest, most garish, most rococo, worst-taste sombrero ever made. Like a vicar who has bought a porno magazine, I slink back on the ship with it, doing my best to hide it from the eyes of the other passengers. In the cabin I read the instructions that come with this hat to end all hats and note that it insists I brush it regularly and never expose it to either sun or rain. Just the thing for rough-riding in the Sierra Madre.

This has been my first visit to Mexico and I hate to admit that I have enjoyed it. I say 'hate' because I feel guilty about the gulf that exists between the haves and have-nots. I am well aware that most Mexicans couldn't afford to spend a single day in glamorous Acapulco. This is not what Mexico is about. But while we have been ashore, I have managed to study some of the local inhabitants, and I've been very impressed by what I saw.

As a people they are full of passion and humour, and it is sad that they have acquired the stigma of being the poor relations of the North Americans. They deserve better and could become a great nation if only they were not held in the tight grip of the Catholic Church. This grip works is such an obvious way that it is surprising nobody has challenged it. The Pope's Ten Steps to Heaven are as follows: (1) the Church forbids contraception; (2) it becomes praiseworthy to have a big family regardless of income; (3) fathers cannot earn enough to support these big families; (4) poverty becomes widespread; (5) being poor breeds insecurity; (6) insecurity breeds fear; (7) the fearful need help; (8) the state is too poor to offer help; (9) only prayers can help; (10) the churches are full of poor people praying for a better life in the next world to make up for the lousy time they are having in this one. Olé!

## DAY 77: BALBOA, PANAMA

AS WE ARRIVE IN PANAMA, dire warnings are issued about the risks of visiting Panama City at night, making it sound like the Sin City of Central America. We all dutifully obey and limit ourselves to the quayside stalls of the hordes of Cuna Indians from the San Blas archipelago who have arrived bearing wondrous native artefacts.

The most exciting Indian offerings are the *molas*. These are colourful cloth rectangles that are normally part of the female costume, but which are now being sold separately as small decorative panels. Cleverly using a complex reverse-appliqué technique, they are a visual delight and many of them have yet to succumb to the vulgarization so common with commercialized tribal art. True, a few of them have already fallen into this trap, but with a discerning eye it is possible to pick out the good examples where this temptation has been resisted, which makes the search even more interesting.

The subject matter of the good *molas* is fascinating and my treasure-hunting urge is now hopelessly out of control. I buy one that shows a large dog biting a huge crescent moon, watched by two smaller dogs; and another that depicts an enormous, spouting whale covered in small crescent moons; and another that shows three massive stingrays with human faces; and another with a small, black, winged human straddling two gigantic parrots that are full of eggs. You can keep your Jackson Pollocks and your Damien Hirsts, this is a joyous fantasy world that I want to share. I may not understand all the tribal symbolism, but these vigorous Cuna compositions cheer me up every time I look at them.

Unlike most local sales-folk around the world, the Cuna Indians are fascinatingly calm and composed. There is no sales pitch, no argument and no haggling. When a tourist asks the price of four, he is simply quoted the single price times four. 'But that's no reduction,' the tourist argues. In response, they smile silently at him. He either has to pay up or push off.

It is a delight to see this tiny remnant of the once great Indian population still behaving with dignity. Although they have come here to generate a little much needed cash from our visit, they have made few concessions. Perhaps this has something to do with the fact that the Cuna are a matriarchal society and, under the control of powerful women, have resisted all attempts to demolish the ancient structure of their tribal society.

The additional fact that they do not inhabit the mainland, with its intrusion of modern technology, but instead still live on the San Blas archipelago – 365 small islands that lie just off the eastern coast of Panama – obviously helps to keep their tribal society intact. The total Cuna population is only forty thousand and they have managed to preserve not only their social customs but also their traditional costumes. Originally the *mola* designs were painted directly onto the naked skin. Then, when they adopted clothing about two centuries ago, the women simply transferred the patterns onto their blouses. Later, when they discovered that these panels were of interest to outsiders, they started making them independently, for their own sake.

I notice that the women who have come to stage this impromptu Cuna market for us still have marvellously decorated legs, although in the dim light it is hard to see the intricate details of the designs that are painted on them. And it seems rude to peer too closely. I only hope that, if they ever start wearing stockings at some time in the future, they will again transfer the patterns of their wonderful body-painting onto their new clothing.

The following day we set off to pass through the extraordinary Panama Canal, the great transcontinental cutting that cost so many thousands of lives to build in the disease-infested jungles. Flocks of pelicans are watching us leave Balboa and as we meet the first patch of dense canal-side vegetation a group of about fifteen black vultures begins to circle over the ship.

The *Arcadia* is so huge that it only just fits into the enormous canal-locks. There are no more than 30 inches to spare on each side, but so efficient is the system of small rail-locomotives tugging us through the locks that we never so much as graze the edges. The cost of passing though the Panama Canal is staggering – over £125,000 for the *Arcadia*. The cost is based on weight, so a journalist who once swam the length of the canal was only charged 36 cents.

We pass new diggings, where, even on a Sunday, teams of men are struggling to keep back the high banks. The lorries all salute us with a chorus of horns, and the massive earth-diggers raise their scoops high in the air and wave them up and down and from side to side, like giant yellow fiddler-crabs. *Arcadia* responds with a deep blast from its hooter. In one short day we pass from the Pacific to the Atlantic and a complete change of mood.

## DAY 79: Curaçao

THERE IS SOMETHING delightfully incongruous about the Dutch East Antilles. The Netherlands and the Caribbean simply don't mix. The result is a fascinating hybrid culture, so odd that when you dock here and walk ashore, you have an uneasy feeling that you are in a space-warp. If it weren't for maps and itineraries, you would have no idea what region of the world you are in.

The 160,000 people here (of more than fifty nationalities) speak their own local patois and, in addition, Dutch (for official use), Spanish (for neighbouring countries) and English (for tourists). The shops sell clogs and Dutch dolls and tourist collectibles which, it has to be said, are the ugliest and most excruciating of anything seen anywhere on this entire world tour. How they can display such bad taste inside the shops when outside them their architecture is the most attractive in the Caribbean is hard to understand.

Another submarine trip, this time along an almost vertical coral wall, provides us with a passing parade of trumpet fish, puffer-fish, parrot-fish, scorpion fish, trigger fish, box fish, bluehead wrasse, blue chromis, sergeant-majors, yellow snappers, tangs and all the rest. If I were rich I would have my own, personal observation submarine and spend day after day exploring the undersea world.

Back in the little capital of Willemstad the yellow, pink, green, blue, red, beige and grey houses with their Amsterdam architectural styles create a strangely Dutch atmosphere here, just north of Venezuela. The story goes that the governor of this small island complained that all the whitewashed houses were giving him a headache in the bright sun. So he ordered all householders to paint them different colours. The result was extremely attractive and the people were delighted, until they learned that the governor also happened to own the local paint shop.

The city is divided into two by the St Anna Bay which, despite its name, looks more like a large canal. This makes Willemstad feel even more like Amsterdam. The two sides of the city are connected by a charmingly antique pontoon bridge, the Queen Emma Bridge, that opens every so often to allow ships to pass through. The *Arcadia* is docked on the landward side of this bridge and I am looking forward to watching from our balcony as the pontoon opens to allow us through and out into the open sea beyond.

As it turns out, I get a chance to see this at close quarters. I have been doing some last-minute shopping and have cut my return to the ship rather fine. I arrive at the bridge, to cross back over it, just in time to see it start its long, wobbly swing to one side. I ask why it is opening so soon. Presumably some smaller ship wants to get through. No, it has opened to let the *Arcadia* through. This is bad news for me as I am on the wrong side of the city. My only hope of regaining the ship, rather that watching it sail off without me, is to find a small boat to get me across to the other side. I spot one that is about to leave and run to catch it. As I do so, my large straw hat blows off and begins rolling like a cartwheel up the edge of the quay. Decisions, decisions. It is my newly purchased, Dutch anti-sun hat and I feel compelled to pursue it, which I proceed to do at high speed, much to the amusement of the locals who are sitting all along the quayside at small, outdoor tables, sipping coffee.

The hat rolls to within inches of the edge of the quay, then away again, repeatedly changing course as I stamp at it with my foot, trying in vain to pin it down. I am receiving a great deal of moral support in this venture, judging by the cheering that accompanies my impromptu flamenco-cum-apache performance. Finally, with one huge leap I slam my foot down and the hat is mine. There is a friendly round of applause. I feel obliged to give them my best Restoration-flourish bow when I see to my horror that the little boat is leaving. My world cruise is about to come to a juddering halt. Luckily, my usual British reserve has already been totally dismantled, so I run and shout and wave my arms about and just manage to clamber on board.

When I am safely back in our cabin, Ramona is unsympathetic. 'Not another hat!' is her only comment. To be fair to her, my hat collection is starting to get out of hand. No, that's not true, it was out of hand two oceans ago. This new one is my twelfth so far. The obsession began in Malaysia. After that I had to buy a coolie hat in every Far Eastern country we visited, to study their subtle national variations. To most people a coolie hat is just a coolie hat, but to me … Perhaps they should have a ship's psychiatrist as well as a ship's doctor on these long voyages. Two and a half months at sea has obviously softened my brain.

'You'll have to pack them, when we get to Southampton,'

says Ramona. I hadn't thought of that. How *do* you pack a collection of coolie hats? I could wear them stacked up on my head, I suppose, but that would look too much like a distraction display and I would have all my luggage searched. On the other hand, if I pack them in the usual way they will end up looking like a set of table mats. Perhaps I should throw them overboard. But then I can imagine the local headlines: 'Mystery ship sinks. Floating hats all that is left of Oriental crew.'

I am still pondering what to do with my ridiculous hats when the *Arcadia* slowly glides out of Willemstad harbour, past the most beautiful sea front in the Caribbean. We are so close to the city centre that we can almost read the menus. I have been told to watch out for the Plaza Hotel, the last building on the sea front, right at the harbour entrance. It claims to be unique in one respect – being the only hotel in the world to be insured against marine collision.

## DAY 81: St Lucia

THE AIR IS HEAVY with incense, which barely disguises the cloud of hashish hanging over the little port of Castries. Even the small article of clothing we buy for our granddaughter reeks of it and we are alarmed at the thought that it may have sniffer-dog appeal when we disembark at Southampton. The large, heavy-featured, charmingly gangling men in their Rasta hats are almost aggressively laid-back. Their smiling, big-eyed women appear to do all the work. The countless little market stalls and shops are all staffed exclusively by these women, who seem too heat-weary to bother with anything but the most cursory sales pitch. The beauty of the steeply rising, richly green hills behind the town is completely at odds with the broken-down shanty feel to the streets.

In the very centre of the town stands a vast Masaab Tree. It has something in common with, of all things, the kangaroo – both were named in the same way. When asked what they were by a foreign visitor, a local inhabitant replied: 'I don't know.' In Aboriginal language this is pronounced 'kan – garoo'; in St Lucia Creole it is 'ma-saab'. The Creole is a strange mixture of other tongues. 'Do-do me amor' means 'Darling, I love you.' In another place there is a tree labelled 'Tourist Tree' *(Bursera simaruba)*. I enquire whether this means it is poisonous. Apparently not, although there is some hesitation in the reply. In fact, it has a red bark that is peeling off in thin flakes and looks exactly like a huge Caucasian who has a bad case of sunburn.

When I point out that it is starting to rain, I am quickly contradicted: 'That is liquid sunshine.' One day they had ten inches of rain in three hours. A very sunny day. An optimistic little island, despite its sauna heat, its torn trousers and its broken pavements, it is proud of its rums and its cockerels, its drive-in volcano and its natural beauty. It also has two Nobel laureates to its credit, one for economics and one for literature. From a population of only 150,000 this is amazing.

There are so many different kinds of rum that it is hard to choose one. In the end it has to be 'Seventh Heaven' because that one contains a magical St Lucian ingredient, an aphrodisiac called 'Bois Bande', made from the bark of the local Bande Tree and known appropriately as 'Stiff Wood'. There is only one catch: by the time you have swallowed enough for the magic to work, you are too legless to do anything about it.

DAY 82: BARBADOS

IN THE MIND, this island is a cricket ground completely surrounded by sandy beaches: golden sands in the west, white in the south and golden-brown in the east. Although there is the usual stinging contrast between the palatial villas of the newcomers and the tiny shacks of the islanders, the shack-dwellers seem much more resigned than usual to this stark inequality.

There is an air of chirpy irreverence about Barbadians that gives them a special, almost childlike appeal. Like child-pirates, they call a machete a 'cutlass'. Picking up two fallen coconuts and holding them in front of his trousers, our local guide calls out: 'Look at my nuts!' Such an action would be unthinkable in, say, Asiatic locations. But here in the Caribbean it has a cheeky schoolboy quality that does nothing but raise a few smiles on the faces of the grey-haired ladies.

Even the political outrages of the Barbadians have a light-hearted quality, like painting the island's famous white stone lion in red, green and gold – a Rastafarian protest. Their attitude to rich celebrities is unusual. There is none of the carping envy that is so common elsewhere: 'We usually only know they've been here when we hear they are leaving.' A quietly friendly country and a good place to live providing your most cerebral occupation is whether or not to have another rum punch.

## DAY 88: FUNCHAL, MADEIRA

WE HAVE CROSSED the Atlantic and this is our last stop before returning home. By now everyone has become so accustomed to the seductive way of life on board that a pang of dejection sweeps through the ship. This will be our last carefree port of call. The next one, Southampton, will be a nightmare of luggage, porters and customs officials. Then, heaven help me, three months of unanswered mail to face when we get home. Better make the most of this last little excursion.

The Madeiran folk-dancing that greets the ship is perilously close to Morris dancing, with its stilted, sexless European cantometrics. Compared with the graceful, sensitive Asiatic dancing, it is clumsily rural; compared with the loose wrigglings of the South Pacific, it is oddly constipated.

Madeira is a steep, forbidding mountain peak, the tip of which peeps out of the sea. There is barely an inch of flat land to be seen. It is a curious fact that there are 50,000 more Madeirans living in South Africa than there are on their home island. Perhaps they relished the long walks on level ground so much that they couldn't face returning to the endless slopes of their birthplace. There is one special feature in its favour, however. For some reason Madeira is one of the best places in the world for exotic flowers, and even in early April they are everywhere, with great heaps of them in the market and intense purple jacaranda trees and vivid flame-coloured African trees all over the city.

Today sees the end of a quaint episode in 'ship scandal'. A fiftyish woman and a man of twenty-one, who had come on board together, were removed from the ship this afternoon, forbidden to return. Last night, the man, after downing bottles of Bollinger like cans of lager, became abusive and was challenged to a fight 'outside' by an outraged passenger. Once on the promenade deck they hurled abuse at one another. This was too much for a massive muscle-man, who strode out, walloped the young man and literally decked him: he was out cold. Today, even after a night to sleep it off, he clearly was not in good shape. Both he and his lady were asked to leave the ship, and peace returned once more, courtesy of a Madeiran ambulance.

### DAY 91: NORTH ATLANTIC

AFTER A FINAL TASTE of the open sea, with 30-foot waves and the roll vying with the pitch to see which can be more unbalancing, we have nearly come full circle; tomorrow we disembark at Southampton. Packing is almost beyond us. Our motley collection of sixteen pieces of luggage has swollen to twenty-one to accommodate our burgeoning collection of ethnic junk. Everything from Indian peacock fans to Bedouin bracelets, Jordanian scent bottles to Vietnamese music boxes, Javanese parasols to Balinese puppets, prayer wheels to decorated gourds, sarongs to grass skirts, native masks to cannibal forks – they all have to be stashed away somehow for the great exodus when over a thousand people will be evicted from the security of their cabins and disgorged onto the threateningly bleak quayside.

A large cruise ship is at best a mobile luxury hotel, at worst a prison for the innocent; at best a condensed city centre, at worst a hospital for the healthy. It is a closed community with no aims. Indeed, being aimless is the whole object of the exercise, as if removing the usual pressures of daily life will somehow cleanse the mind. Not for me. For me a still mind is a dead mind. When I should have been gazing blankly at the waves, I was in reality checking the maximum distance that flying fish, disturbed by the prow of our ship, can glide through the air before crashing back into the sea. Groups of leaping dolphins, soaring albatrosses, a passing turtle and even the occasional killer-whale fins glimpsed in the oceans as we glide by, have all offered small goals that could be scored against the expensive blandness of the daily routine. And, of course, passenger-watching has its inevitable appeal.

Now it's over and, after visiting twenty-one countries in ninety-two days, we will be back to our own small patch of earth with slightly less local bias than when we left. In the end, that is the great gain – the ability to wake up each morning knowing a little more clearly what it is like to be waking up in twenty-one other nations around the world.

———◦∞◦———

# AFTERWORD

---

ALTHOUGH THE SHORT CHAPTERS in this book are fragmentary and episodic, and a great deal has inevitably been omitted, the intention throughout has to been to convey the wonderfully varied pleasures available to anyone living on this small planet who manages to maintain an inquisitive eye, a childlike wonder and a sense of humour. It is true that the ageing process always involves an increase in rigid thinking, in firmly held opinions and in hardened attitudes. But although we cannot defeat physical ageing to remain young in body, we can do a great deal to stay young in mind. The trick is to never stop asking questions and never stop exploring, whether it be new places or new ideas. And it helps to perform at least one perversely eccentric act each day, no matter how small. Nearly all the great discoveries made by mankind have come from exploiting a lucky accident. But you stand no chance of encountering such an accident if your life is too neatly organized and routine-dominated. A search for novelty cannot guarantee exciting discoveries, but you can be certain that without it there will be none.

And please don't fall for that propaganda about requiring advanced technical skills in order to be able to unravel the mysteries of the universe. It is true that in some specialist fields they are essential, but it is amazing how much is sitting out there, just waiting to be discovered, simply by using the naked eye.

## PUBLICATIONS BY DESMOND MORRIS RELATING TO THE TRAVELS DESCRIBED IN THIS BOOK

### 1. EXPLORING THE MALTESE ISLANDS (1968–1974)
1969. *THE HUMAN ZOO*. JONATHAN CAPE, LONDON.
1971. *INTIMATE BEHAVIOUR*. JONATHAN CAPE, LONDON.

### 2. EXPLORING LANZAROTE (1974)
1974. 'THE IDOL OF TEJIA' IN: *ILLUSTRATED LONDON NEWS*. AUGUST, P. 43.

### 3. AROUND EUROPE IN SEARCH OF GESTURES (1975–1976)
1979. *GESTURES: THEIR ORIGINS AND DISTRIBUTION* (WITH PETER COLLETT, PETER MARSH AND MARIE O'SHAUGHNESSY). JONATHAN CAPE, LONDON.

### 4. MANWATCHING IN ITALY (1977)
1977. *MANWATCHING: A FIELD-GUIDE TO HUMAN BEHAVIOUR*. JONATHAN CAPE, LONDON.

### 5. THE GREAT PACIFIC CRUISE (1978)
1978. 'THE GREAT PACIFIC CRUISE' IN: *VOGUE* 135, NO. 2166. 1 SEPT 1978. P. 212–214, 232.

## 6. EXPLORING GIBRALTAR (1978)
1979. 'MONKEY BUSINESS' IN: *High Life: British Airways In-flight Magazine.* January 1979.

## 7. TRAVELS FOR *THE SOCCER TRIBE* (1979–1980)
1981. *THE SOCCER TRIBE.* Jonathan Cape, London.

## 8. IN AFRICA FOR *THE HUMAN RACE* (1981)
1982. INTRODUCTION TO *THE HUMAN RACE.* Thames Methuen, London. (Book written by Terence Dixon and Martin Lucas.)

## 10. TRAVELS FOR *THE HUMAN ANIMAL* (1993–1994)
1994. *THE HUMAN ANIMAL: A PERSONAL VIEW OF THE HUMAN SPECIES.* BBC Books, London.

## 11. TRAVELS FOR *THE HUMAN SEXES* (1996)
1997. *THE HUMAN SEXES: A NATURAL HISTORY OF MAN AND WOMAN.* Network Books, London.

# INDEX

―――∽◦◦◦∼―――